Islamic Messianism

Islamic Messianism

The Idea of Mahdi in Twelver Shi'ism

Abdulaziz Abdulhussein Sachedina

State University of New York Press

ALBANY

Published by

State University of New York Press, Albany
© 1981 State University of New York

All rights reserved
Printed in the United States of America

For information, address State University of New York
Press, State University Plaza, Albany, N.Y., 12246

Library of Congress Cataloging in Publication Data

Sachedina, Abdulaziz Abdulhussein, 1952-
Islamic messianism.
Bibliography and Index
1. Mahdism. I. Title.
BP 166.93.S22297'.2380-16767
ISBN 0-87395-442-4
ISBN 0-87395-458-0 (pbk.)

To
Fatima

Contents

Transliteration

Transliteration of Arabic and Persian terms and phrases into English in the present work follows in general the method of the Library of Congress as outlined in the *Cataloguing Service Bulletin,* 49 (December, 1958), except for the omission of diacritical long marks and dots.

Preface

"No doubt an Imam will rise—an Imam who will govern according to the name of God and the blessings."

For more than a millenium the idea of the future coming of the Mahdi has provided Shiʻi piety with a unique aspiration in the redemption through the appearance of the twelfth Imam. Modern western scholars have written virtually nothing on the subject of the Mahdi idea in Imamite Shiʻism, and this became a motive behind the present work which grew out of a doctoral dissertation submitted to the University of Toronto in 1976. I felt it necessary to examine the vast literature on this subject and make my findings available for other scholars without losing sight of the rigorous demands of modern scholarship. The extent to which I have been able to achieve this purpose was due in large measure to the assistance I have received from my professors and from many friends and colleagues in Toronto, Mashhad in Iran and Najaf in Iraq.

I wish to express my deepest appreciation and gratitude to Professors G.M. Wickens and R.M. Savory who kindly read revised and expanded versions of my work and offered many valuable suggestions and incisive critical comments that guided my research. I also wish to thank Professor M.E. Marmura who kindly agreed to comment on the chapter on Shiʻite theology. I am also grateful to Professors Wilfrid Madelung, W.M. Watt and Muhsin Mahdi for having read the work and made some substantial comments pertaining to the theological problems discussed therein.

I am also indebted to Sayyid Fadil al-Malani of Mashhad and Sayyid Muhammad Baqir al-Khirsan of Najaf who were particularly helpful on problems of *kalam*, while Professor Wa'izzada Khurasani helped with many obscurely worded *hadith* reports. I would also like to acknowledge the help of various professors at the Faculty of Theology and Islamic Studies at the University of Mashhad with whom I had many useful discussions related to this book. In Charlottesville, my colleagues at the Department of Religious Studies, Professors Victor W. Turner and Kyle P. Mc-Carter read the entire work and made numerous and pertinent suggestions for improving it. In preparing this study for publication, I received much encouragement from William D. Eastman, director of the State University of New York Press.

Finally, I am forever indebted to my wife, Fatima Sachedina, for her patience and moral encouragement throughout my years of study and research in Iran, Iraq, Canada and the United States.

Abdulaziz Abdulhussein Sachedina

Department of Religious Studies
University of Virginia, Charlottesville
Muharram, 1401
Aban, 1359
November, 1980

1. Introduction: The Islamic Messiah, al-Mahdi

In recent years the general reader will have seen much about Iranian Muslims, who follow a particular branch of Shi'ite Islam, which maintains belief in the appearance of a messianic savior from among the descendants of Muhammad, the Prophet of Islam. The essence of Shi'ite Islam is a chiliastic vision of history expressed in terms of radical social protest in the face of political oppression. The Shi'i expectation for the end of tyranny and wickedness through the establishment of justice by a descendant of the Prophet means not merely a hope for a better future, but also a re-evaluation of present social and historic life. Current social and political circumstances are expected to change for the better in the light of what is going to happen when the Savior of Islam appears. It is the study of the key concept of the Savior Imam, the Mahdi (divinely guided), as taught by the Imamite or Twelver Shi'is (believers in the line of twelve Imams) with which we shall be concerned in this book.

The notion of an expected deliverer, who is to come and humble or destroy the forces of wickedness and establish the rule of justice and equity on earth, is shared by all major religions of the world. Christians, Jews, and Zoroastrians, who, at different times, were subjected to the rule of those who did not share their religious heritage, cherished their traditions concerning a Messiah or Saoshyant of a divinely chosen line. Such a deliverer was expected to come or return, in God's time, to end the sufferings of the faithful and the rule of enemies of God and establish His kingdom on earth. Although the terms "messiah" and "messianism" have a specifically Judaeo-Christian ring and imply a whole series of Jewish-Christian doctrines, it is, nevertheless, perfectly permissible to employ the terms in an Islamic context, if we are quite certain at the outset in what sense we are using them. As a simple matter of fact, the Christian, Jewish, and Islamic traditions differ in the way the formula of an expected deliverer is employed. The Christians think of a Second Coming, the Jews of one who is yet to come, while the Muslims conceive of a person who will "appear" (*zuhur*) or "rise" *qiyam*) against existing intolerable secular authority. The term "messianism" in the Islamic context is frequently used to translate the important concept of an eschatological figure, the Mahdi, who as the foreordained leader "will rise" to launch a great social transformation in order to restore and adjust all things under divine guidance. The Islamic messiah, thus, embodies the aspirations of his followers in the restoration of the purity of the Faith which will bring true and uncorrupted guidance to all mankind, creating a just social order and a world free from oppression in which the Islamic revelation will be the norm for all nations.

Although the similarity of Islamic messianism to Judaeo-Christian ideas of the Messiah has been noted, the idea of the Mahdi as held by Muslims has a distinctive Islamic coloring. The Islamic doctrine of salvation does not conceive of man as a sinner who must be saved through spiritual regeneration. Rather it holds that man is not dead in sin, so he needs no spiritual rebirth. Nor does the doctrine conceive of its people's salvation in nationalistic terms, with the assurance of the realization of the kingdom of God in a promised land by a unique, autonomous community. The basic emphasis of Islamic salvation lies instead in the historical responsibility of its followers, namely, the establishment of the ideal religio-political community, the *umma*, with a worldwide membership of all those who believe in God and His revelation through Muhammad.

This responsibility carried within itself the revolutionary challenge of Islam to any inimical order which might hamper its realization. The seeds of this responsibility, which were to bear fruits of rebellion throughout Islamic history in the persistent aspiration of its followers for a more just future, were sown by the Prophet himself. Muhammad was not only the founder of a new religion, but also the guardian of a new social order. His message, embodied in the Qur'an, provided tremendous spiritual as well as socio-political impetus for the creation of a cosmopolitan, just society. Consequently, in the years following the Prophet's death a group of Muslims emerged who, dissatisfied with the state of affairs under the Caliphate, looked backward to the early period of Islam, which was dominated by the brilliant figure of Muhammad, the

Prophet and the statesman, and which came to be regarded as the only ideal epoch in Islamic history, unadulterated by the corrupt and worldly rulers of the expanding Islamic empire. This idealization of the Prophet himself gave rise to the notion of his being something more than an ordinary man; he must have been divinely chosen and hence the true leader who could guide his people to salvation. Owing to the feeling of this special status of the Prophet, some of his followers began to look forward to the rule of an individual from among his descendants "whose name will be also Muhammad, whose *kunya*, patronymic, will also be like that of the Apostle of God, and who will fill the earth with equity and justice, as it has been filled with injustice, oppression and tyranny."[1] As a result, although the concept of Islamic salvation as taught by the Qur'an had not envisaged the appearance of the redeemer Mahdi to guide the community of the believers to the pristine Islam in the last days, it was, in all probability, the personal devotion of the faithful to the Prophet that made them await the advent of a divinely guided savior from his family *(ahl al-bayt)*.

The growth of such a hope among the group which had been wronged and oppressed was the inevitable outcome of the consistent stress in Islam on the realization of the just society under the guidance of divine revelation. With the establishment in Islam of various dynasties which failed to promote the Islamic ideal, the need for a deliverer became imperative; those who desired the appearance of the messianic Imam were generally the ones who sympathized with the claims of the descendants of the Prophet as being heirs to the prophetic mission. These were the early Shi'ites. The most important factor in the development of Shi'ism was the idea of a messianic Imam who promised the end of corruption and wickedness. Thus the belief in the appearance of the Islamic messiah became a salient feature of Shi'ite Islam, especially Imami Shi'ism, where the conviction of the advent of the Mahdi, the twelfth Imam, continues to be expressed in the most repeated Shi'i prayer: "May God hasten release from suffering through his (the Imam's) rise."

Shi'ism and the Concept of the Messianic Imam

The division of Islam into Shi'i and Sunni was partly the result of a difference in the understanding of the conception of salvation by the two factions. Probably for this reason we cannot speak about Shi'a or Sunni

[3]

in the early years of Islam, when systematic exposition of Islamic doctrines had not been achieved. The religious principles set forth in the Qur'an did not yet form an integrated focus for the Muslim doctors in interpreting, formulating and crystallizing their creed. The whole doctrinal development was gradual. Hence, the Qur'anic teachings about salvation had to wait on historical events, and this fact undoubtedly had a major impact on their formulation. If the Islamic doctrine of salvation was conceived in the formation of an ideal religio-political community living under a fitting legal and social system of Islam on earth, then such an ideal was dependent on the leadership which could assure its realization. If not immediately following the Prophet's death, as the Shi'ites assert, at least in subsequent decades the question of Islamic leadership was the crucial issue which divided the Muslims into various factions. The doctrine of salvation was interwoven with the divine guidance through the appointed mediatorship of the Prophet, who was responsible for delivering the message.

The early years of Islam were characterized by a constant succession of victories of the Muslim army under the Caliphate; consequently, there does not seem to be any debate on who should be responsible to lead the community toward salvation after the Prophet's death. But as this period reached its end, and the civil wars broke out after the murder of Muhammad's third successor in A.D. 656, the Muslims were confronted with an unfulfilled idea of a just order, which gave rise to a discussion of the necessity of a qualified leadership to assume the Imamate of the *umma*, on whom depended the establishment of a true Islamic order. Most of these early discussions on the Imamate took at first sight political form, but eventually the debate encompassed the religious implications of salvation. This is true of all Islamic concepts, since Islam as a religious phenomenon was subsequent to Islam as a political reality. The rise of several individuals as the leaders, Imams, and the sympathetic and even enthusiastic following that they mustered clearly show an attempt to visualize the manner in which Muslim society must be ordered to fulfill its historical responsibility: the formation of a just society, including its political organization. During the years following the outbreak of civil wars, the two main answers offered to the crucial question of Islamic salvation were given by the two main opposing factions of the Muslims. These responses would, at a later time, characterize the two groups with their sectarian epithets: the Sunnites and the Shi'ites.

Following the end of the earlier caliphate of the "Rightly Guided" (A.D. 680), the Sunnites or, as their Islamic title goes, *ahl al-sunna wa al-jama'a* (people of the custom and community), looked upon salvation as possible only through the allegiance and loyalty of all believers in the community. As long as the community continued to be fully committed to the promulgation and observance of the Law (Shari'a), its salvation was guaranteed regardless of the qualities or, as it was later held, descent of the leaders who headed the community. After all, the leader, as conceived by later Sunni theorists, was merely a protector of the Law, and this function was vested in him through the process of allegiance paid by the members of the community. The solution offered by the Sunnites was, in fact, a simple expression of recognition of a historical reality, namely, that the leadership of the Muslims after the early period of the Rightly Guided caliphs, which was idealized by them as the golden age of Islam, depended not on the individual on whom it was conferred; rather, it was subject to the commitment and loyalty granted by the community to that leader. Thus, in the final analysis, it was acceptance of the tradition by the community and its membership which guaranteed salvation.

The Shi'ites, on the other hand, did not find the community allegiance, as maintained by their opponents, capable of ensuring the salvation that Islam had envisaged. From the early days of the civil war in A.D. 656, some Muslims not only thought about the question of leadership in political terms, but also laid religious emphasis on it. To begin with, they maintained that Muhammad himself was a charismatic leader, who held both spiritual and temporal power. His spiritual authority included the power to interpret the message embodied in the Qur'an without corrupting the revelation. Islam, in order to continue its function of directing the faithful toward salvation, was in need of a leader who could perform the Prophet's dual role authoritatively. In other words, only another charismatic leader could succeed the Prophet and accomplish the creation of an ideal Islamic society. Who could be better qualified for such a crucial task than his own family members, who would have inherited his charisma? The notional exaltation of the Prophet and his rightful successor as a second cause, in addition to the hope of the ill-treated mentioned earlier, gave rise to the very concept of messianic leadership from among the descendants of the Prophet, an Imam who could save the believers. In all likelihood, the movement began immediately after the death of the Prophet with the formation of the party *(shi'a)* of 'Ali, Muhammad's cousin and son-in-law, which upheld 'Ali's succession to the Prophet. The party of 'Ali became the nucleus of the Shi'a movement. During the last years of 'Ali's caliphate and the beginning of the Umayyad rule, the group had been fairly small, centered at Kufa in Iraq. It is significant to note that Kufa, which had been 'Ali's capital during his caliphate (35–40/656–61), had gained much political, economic, and intellectual importance in the eastern portion of the Islamic lands. The Shi'a in Kufa had looked upon 'Ali and his family as the rightful candidates for the leadership of the community and had championed their cause as restorers of true Islamic polity. This group had also symbolized 'Ali as the leader standing for justice against the central authorities. As a result of such claims, a merely political *shi'a* of Kufa gradually became a powerful group and gained widespread importance in different parts of the eastern lands of the caliphate, especially in an Arab garrison town of Qumm in the west Iranian highlands. The *shi'a* took advantage of the intimate historical relationship of 'Ali with Muhammad and of the old Arab tribal concept of *ahl al-bayt* (people of the household)—the family from whom chiefs were chosen—and zealously supported the candidacy of the 'Alids, who, in fact, were the sole progeny of Muhammad through his daughter Fatima. This support for the leadership of the 'Alids, at least in the beginning, did not imply any religious underpinning. However, it is important to understand that this formative period in Shi'ism helps one to comprehend the following century when the idea of the Imam was taking shape and poising itself for the ninth and tenth centuries; it is also gratifying to discover that some twentieth century problems facing the Shi'ites were already anticipated towards the end of the tenth century. The claim for leadership of the 'Alids became an exaggerated belief expressed in pious terms of the traditions attributed to the Prophet, and only gradually became part of the cardinal doctrine of the Imamate, the pivot on which the complete Shi'ite creed rotates. The entire spiritual edifice of the Shi'a was built on the *walaya* (love and devotion) of 'Ali, who became the first Shi'a Imam. As a matter of fact, the *walaya* of 'Ali became the sole criterion for judging true faith. Faith *(iman)* was conceived in terms of personal devotion to 'Ali and what he symbolized, as far as Islamic justice was concerned. Salvation was impossible if a person failed to acknowledge the true Imam of his time, to whom devotion and obedience was incumbent since he alone could bring a true Islamic rule of justice and equity in the world, the main function attributed to the Islamic messiah, al-Mahdi.

The Shi'i conception of salvation was bound to meet with much resistance, since it not only demanded the recognition of the rightful Imam with a messianic role, but more importantly, it also challenged the right of the existing regime to rule. The latter issue became a rallying point for all those who thought they had been discriminated against or maltreated by the ruling house. Thus early Shi'ites, under the Umayyads, were united in their recognition of 'Ali as the Imam after the Prophet, and in their aspiration for a just order under the command of 'Ali, by opposing the Caliphate. As a result, from its inception Shi'ism became the traditional opposition party, and as such several protest movements were organized under its wide range of leaders from among the members of the *ahl al-bayt*, who were able to arouse a genuine religious urge in their followers to achieve political goals. Thus messianic Shi'ism was a distinguishable feature of all early revolutions that took place in different regions of Islamic lands under different leaders. The notion of the divinely guided savior Imam, the Mahdi, who was believed to have been equally endowed with divine knowledge as the Prophet had been, seized the imaginations of all those who were deprived of their rights under the existing regimes.

However, the Shi'i attempts at direct political action were met with severe resistance, and very early their political experiences resulted in failure, a fact which caused further factionalism among them. On the one hand, some insisted on armed resistance to the oppressive rule of the Caliphate. These were the radical Shi'ites, who were sometimes, because of the extravagant calims that they made for their Imams, known as *ghulat* (extremists). They regarded the Sunni caliphs as cursed usurpers and believed that justice on earth could be hoped for only when the rightful Imams from among the descendants of Fatima, the Prophet's daughter and 'Ali's wife, could and would rule with true guidance from a purified Islam. On the other hand, some Shi'ites, having seen the futility of direct political action, were prepared to postpone the restoration of true Islamic rule beyond the visible future. The adoption of the moderating trend by this group was in no way a compromise of their stance as far as the question of the Imamate was concerned. Even this group insisted on allegiance and obedience to the Imams springing from the descendants of 'Ali and Fatima. It was probably the murder at Karbala'

[7]

of al-Husayn (61/680), the younger son of 'Ali, by Umayyad troops, and later the failure of the revolt at Kufa of Zayd (122/740), al-Husayn's grandson, which clearly marked the turn toward a quietist attitude by this group, who had until that time been willing to fight for their rights. The idea of passion seized the imagination of this group and gave rise to the peculiar religious doctrine of the martyrdom of all the Imams at the instigation of the caliphs, until the line reached the last Imam, who disappeared in A.D. 873 in order to be saved from the same fate. The latter, according to Shi'ite belief, will reappear as the Messianic Imam to wipe out injustice on earth.

The radical Shi'ites had become so strong by the middle of the eighth century that one of their sub-divisions was able to help organize an 'Abbasid revolution which was successful in establishing the dynastic caliphate of the house of 'Abbas, the Prophet's uncle; but the caliphate turned the tables against the revolutionary expectation of its Shi'i supporters and adhered to Sunnism. The factor that contributed to the Shi'i disappointment was the absence of a concrete Shi'ite ideology until the times of the great Shi'i Imam Ja'far al-Sadiq (d. 148/765), a descendant of 'Ali through his son al-Husayn, at the time of the 'Abbasid victory. Under this Imam the Shi'ite doctrine of the Imamate was formulated. The confused and diverse aspects of the Shi'i attempts to establish an 'Alid caliphate at the time of the 'Abbasid revolution corroborate the fact that the Shi'i efforts were still lacking in a concrete ideology.[2] It is, however, significant to note that Ja'far al-Sadiq had been greatly responsible for the moderation and disciplining of radical elements among the Shi'ites,[3] and he was, in all probability, the person who provided Shi'ism with a sectarian ideology as well as the distinguishing mark of being "Ja'fari," related to Ja'far al-Sadiq. As a result, Ja'far al-Sadiq has been given prominence in all Shi'ite traditions, whether radical or moderate.

The moderate Shi'ites, whose Imams had refrained from active participation in politics, continued to uphold the Imamate of the descendants of al-Husayn until the line reached the twelfth, who was believed to be the *Qa'im*, "the chief redresser of wrongs" committed against the family of the Prophet, and the Hidden Imam, whose return was awaited. Thus they were known as Imamites or Twelvers. During this period of political quietism they continued their opposition, although, compared to their radical counterparts, they posed little threat to the ruling dynasty. Their belief in the doctrine of the hidden messianic leader who

[*8*]

would rise only when God would command him to do so, in addition to their unwillingness to go along with this quest for their martyrdom and death in the face of political oppression (similar to the fate of the Imams who were rejected and persecuted), encouraged moderation as the accepted way of living for many Shi'ites of this school. The disappearance of the twelfth Imam in A.D. 873 may have in effect marked the beginning of the accentuation of the title Mahdi, to designate an eschatalogical leader, unlike its early designation merely for a true Islamic ruler. Consequently, it is in the Imamite form of Shi'ism that we ought to study Islamic messianism, because only this school of Shi'ism continued to cherish chiliastic hopes, perpetuated in the peculiar vision of Islamic history as culminating with the rise of the messianic Imam. While belief in the future coming of an Imam is a salient feature of all Shi'ite sects in Islam, in Imami Shi'ism the belief in the messianic Imam becomes not only a basic tenet of the creed, but also the foundation on which the entire spiritual edifice of the Imamite religion rests. It is the acknowledgment of this Imam which can ensure salvation.

Early Shi'ite Sects and the Concept of the Mahdi

All groups with Shi'i sympathies had entertained chiliastic hopes and had asserted the Mahdiism of their Imams. Although the title Mahdi was used for the first time for 'Ali and al-Husayn among the Shi'i Imams merely as a designation for the righteous Islamic ruler,[4] its usage in the messianic context seems to have been applied by al-Mukhtar b. Abi 'Ubayd al-Thaqafi to Muhammad b. al-Hanafiyya, a son of 'Ali by a woman other than Fatima, in 66/685—86, in his rebellion against 'Abd Allah b. al-Zubayr. The latter had challenged the Umayyad power and had turned for his main support to Iraq, where the Shi'i Imams were actively engaged in their anti-Umayyad agitation. Al-Mukhtar was a man with Shi'i sympathies and had used the martyrdom of al Husayn as a basis for his rebellion in Kufa, which was inhabited by people of different races and creeds, who were united in their dislike of the Umayyads. In such troubled circumstances al-Mukhtar's call for war against the "wicked" became a rallying point for the discontented, who joined him in this revolt in the name of Ibn al-Hanafiyya. The whole episode of the revolt in Kufa shows the extent to which any shrewd and ambitious person like al-Mukhtar could manipulate the genuine religious devotions of ordinary men in the name of the son of 'Ali, who probably had nothing to do with the uprising. It also indicates the extreme fluidity at the time of religio-political parties, whose organizers did not hesitate to introduce elements from other non-Islamic traditions which conceived of the messianic leaders as semi-divine individuals.

This revolt was suppressed by the Umayyads and actually brought to an end by Mus'ab, son of al-Zubayr (who represented his brother 'Abd Allah in Iraq), who defeated and eventually killed al-Mukhtar in the year A.D. 687. Ibn al-Hanafiyya, who seems to have declined the extravagant claims made for him by al-Mukhtar, died in 81/700−01 without achieving anything significant. But the aftermath of the movement was far-reaching. Many of the adherents of this movement did not accept the death of Ibn al-Hanafiyya as a reality, and instead maintained that he was in hiding and would eventually return and "fill this world with justice and equity, as it is now filled with injustice and oppression." These were the Kaysaniyya, who seem to have been named almost certainly after a follower and the chief of al-Mukhtar's body-guard by the name of Kaysan Abu 'Amra,[5] who must have shaped the Kaysanite doctrines.

The Kaysanites were active during the latter part of the Umayyad period, and they were probably the first Shi'ite faction to conceive of their Imam in the messianic terms which subsequently came to be held by other Shi'ites in regard to their Imams. This was the beginning of the two central beliefs in the idea of Mahdi, the *ghayba* (occultation) and the *raj'a* (return) of the Islamic messiah at the appropriate time. It was under the historical impact of the Umayyad Caliphate that such tenets were evolved, more particularly, when the situation was beyond the control of those who were demanding Islamic egalitarianism. The belief in the occultation of the savior Imam and his eventual return at a favourable time helped the Shi'ites to endure under difficult circumstances and to hope for reform pending the return of the Mahdi. They looked forward to the promised events accompanying the emergence of the hidden Imam which would adjust the present unbearable historical circumstances in favor of the oppressed who remained loyal to the Imam. The messianic expectation of these Shi'ites, consequently, did not require them to oppose the establishment actively; rather, the absence of any information on the exact time when the hidden Imam would appear required the Shi'ites to be on the alert at all times. In other words, they had to remain prepared and also pave the way for the Mahdi's coming by constantly re-evaluating contemporary historical life on the basis of the signs foretold regarding Mahdi's reappearance.

Among the Kaysanites were the poets Kuthayyir (d. A.D. 723) and Sayyid al-Himyari (d. A.D. 789), who were involved in propagating the messianism of Ibn al-Hanafiyya, after the latter's death. Kuthayyir had visited the Umayyad court in Damascus and was also connected with the sub-sect of the Kaysaniyya, the Karbiyya who were the followers of a person called Ibn Karb. Both these poets had maintained that their Imam Ibn al-Hanafiyya had not died, was in concealment at mount Radwa, and would return at the appropriate time to establish the true Islamic rule. Sayyid al-Himyari later turned to Ja'far al-Sadiq. The last decades of the Umayyad rule were marked by several Shi'i revolutions and uprisings headed by 'Alids or other members of the Hashimite clan and demanding a new and more adequately just social order. Even the 'Abbasid revolution was based largely on Kaysani-Shi'i expectations. The rebellion of al-Mukhtar and then of 'Abd Allah b. Mu'awiya (d. A.D. 747), a descendant of Abu Talib, 'Ali's father, formed the nucleus of the 'Abbasid revolt. Although both abandoned their messianic role after being established as caliphs and adopting Sunnism, they nevertheless persisted in assuming messianic titles with religious connotations in the hope that the office of caliphate would have some semblance to the ideals of the Shi'i Imamate and its function of restoring the purity of Islam. In fact, al-Mansur (A.D. 754–75) not only adopted religious titles for himself, but conferred the title of al-Mahdi, the expected deliverer of Islam, on his successor.[6] Even after the great disappointment for the Shi'ites following the 'Abbasid victory, the Shi'i hopes continued to run high, and consequently almost all Imams from this time onward were believed to be the Mahdi and not to have died; their return was expected.

Following Ibn al-Hanafiyya, the second prominent person among the 'Alids for whom the messianic epithet of al-Mahdi was used was Muhammad al-Nafs al-Zakiyya (the pure soul) (100–45/718–62), a descendant of 'Ali through his son al-Hasan (50/670). He seems to have been considered as the Mahdi at a very early age by his family.[7] His adherents asserted that he was the one who would accomplish the mission of Islam by restoring justice in the world. On his death they claimed he had not died but was in concealment in one of the hills on the way to Mecca from Najd, namely 'Ilmiyya, and would return. In fact, even some

[*11*]

of the Zaydites, who upheld the Imamate of Zayd, the great grandson of 'Ali, who led a futile insurrection in Kufa in A.D. 740, awaited the return of al-Nafs al-Zakiyya.

Among the followers of Muhammad al-Baqir (d. 113/731−32), the grandson of al-Husayn and the Imam of the moderate Shi'ites, who also was held to be the Mahdi by the Baqiriyya faction of the Shi'ites, there were those who were opposed to the claims of al-Nafs al-Zakiyya. On the death of al-Baqir in 731−32 some of his adherents seceded and supported the claims of al-Nafs al-Zakiyya. But Ja'far al-Sadiq, who was acknowledged as the Imam after al-Baqir by a majority of the Shi'ites, refused to support the cause of his cousin al-Nafs al-Zakiyya and his brother Ibrahim. Al-Sadiq was one of the most respected leaders of the 'Alids at the time and thus was supported by the rest of the Shi'ites on al-Nafs al-Zakiyya's death.

On the death of al-Sadiq (A.D. 765), a faction of the Shi'ites, headed by a person named 'Ajlan b. Nawus from Basra and thus called after him al-Nawusiyya,[8] believed al-Sadiq to be the Mahdi. The Nawusites believed that the latter had not died and would return to establish justice and equity on earth. Again, from this period onwards, it appears that only the Imams from the line of al-Husayn were proclaimed to be the Mahdi whose return was awaited. Probably at this time, following the success of the 'Abbasid cause in manipulating Shi'ite sympathies, the role of the messianic Imam was limited to the descendants of Fatima through al-Husayn only, although several individuals from the descendants of al-Hasan also were able to assume the role of the savior Imam. But the descendants of al-Husayn, partly because of the latter's resistance to the Umayyads and his martyrdom in Karbala', enjoyed greater prestige and influence than the descendants of al-Hasan, who had abdicated his right to the caliphate in favor of the Umayyad Mu'awiya. Thus al-Husayn became the symbol of resistance and martyrdom in the face of political turmoil throughout Shi'ite history.

Another faction of the Shi'ites, namely al-Musawiyya, maintained the Mahdiism of Musa al-Kazim, the son of al-Sadiq, who had died in 183/ 799−800 in the prison of the 'Abbasid Harun al-Rashid, and they awaited his return. In fact, numerous factions believed in the Mahdiism of al-Kazim. Still another faction believed in the Mahdiism of Isma'il, another son of al-Sadiq, and claimed his immortality, and others proclaimed the son of Isma'il, Muhammad, as the Mahdi who would not die until he had conquered the world, he being the promised ruler to come in due time. This was the beginning of the Isma'ili mission which eventually developed into a radical social, economic, intellectual, and religious revolution culminating in the tenth century with the appearance of a descendant of Muhammad b. Isma'il who claimed to be the legitimate ruler of the Muslims in North Africa. He proclaimed himself as the long awaited Fatimid Mahdi, who would initiate an era of the ideal Islamic rule. Later on the Fatimids, as they came to be known, explained the idea of the Mahdi not as the title of a particular messianic Imam, but as a collective designation for the line of Imams from the descendants of Fatima, "who are like one and the same person, only appearing in different bodies and states although being in spirit one and the same all through the ages."⁹ It is important to note that the first ruler of the Fatimid dynasty, al-Mahdi, did not appear until after the twelfth Imam of the Husaynid line (as recognized by the moderate Shi'ites, who were the adversaries of the Isma'ilis) was declared to be the Hidden Imam around 873.

The belief in the Mahdiism of all the descendants of al-Husayn after al-Sadiq demonstrates the fact that within the framework of the Mahdi idea, which evolved in the political turmoil of the Caliphate, was embedded the never-relinquished Shi'i demand for the fulfillment of a true Islamic justice under the command of the Husaynid Imam. In this perspective one can apprehend on the one hand the expectation of each Shi'i generation, namely, the appearance of the messianic Imam in their lifetime to redress their grievances against the growing political turmoil of the period, and on the other hand, the reason why each Husaynid Imam declined the extravagant claims made for him by his overzealous disciples and adopted a posture of quietism, moderation, and even accommodation in order to win tolerance from the Sunnite majority as exemplifying a minor deviation.¹⁰ The moderate Shi'ites, who were later on to form the bulk of the Shi'ites maintaining the Imamate of the twelve Imams, although insisting on the exalted status of the Imams and allegiance to the twelve successors of the Prophet, maintained relations with the community at large. The Imamite accommodation also warranted their continuity and, indirectly, their pervasive influence in gaining a recognition for the elevated position of the *ahl al-bayt* (the family of the Prophet) in Sunnite circles. The *walaya* or love and devotion to that family was given an official status in the personal piety of all Muslims, and the idea of the appearance of the Mahdi from among the descendants of Fatima through her son al-Husayn became a widespread Islamic belief. The Sunnites, however, expect the Mahdi to be the ultimate Caliph of the Prophet and do not consider the belief in the restorer of Islamic purity as an essential part of their creed, as the Shi'ites do. Ibn Khaldun (d. A.D. 1405) in his *Muqaddima* has summarized the Sunnite position on the question of the future restorer of the faith in the following terms:

> It has been well known (and generally accepted) by all Muslims in every epoch, that at the end of time a man from the family (of the Prophet) will without fail make his appearance, one who will strengthen Islam and make justice triumph. Muslims will follow him, and he will gain domination over the Muslim realm. He will be called the Mahdi. Following him, the Antichrist will appear, together with all the subsequent signs of the Hour (the Day of Judgement), as established in (the sound traditions of the *Sahih* [authoritative collections of the Prophetic sayings recognized by the Sunnites].[11]

Ja'far al-Sadiq and Imami Shi'ism

Although al-Baqir was the first Imam among the descendants of al-Husayn to be considered Mahdi, it was with al-Sadiq and his successors that the idea of the messianic role of the 'Alid Imams became a distinctive feature of later Shi'ism. The anti-Umayyad revolts and wars had begun in al-Baqir's time. The Umayyad family itself was occupied with internal disputes regarding succession, which to a certain extent left the Shi'i Imam alone to prepare ground for the Shi'i doctrinal formulations. It is significant that under al-Baqir's successor, al-Sadiq, the sectarian doctrine of the Imamate was formulated. In the political turmoil of the period which marked the end of the Umayyad and the beginning of the 'Abbasid rule, al-Sadiq had great opportunities to propagate Shi'i viewpoints without any inhibition, and to modify the radical tone of early Shi'ism into a more sober expectation as far as the rise of the divinely appointed leader was concerned. Apart from the political upheavals, it was al-Sadiq's heritage which contributed tremendously to the shaping of the developing Shi'i school.

Al-Sadiq's grandfather, 'Ali b. al-Husayn, had a reputation as an eminent scholar, besides being a pious and righteous person. He is even cited in the Sunnite *isnads* (chain of transmitters), as having related traditions on the authority of his father al-Husayn, his uncle al-Hasan, Ibn 'Abbas, one of the best known early authorities on Islamic religion, and others.[12] His son Muhammad, known as al-Baqir, meaning the one who splits open (knowledge), because of his profound knowledge of Islamic sciences, inherited his father's piety and knowledge, and is equally known in the Sunnite *isnads*. With al-Baqir began the period in which much attention was given to the interpretation of the Qur'an.[13] The disciples of this Imam seem to have maintained the belief that only the Imams from the household of the Prophet knew the full implications of the Qur'anic verses, and consequently, they alone were endowed with the secret knowledge of the revelation. The belief that the Imams were the "speaking *(al-natiq)* Qur'an," who knew the esoteric interpretation of the Book, most probably began during al-Baqir's time. Thus al-Sadiq had inherited from both his father and grandfather the basic Islamic sciences, which under him reached a level of systematic exposition. He had also inherited their political quietism following the murder of al-Husayn in Karbala'. It is not without reason that al-Sadiq did not support the direct political action of his cousins and also declined an invitation to accept the caliphate at the time the 'Abbasid assumed power.[14] Al-Sadiq's refusal to accept any political office was an indication of his efforts to re-orient his followers' expectation concerning the true Islamic rule by a descendant of al-Husayn. The failure of most of the Shi'i revolts to achieve any concrete results in favor of the family of the Prophet was an important factor which had contributed to the adoption of a policy of quiescence and the acceptance of existing circumstances despite their various shortcomings. Nevertheless, the notion of the savior Imam dramatized the expectations of the Shi'ites, who were now told by their leaders to remain on the alert because it was possible that the Mahdi might appear and summon the faithful to arms to launch the great insurrection under his command to deliver humanity from misery and distress. No one was told "when" such an insurrection would take place, since its knowledge was with God alone.

Both Muhammad al-Baqir and Ja'far al-Sadiq were, at various times, approached by their followers and assured of their support if they wanted to rise against the existing regime.[15] The Imams had to appease the impatience of their Shi'a by saying that while it was true that all the Imams were Qa'im and thus capable of overthrowing unjust rule, the

eschatalogical Qa'im would be the one who would appear after concealment to wipe out injustice, only when God would command him to do so.

Al-Sadiq's endeavors to discipline his followers' overzealous claims for
their Imams is well attested in his disowning of his fanatical supporter
Abu al-Khattab (executed in 138/755–56). The latter asserted that al-
Sadiq had transferred his authority to him by designating him to be his
wasi and *qayyim* (deputy or executor of his will) and entrusting to him the
Greatest Name of God *(al-ism al-a'zam)*, which was supposed to empower
its possessor with extraordinary strength in comprehending hidden matters.[16] The delay in fulfillment of the Shi'i dream of Islamic
egalitarianism had given rise to many esoteric pronouncements attributed to an Imam, especially al-Sadiq, which darkly foretold events to
come. The attribution of such esoteric knowledge to the Imams was, in
some measure, the belief in the special knowledge of the messianic
leader, who was held to have been endowed with divine knowledge with
the assistance of which he could perceive the destiny of his followers.
When the Imams themselves declined such knowledge, as they often did,
an ambitious and popular disciple like Abu al-Khattab could claim to be
heir to that knowledge in order to rally Shi'i support for radical action.
The extent to which such disciples were a threat to the moderating
trends initiated by al-Sadiq, in a period which called for much restraint
and prudence on the part of the latter, can be measured by considering
what he said about Abu al-Khattab: "I dread him all the time, whether I
stand, or sit, or lie in my bed. May God make him taste the heat of
iron."[17] Without considering the period of al-Sadiq it is difficult to understand why the Imam considered disciples like Abu al-Khattab a continuous source of fear to him.

Al-Sadiq's prominence among the descendants of 'Ali, his being accepted by all the Shi'ites as their Imam, including even those who had
followed radicalism in their attempt to establish 'Alid rule later on like
the Isma'ilis, and his being enlisted as an authentic transmitter of the
traditions in the Sunnite *isnads*, all suggest that it was almost certainly
under his leadership that moderate Shi'ism, with its veneration of the
family of the Prophet, became accepted by the Sunnite majority as a
possible interpretation of Islamic piety. His attitude toward politics became the cornerstone of the Imamite political theory, which, in the absence of the political discretion of the Hidden Imam, did not teach its
followers to overthrow the tyrannical rulers and replace them by the

Imam; rather, and prudently, the leadership of the community was divided into temporal and spiritual spheres. The former was vested in the ruling dynasty, which in theory required proper *nass* (designation) by the Prophet, but was acceptable as long as its sphere of action was limited to the execution of the Law. The spiritual sphere too required a clear designation, also by the Prophet, since the holder of spiritual authority was empowered to interpret the message and elaborate on it without committing error. This latter aspect was secured through the principle of special inheritance of the prophetic knowledge. The spiritual authority, according to the Shi'ite teaching, was available in 'Ali from the day the Prophet died, since he became the Imam and the only true *amir* of the faithful through the Prophet's designation; this leadership would be available in the line of the Imams, who are all clearly designated by the preceding Imams. When the messianic Imam appears, the temporal and spiritual authorities will merge in his person; like the Prophet, he will uniquely unite the two spheres of the ideal Islamic rule. Thus the idea of Imamate by designation among the 'Alids, continuing through all political circumstances, was complemented by that of an Imamate based not primarily on political claim, but on the special privilege of possessing the prophetic knowledge.[18]

The period of al-Sadiq's Imamate coincided with a period of intellectual activity in Islam, especially the systematization of the Law through collection of the *hadith* literature. The eminent figures of Abu Hanifa (d. 150/768) and Malik (d. 179/795) were occupied by the attempt to fulfill this need. Al-Sadiq's Fatimid ancestry, and his claim to the special designation with all its implications, greatly enhanced his prominence in Medina, and he in effect became the fountainhead not only of the Ja'fari school of Islamic law, but of all Shi'i intellectual as well as traditional sciences. Al-Sadiq's prestigious and generally recognized Imamate gave ultimate recognition to the line of the Husaynid Imams, among whom the twelfth and the last was declared to be the awaited messianic Imam, the Qa'im al-Mahdi.[19]

The Imami Shi'i Doctrine of Imamate

It is plausible to maintain that from the time of al-Sadiq, following the failure of the 'Abbasid revolution to establish a truly 'Alid caliphate, Shi'ism began to develop a concrete ideology and even to cultivate its own form of personal piety, which made it a distinct sect with its own interpretation of Islamic concepts. Although al-Sadiq's esteemed position had managed to keep the Shi'ites as members of the community at large, one point, however, became a source of dispute between the Shi'ites and the Sunnites. The Shi'ites had insisted that no law could become binding on the community if its reliability was not assured by the presence of an authoritative and rightful successor of the Prophet. The community as a whole could not verify the authenticity of a particular law; rather, the validity depended on its verification by the true 'Alid Imam. Thus, however close the Shi'ites moved to the Sunnites in observing the precepts of the Law, the cardinal doctrine of the Imamate and the insistence on intense devotion to the holders of this office became obstacles to the full assimilation of Ja'fari Shi'ism into Sunnism.

The doctrine of the Imamate, to be discussed presently, was the later systematization of what was known to the early adherents of this school as the idea of the messianic savior of the Islamic peoples. The evolution of the doctrine of the Imamate, from a simple notion of a leader who would bring Islamic justice to the oppressed, to a highly complex concept of the eschatalogical Hidden Imam, provides an outline of the history of Shi'ism in Islam. In the beginning, because of the unbearable political as well as social circumstances, a group of Muslims had come to look forward to a charismatic leader, not unlike the Prophet himself, who would right all wrongs and deliver the community from misery and distress. The fulfillment of such an expectation was believed to be possible only through a relative of the Prophet, more precisely a descendant of 'Ali and Fatima. But very soon such hopes were frustrated by a series of failures and by the martyrdom of the religious leaders who had attempted to redress the grievances of their supporters by rising against the authorities. This marked the beginnings of the development of a religious emphasis in the role of 'Alid Imams, who were now held to be in concealment and whose return was confidently expected. The belief in the hidden messiahs was a clear shift in the Imam's temporal role as it had been stressed so far. The Imams were now believed to possess divine knowledge which enabled them to predict future events, including the proper time for the messianic Imam to strike. The highly speculative aspects of the doctrine of the Imamate should be attributed to the circumstances in which the Imams manifested political quietism but did not object to certain extravagant claims made for them by their fanatical associates. These claims included the possession of esoteric knowledge inherited through designation by the Imam. Later on, the very question of designation became one of the pillars of the Imamite doctrine of the Imamate. Following is a summary of the Imami Shi'i doctrine of the Imamate.

The Imamite authors, in their exposition of the Shi'ite creed, divide the Principles of Religion *(usul al-din)* into five tenets:

1. *al-tawhid*: The affirmation of the Unity of God *(al-iqrar bi'l-wahda)*.
2. *al-'adl*: Belief in the Justice of God.
3. *al-nubuwwa*: Belief in Prophecy.
4. *al-imama*: Belief in the Imamate.
5. *al-ma'ad*: Belief in the Day of Judgment.

In four of these principles, that is 1, 2, 3, and 5, the Imamites in general share a common ground with the Sunnites, although there are differences on points of detail. With respect to the second principle, *al-'adl*, the Imamite position is similar to that of the Mu'tazilites. In the third/ninth and the fourth/tenth centuries, when the theological exposition of the Imamite school was being worked out, its theologians adopted an essentially Mu'tazilite theological doctrine; but they refused any identification with the Mu'tazilite theologians. *Al-'adl* means that God is infinitely removed from every evil act and from being remiss in what is declared as incumbent. *Al-'adl* depends on the knowledge of good and evil as determined by reason; reason guides a person to such knowledge, and asserts that good is good in itself, and evil is evil in itself, whether the lawgiver pronounces it so or not.[20] The fourth principle, *al-imama*, the Sunnites do not consider as *asl*, a fundamental principle of religion,[21] while the Shi'ites make it their central and cardinal principle. In fact, the foundation of the Shi'ite creed is based on the principle of *al-imama*.

The Shi'ite Imam, unlike the Sunnite caliph, is regarded as designated by God. God alone appoints the Imams, one by one, in accordance with the testament *(wasiyya)* revealed to the Prophet, which announces the names of those who will succeed him. The *wasiyya* was brought down by Gabriel to the Prophet, who dictated it to 'Ali, and the text, its transcription, etc., were witnessed by Gabriel and other angels of the first rank who had accompanied him on this occasion. The testament had several golden seals on it, which were opened by each Imam beginning with 'Ali down to the last Imam al-Mahdi. Each Imam after breaking the seal was required to follow the instructions therein. Thus the first three Imams,

'Ali, al-Hasan, and al-Husayn, chose to resist the Umayyad, while the other Imams chose political quietism until the rising of messianic Imam al-Mahdi, in compliance with the instructions in the testament.[22]

The Imamate is the convenant *('ahd)* of God and His Prophet with the persons specified by their names in the testament. No Prophet is sent without a successor among his own progeny, who are the true heirs to the prophetic knowledge which the Imams were asserted to have inherited from the Prophet and 'Ali.[23] The Imamate possesses the status of the prophets and the inheritance of their legatees *(al-awsiya')*. It is the deputyship of God *(khilafat allah)* and the vicarship of the Prophet *(khilafat al-rasul)*; it is the position of the *amir al-mu'minin,* which entails the responsibility of administering justice and conducting the religious life of the *umma.* Consequently the Imamate, like the prophethood *(al-nubuwwa)*, has to be announced at the set time, for the guidance of mankind by the will of God. The leadership of the Imam resembles that of the Prophet himself in its temporal and spiritual aspects; this means that the Imam is equal to the Prophet in all respects except that the Prophet, and 'Ali among the Imams, hold a special excellence over the other Imams in the methods of comprehending the lawful and unlawful *(al-halal wa al-haram)* in the Faith. The Imam, like the Prophet, is endowed with special knowledge and has inherited the knowledge of all the ancient prophets and their legatees. In this way, the Imam is the link with the way of guidance, and without acknowledging him a person seeking guidance cannot obtain it.

The Imam, like the Prophet, is blessed with special grace *(lutf)* from God, which renders him immune to sin *(ma'sum)* before God makes him His witness *(shahid)* to the people and His proof *(hujja)* for them.

The Imam is *shahid* in the sense that he is the one who will be called upon to bear witness on the day of Judgment to what was revealed to the Prophet. He will also bear witness to those who acknowledged him and those who charged him with falsehood. 'Ali is *shahid* in the sense that he acknowledged the prophethood of Muhammad. There is one witness in every century among the Imams who act as witnesses for the people, and the Prophet is the witness for the Imam.[24]

The Imam as the *hujja* is the receiver of special qualities which entitle him to bear witness against those who refuse to accept the authority of God and to follow His injunctions. He is the only person who stands as a proof of His existence and the existence of His revelation on earth. On the Day of Judgment God will present his *hujja* in order to refute the sinners who would claim that they did not know a person who gave them the example of saintliness.[25]

The special mark of the Imam, as it was known to the late Imamites, was *'isma* (infallibility). Whereas the Sunnite theologians considered infallibility to be a peculiar quality of the Prophet, the Shi'ite theologians contended that since the Imamate was intended for the continuation of the mission of the Prophet and the guidance of mankind after him, the community could not afford to accept a fallible successor to this divine institution; therefore, the Imam had to be protected from sin like the Prophet. The difference between the two creeds became marked when the Shi'ite Imam was asserted to have possessed the light of God, which was passed on to him by the Prophet. This light attracted the people and made them advance toward him. By becoming a partner in the Prophetic light, the Imam, as its possessor, attained all sorts of transcendental distinctions such as "the tree of prophethood, and house of mercy; . . . the keys of wisdom, the essence of knowledge, and locus of apostleship, the frequenting place of angels and repositories of the secret of God."[26]

In addition to the Prophetic light, the Imam is heir to the Prophetic weapons *(al-silah)*, which resemble the ark *(al-tabut)* of the Israelites in that in whichever house the ark was found, prophethood was there, and in whichever house the weapons of the Prophet were found, the Imamate was there. The Prophet, according to the Twelvers, left his sword, coat of mail, and a short spear *('anaza)* to 'Ali. The possession of the Prophet's sword was considered to be the most crucial factor in deciding the Imamate and the obedience to the Imam. This sword was named *dhu al-fiqar* (endowed with piercing quality) and was believed to have been brought by Gabriel from the heavens. The coat of mail of the Prophet was known as *dhat al-fudul* (endowed with favors). This will be worn by the Qa'im when he rises and will fit him alone. The weapons of the Prophet and his knowledge remain in the same house; hence the Imam inherits both his knowledge and the weapons which he hands over to the succeeding Imam when he dies. This also means that the Imam does not die without seeing his successor, to whom he entrusts "the Books *(al-kutub)*, the knowledge *(al-'ilm)*, and the weapons *(al-silah)*."[27]

The books that the Imam inherits from his predecessor include (i) *al-Jami'a* (the Comprehensive), (ii) *Mushaf Fatima* (the Prophetic Scroll of Fatima), and (iii) *al-Jafr*.

(i) *al-Jami'a* is described as a scroll seventy cubits long, one cubit being as long as the Prophet's forearm. It was written by 'Ali under the dictation of the Prophet and contains instructions about the lawful and unlawful and all the judgments that people need to know down to the smallest detail.

(ii) *Mushaf Fatima* is described as a scroll three times the size of the Qur'an. The circumstances of its compilation are recounted by Ja'far al-Sadiq. He relates that when Fatima was in great sorrow after the death of her father, the Prophet, God sent an angel to console her. She heard the angel's voice speaking to her. She once complained to 'Ali about this strange event, and he asked her to inform him whenever she heard the voice. She did so and he wrote down everything the angel told her. The *Mushaf* does not say anything about what is lawful and what is unlawful but relates future events. Comparing it to the Qur'an, the Imam says it contains nothing which was in the Qur'an. It also contains the last will of Fatima and is accompanied by the weapons of the Prophet. Another feature of the *Mushaf* is that it contains the names of all those who would rule the world, together with their fathers' names.

(iii) *al-Jafr* is described as a pot made of cow-hide, in which was inscribed the knowledge of the Prophets, their legatees, and the learned persons among the Israelites. There were two kinds of *Jafr*: the White *(al-abyad) Jafr*, which contained the Psalms of David, the Torah of Moses, the Gospel of Jesus, the scrolls *(suhuf)* of Abraham, all knowledge of the lawful and unlawful, and the *Mushaf Fatima*; and the Red *(al-ahmar) Jafr*, which seems to have been a leather bag which contained the weapons which will be opened by the Master of the Sword *(sahib al-sayf)*, that is, the messianic Imam, in order to take revenge when he rises.

The heritage of the Imam thus guarantees the survival of religion in his person. He alone is endowed with the power of interpreting religion at different times, and "the earth cannot be set aright except by the Imam." As a result, a person who dies without acknowledging his Imam dies a death of ignorance. Besides belief in the Unity of God, the Prophecy, and the Day of Judgment, it is incumbent to believe in the Imamate of the rightful Imam, the Master of the Age *(sahib al-zaman)*, who is the infallible leader and the protector of the Religion. The soul cannot be saved without the knowledge of the Imam of the Age. Ja'far al-sadiq was once asked, "Is it obligatory for every person to acknowledge his Imam?" He replied, "God, the Exalted and Glorius, sent the

Prophet (peace be on him and his progeny) to all mankind and made him His Proof to all his creation on earth. Thus those who believe in God and the Prophet and follow him and confirm his prophethood, should also acknowledge the Imam among us."[28]

Since the believers cannot find a way to salvation without the Imam, God, who is just and has created the universe with a purpose, will not abandon the world to survive without such a leader. It is incongruous to support that God would impose duties of the Law *(taklif)* without proper guidance as to its performance. The duties are imposed in order to attain great reward, which is the goal of creation. But it is through the Prophet and the Imams that advancement toward reward comes about. Thus the Imam is responsible for elucidating the duties which constitute the religious injunctions. As a consequence, as long as the duties remain imposed, the Imam coexists with them to enable the believer, on whom the *taklif* is imposed *(mukallaf)*, to perform the religious duties. This means there is an Imam in every age, be he manifest *(zahir)* or concealed *(mastur)*, who has the knowledge of the lawful and the unlawful in Islam, and who calls people to the way of God. But there are times when the world can be without a manifest Imam; this is so when God is enraged at the people, who are unable to see the Imam in occultation, although he sees them.[29] Occultation *(ghayba)* is a state chosen by God for the Imam who is in danger of being slain by his enemies. Thus the twelfth Imam, Muhammad b. al-Hasan al-'Askari, went into occultation in the year 260/873−74 and will continue to live in this state for as long as God deems it necessary; then He will command him to reappear and take control of the world in order to restore justice and equity. During this period of concealment the Imam is not completely cut off from his followers but has spokesmen, in the person of learned jurists, who can act on his behalf and guide the Shi'ites in their religious matters.

The doctrine of the Imamate as maintained by the Imamites clearly shows its development from a simple exaggerated belief in the messianic role of the savior Imam to a dogma of the religious leadership with all its theological complexities. This development was an inevitable outcome of the Shi'ite experiments at establishing an 'Alid caliphate, which met with formidable resistance and which resulted in political failures. Ironically, these failures laid the ground for the religious development in Shi'ism, ensuring its existence under numerous vicissitudes in the face of Sunnite repression.

Historical Background to the Disappearance of the Twelfth
Imam

The twelfth Imam, Muhammad al-Mahdi (b. 256/869), disappeared in
Samarra, the new 'Abbasid capital some sixty miles north of Baghdad, in
the year 260/873–74. Consequently, the period preceding the occultation of the moderate Shi'i Imamate coincides with Samarra period of the
'Abbasid caliphate (836–92). Although a gradual decline of the power of
the caliphs and the rise of warlords ruling through their troops had set
in earlier, the Samarra period witnessed the total breakdown of caliphal
authority. This period marked the crucial days of Imamite history, since
the question of the Imamate had once again given rise to dissent within
the Shi'ite group. In all probability, it was the confused situation caused
by the 'Abbasid atrocities committed against the descendants of al-Sadiq
on one hand, and the confusion over the succession of the Imam Hasan
al-'Askari (d. 260/873–74) in Samarra on the other, which became an
important factor contributing to the theory of the occult Imamate of the
Imami Shi'ism.

Medina had remained the intellectual as well as the religious center of
moderate Shi'ites following the leadership of al-Baqir and al-Sadiq,
known together as al-Sadiqayn—the two Sadiqs. The 'Abbasid caliphs
had, it appears, always looked upon the 'Alid leadership in Medina with
suspicion. The 'Alid Imams had not taken active part in politics following al-Husayn's martyrdom in Karbala'. From al-Sadiq's time there was a
definite shift in the role of the Imam, and a period of reorientation of
the belief in the Imamate toward pacific religious leadership seems to
have begun at this time. The 'Alid Imamate, more particularly the
Husaynid line, began to be conceived as a divinely designated authority
based on peculiar religious qualifications, not on a political claim. As
such, the Imamate could continue to perform its function through all
political circumstances, and the adherents of the Imam could live under
existing temporal authority, without demanding the overthrow of the
illegitimate caliphate, pending the return of the messianic Imam, al-
Qa'im al-Mahdi.

The 'Abbasids, who had come to power through a revolution based on
the manipulation of the Shi'i ideal of the messianic Imam, found it
expedient to cling to the latter ideal, even after adopting Sunnism, in
order to strengthen the caliph's authority. The 'Abbasids sought to give

their authority a thoroughly religious coloring, particularly in the face of the probable challenge posed by the 'Alid Imams in the religious center of Islam, Medina, as the true and rightful heirs to the divine knowledge. It is plausible to maintain that for this reason, beginning with Musa al-Kazim (d. 183/799–800), al-Sadiq's successor, who was accepted by a majority of the Shi'ites following much dispute over the latter's succession, all Imams were either imprisoned as politically suspect or kept under surveillance in the 'Abbasid capital, wherever it happened to be, away from Medina. Al-Kazim spent most of his time in Harun al-Rashid's prison in Baghdad, where he died in 800. His son 'Ali al-Rida, who had been appointed as heir to the caliphate by al-Ma'mun, also died in mysterious circumstances in Tus, Khurasan in 202/817–18.[30] His son Muhammad al-Jawad, who was only eight or nine when he succeeded his father, was kept under close watch in Baghdad under al-Ma'mun. Later on he was allowed to return to Medina by the latter, where he remained until summoned by al-Mu'tasim in A.D. 834. In the following year he died in Baghdad and was succeeded by his son 'Ali al-Hadi, who too was not more than nine years of age. But the long Imamate of al-Hadi and probably the absence of any other prominent 'Alid at this time rendered him more widely acknowledged as Imam than had been his father. This Imam and his successor Hasan al-'Askari, known together as al-'Askariyayn, the two 'Askaris, were contemporaries of the caliphs in Samarra and witnesses of the complete deterioration of the 'Abbasid caliphate.

The Breakdown of the 'Abbasid Caliphate and the last 'Alid Imams (836–74)

'Ali b. Muhammad al-Hadi, also known as al-Naqi (the immaculate) and al-'Askari (because of his confinement to al-'Askar [cantonment of the army], another name for Samarra), was a contemporary of the six caliphs subsequent to al-Ma'mun's death in A.D. 833: al-Mu'tasim (d. 227/841–42), al-Wathiq (d. 232/846–47), al-Mutawakkil (d. 247/861–62), al-Muntasir (d. 248/862–63), al-Musta'in (d. 252/866–67), and al-Mu'tazz (d. 255/868–69). With the accession of al-Mutawakkil (232/846–47) the 'Abbasid caliphate entered on a new phase of its religious policy which brought about significant changes in the outlook of the Shi'ites. The 'Alid Imams had realized the futility of any attempt to

[25]

establish an 'Alid caliphate, especially after what had befallen 'Ali al-Rida in 817. Consequently, they seem to have encouraged the idea of the *future* establishment of the legitimate caliphate, after the return of the Imam in concealment. The idea of the hidden Imam functioning through his personal representatives, his *safir*, or his agent *(wakil)*, must be attributed to the Samarra period when the Imams were for the greater part of their lives kept under surveillance or incarcerated. As a matter of fact, in the *Ithbat al-Wasiyya,* which is alleged to have been written by the historian al-Mas'udi (d. 344/955—56), there is an account indicating a gradual development of the custom which had arisen for the Imams in Samarra to communicate with their followers through an agent. The account describes the way al-Hadi at Samarra used rarely to mix with the people and was not in contact with anyone except his immediate family and associates. When al-'Askari, his son, succeeded him, most of the time he used to talk with the Shi'ites behind a curtain so that they should prepare themselves for the occultation of the Imam after him.[31]

The Samarra period also dealt a great blow to the alleged 'Abbasid ideal of establishing the Islamic form of government to create an all powerful caliphate congruent with the Shi'i political theory, which was carried to its logical conclusion by al-Ma'mun, who even adopted the title *"imam"* to signify his theocratic authority.[32] The caliphs after al-Mutawakkil's death in 861 had been reduced to mere puppets of their army generals, who were often able to appoint and depose them at will. The long Imamate of al-Hadi (A.D. 835—68) had witnessed the dwindling authority of the caliphs as well as their fruitless attempt to reassert their supremacy. As a consequence, he and his successor al-'Askari, assisted by their intimate associates, who were in closer contact with the Shi'ites in Baghdad and other cities in the empire and who were also able to penetrate the governmental level, probably realized that the rise of the 'Alid Imam as the Qa'im and Mahdi in the immediate future "would not and could not change the course of events, and would only risk further disturbance and disunity in the Muslim community for no real gain."[33] The aspirations of the Shi'i masses for a more just future under the legitimate rule of the Shi'i Imam, at this time, proved incapable of arousing an effective opposition to the growing political turmoil of Samarra period. Hence, the postponement of the revolution expected to be led by the Qa'im to transform the contemporary political scene became inevitable, and the expression "near future" became a truly religious term for "unspecified" future time. The historical events of the past hundred years had taught at least the moderate Shi'ite leaders, and gradually their adherents, that the overthrow of the existing circumstances to create an ideal Islamic society would have to wait until the messianic restorer of faith could rise under divine guidance. God alone could guarantee the Mahdi's success.

Under al-Mutawakkil the policy of reconciliation with the 'Alids was at once abandoned. The demolition of al-Husayn's mausoleum at Karbala' in 236/851 was meant to convey both to the Imams and to their adherents, who held the visit to this mausoleum as a highly meritorious act, the extent to which al-Mutawakkil was going to reverse al-Ma'mun's pro-'Alid line. In 243/857, as a result of certain false charges that were made against al-Hadi by his governor in Medina, al-Mutawakkil ordered one of his officers to invite the Imam from Medina to Samarra. The charges made against this Imam were no different from those made against his predecessors, namely, that the Imam was collecting forces to rebel against the government, or that he had a large following who could overthrow the Caliph's rule on his orders. Al-Hadi complied with the order received in the form of an invitation and came to Samarra, where he was kept under surveillance. Presumably, the government did not suspect serious danger from him, because he was allowed to receive visits from his Shi'a and to move freely within the city limits. Yet al-Mutawakkil tried by all possible means to trouble and dishonor him. Many times he called the Imam to his presence with the aim of killing him or disgracing him and often had his house searched. But by this time, it appears that the 'Alid Imam had been recognized as a pious and learned authority and killing him might have aroused further anti-government sentiment among the Shi'ites. Ibn Khallikan relates an account of one of these searches in which al-Mutawakkil, having received information that al-Hadi had weapons and anti-government letters from his Shi'a concealed in his house, sent some soldiers of the Turkish guard to break in on him at night. The soldiers found the Imam alone in his room praying and reciting verses from the Qur'an, with his face in the direction of Mecca. They arrested him in that state and brought him before the caliph who was engaged in drinking wine. Al-Mutawakkil received him courteously and was informed about the falseness of the report concerning weapons and letters. The caliph then offered the Imam a drink from his cup, on which the Imam asked to be excused from drinking. The Caliph then insisted that he should sing some lines, but the Imam chose to recite some verses, the moral theme of which made the Caliph and his courtiers weep. He finally asked the Imam if he were in debt and the Imam replied he was indebted to the amount of four thousand dinars. This al-Mutawakkil paid and sent him home.[34]

The report by Ibn Khallikan shows the pressures to which the Imams were subjected in Samarra. Al-Mutawakkil's ill-treatment of the 'Alids was not confined to Iraq. Even the 'Alids in the Hijaz lived in a pitiful condition, as described by Abu al-Faraj al-Isfahani in his book entitled *Maqatil al-Talibiyyin* (The Circumstances of the Murders of the Descendants of 'Ali b. Abi Talib). The latter work is an extremely important and indispensable source for the study of various Shi'i revolts under the Caliphate. In his account of those 'Alids who were killed under al-Mutawakkil, he prefaces his list with comments on the latter's enmity toward the family of the Prophet and states that their womenfolk in the Hijaz had no veils with which to cover themselves. Many of them had only one veil, which they shared with each other at the time of daily prayers.[35]

The murder of al-Mutawakkil in 247/861−62 was followed by the short reign of al-Muntasir, who repealed the anti-'Alid measures of his father. His successor, al-Musta'in (862−66), also followed in his footsteps, and the Imam al-Hadi continued to live with more freedom during these years. It must have been during these years that he appointed 'Uthman al-'Amri (d. 260 or 261/274−75) as his personal representative and agent in Baghdad. 'Uthman was also subsequently confirmed in this office by al-'Askari and the last Imam. The function of guiding and organizing the central structure of the moderate Shi'ites was gradually being handed over to the agents, who continued the strategy of the Imams as far as political quietism was concerned, and who were to a large measure responsible for the later elaboration and crystallization of the doctrine of the Hidden Imam as apprehended by the Imamites. During the caliphate of al-Mu'tazz (866−69), the 'Abbasid suspicion of the Imam's activities once again put restraints on al-Hadi's freedom of movement until the Imam died, as the Shi'ites assert, of poison administered by the caliph in 254/868.

The Samarra period was drawing to a close after al-Mu'tazz, who was followed by al-Muhtadi (255/869) and al-Mu'tamid (256/870), the latter being the last caliph to reside in Samarra. After being proclaimed caliph in A.D. 870, al-Mu'tamid decided to return to Baghdad in A.D. 892, in order to control the political ambitions of his brother and regent al-Muwaffaq, who had become the real master in the old capital. The empire had been disintegrating and the central government was unable to establish effective control of the provinces due, on one hand, to the rise of Zanj in southern Iraq, and on the other, to the encroachments of provincial leaders in the Persian provinces and in Egypt and Syria. Al-Hadi's successor al-'Askari (b. 232/845) was contemporary to this period of general anarchy and confusion in the 'Abbasid caliphate. Under these circumstances, and given the anti-'Alid attitude of al-Mu'tamid, al-'Askari was denied even the minimum freedom of receiving visitors after his father's death in A.D. 868, when he became the Imam at the age of twenty-two.

During the seven years of his Imamate, al-'Askari lived in hiding and dissimulation *(taqiyya)*. The Shi'ites had from the early period, it seems, developed dissimulation of their true beliefs in order to protect themselves against the Sunni majorities or Sunnite governments. The Imams had encouraged the employment of *taqiyya* and had even declared it to be an incumbent act on their followers, so as not to press for the establishment of the 'Alid rule and the overthrow of the illegitimate caliphate. Most probably through the application of this principle the moderate Shi'ites avoided expressing their true opinions publicly in such a way as to cause misunderstanding and enmity and remained eager to identify themselves socially with the Muslim community. For some time al-'Askari was also imprisoned and then set free. On the whole, al-Mu'tamid had adopted the inflexible and intolerant attitude of his father al-Mutawakkil toward the 'Alid Imam, who had to assume the arduous responsibilities of the Shi'i leadership under more strict surveillance than that of his father.

The institution of the *wikala* (deputyship) was the consequence of the inability of the Imam to receive his followers or communicate with them in person. Thus al-'Askari appointed his personal representative for the purpose of guiding the Shi'ites in religious matters and receiving the fifth *(al-khums)*, a tax intended for pious purposes and particularly for descendants of the Prophet, to be administered by the Imam. The meetings between the agents, who mostly resided in the merchant quarter of Baghdad, al-Karkh, a stronghold of the Shi'ites, and the Imams were kept to the minimum and were highly secret. In order to avoid drawing the attention of the government officials, the agents adopted trades. Hence, for instance, 'Uthman al-'Amri plied the trade of a seller of cooking fat and had consequently acquired the nickname of al-Samman. This was the way to hide his true identity as the agent of the Imam. The Shi'ites used to bring their dues to the Imam to 'Uthman, who would hide them in cooking fat containers and take them to al-'Askari under dissimulation and with apprehension.[36]

Following the death of al-'Askari in A.D. 874, the central organization of the deputyship was the only way through which the Imams at Samarra could foresee the continuation of their teachings, and even more so when the question of the successor of al-'Askari was in dispute. The institution of the deputyship also prepared the ground for the Shi'i jurists to assume the religious leadership of the Imami Shi'ites in the absence of the twelfth Imam, who became the Hidden Imam and was declared to be the promised Islamic messiah. The deputyship also ensured the survival of the Imamite religion in the vicissitudes of the following centuries. Indeed, the 'Abbasid atrocities and their inflexible attitude toward the 'Alid Imams had taught the moderate Shi'ites to prepare for a period when direct communication with the Imam would become impossible. The successor of al-'Askari was declared to be in occultation, and the guardianship of the nascent Imamite community was left in the hands of these agents, who were believed to have been directly appointed by al-'Askari and his successor, Muhammad al-Mahdi, and who maintained that community's religious as well as its social structure. The study of the Imamite messianic phenomenon is actually the study of the elaboration, systematization, and crystallization of the Imamite doctrine of the Mahdi Imam by his directly appointed agents, followed by his indirect spokesmen among his adherents, the Shi'ite jurists *(mujtahidun)*.

The Social and Political Stratification of the Early Imamite Doctors: al-Kulayni to Tusi

The primary sources studied in this work are the product of the intellectual endeavors of Imamite jurists who lived as a minority in the Sunnite circles and who were faced with challenges from within and without. These challenges initiated an intellectual movement within the Imamite school towards the sifting, systematizing, and arranging of the *hadith* reports which played a crucial role in the evolution of the doctrine of the

Hidden Imam. We can safely assume that the issues discussed by these doctors were real issues which engaged the intellectual as well as social energies of the scholars, who not only refrained from advancing certain fixed ideas about the twelfth Imam dogmatically, but remained open to adjust and amend their views in the light of the cirticisms leveled against them by their adversaries and even their own fellow Imamites. The period posed challenges not only to Shi'ite doctors; even the Sunnite scholars were engaged in a similar intellectual activity in vindication of their doctrinal position. However, a substantial difference between the two intellectual movements greatly accelerated the systematizing of their respective creeds. While Sunnism was afforded protection and encouragement as the official creed by almost all major ruling houses and possessed, therefore, the necessary means and possibilities to adjust itself under the impact of ever-changing social and political realities of the age, Shi'ism, on the contrary, was compelled to lead a *taqiyya*-oriented existence in the Sunni milieu. As a result, the Shi'i intellectual activities were diverted towards a predominantly theoretical consideration of their doctrines. Even then, such formulations had to wait for a relatively safe and favorable period, which came about with the establishment of the Shi'i Buyid dynasty (320–447/932–1055). Nevertheless, the establishment of the Buyids and their patronage of Shi'ism was not directly responsible for the intellectual prominence and the refinement of the Imamite doctrines during this period. In all probability, the discontinuation of the Imamate and the developments of the preceding period of the deputyship *(wikala)* of the prominent Shi'i personages between A.D. 873–941 (the period of the Short Occultation) were the main factors that contributed to the remarkable literary output of the Imamite doctors. The period of the deputyship will be dealt with in detail in Chapter III. At this juncture, it is relevant to review in brief the authors of our primary sources and correlate the trend in their ideas with their social and political environment.

It is important to note that most of the Shi'i doctors lived and produced their works in Baghdad between the fourth/tenth and fifth/eleventh centuries. Much earlier than that, from the time of Ja'far al-Sadiq on, most of the Shi'i Imams had spent some time in Baghdad, and two of them, the seventh and the ninth Imams, had died there. The latter were buried in the cemetery of the Quraysh in the Karkh quarter of Baghdad. The Karkh was inhabited by the old Shi'i families of Kufa and was a center of trade as well as of Shi'ism. Shi'ite scholars from the early days of the foundation of Baghdad had either frequented or sojourned in this capital of the 'Abbasid caliphate. In the course of many years they had established a relationship with the caliphal court and the vizierate, more particularly during the Barmakid ascendancy.[37] The Shi'ites of Baghdad figured prominently as the old mercantile class of Iraq, who were also partly responsible for the protection and patronage of a number of Shi'i scholars. These scholars included early figures like Hisham b. al-Hakam, 'Ali b. Yaqtin and his progeny, the Nawbakhtis, the Quluyas, the Iskafis, and the Sharifs Ahmad, al-Radi and al-Murtada, among the later eminent families, who had all lived in Baghdad. Some of these families formed the upper bourgeoisie and supported many discontent non-Arab *mawalis* of Kufa in the reactionary milieu of Baghdad. As years passed the presence and concentration of the Shi'ites in that region became more felt, until between the third/ninth and fifth/ eleventh centuries it became a most influential center under the leadership of the Imamite doctors. As will be seen in Chapter III, the deputies of the twelfth Imam during the Short Occultation, who had become the focus of the Imamites, lived in Baghdad, and their graves are located in the old section of the city where even today the Shi'ites are mostly concentrated.

Among the Islamic sciences, *hadith* attracted numerous Muslim scholars to Baghdad. *Hadith* is a transmitted science, and those who compile these reports were required to "hear" them and obtain permission *(ijaza)* to record them on the authority of the transmitters. Hence, Baghdad, as a frequenting place of Muslim scholars from all over the Islamic empire, was an ideal place for perusal of *hadith* as well as for personal contact with the author. This also facilitated the process of collecting and compiling the *hadith*. In Baghdad, more than any other center of Islamic learning, the science of *hadith* was cultivated during this epoch. It can be plausibly maintained that all the transmitted sciences, especially *hadith*, including the *hadith* of the *ahl al-bayt*, were collected by the traditionists of Baghdad.

Apart from the transmitters of *hadith* in the eighth and ninth centuries who were native to Baghdad, there were many like al-Kulayni, the renowned Imamite traditionist of Rayy, who migrated there. Al-Kulayni was the leader of the Imamites during the last years of his life in Rayy, and in Qumm. The latter city was at that time an important center of

Shi'ite learning, whence the majority of al-Kulayni's transmitters were derived. Al-Kulayni migrated to Baghdad, it seems, to spread the Imamite *hadith*, which he had compiled under the title of *al-Kafi*. This compilation took some twenty years to finish and was probably completed in Rayy. But *al-Kafi* was spread and taught by the transmitters like al-Nu'mani (the author of the earliest book of *Ghayba*) and others to whom al-Kulayni had read his work. Al-Kulayni's contribution was similar to the work produced by al-Bukhari (d. 256/870) in the Sunnite circles, which greatly assisted subsequent scholars towards sifting, systematizing, and classifying the *hadith* literature and using it for the doctrinal formulations of their respective creeds.

The Shi'i *hadith* from the early days of the caliphate had two important centers—Kufa and Qumm—but Baghdad was the convergence point for these two branches. Moreover, Kufa was always in touch with Medina, while Qumm remained in close contact with Kufa. Thus among the associates of the Imam Ja'far al-Sadiq one finds several Kufis and also some Qummis.[38] Qumm remained an important center for other eastern cities of Khurasan, like Nishapur and Samarqand, where there existed centers of Shi'ite learning. Through the study of the transmitters of *hadith* in the compilations of the Qumm school, such as that of Ibn Babuya, one can detect a third school of Imamite *hadith*, namely, the Khurasan school, fairly independent of Qumm. However, the traditionists of all these centers used to meet from time to time and transmit their *hadith* in Baghdad, where these transmitters frequently settled permanently to benefit from the great teachers of the Imamite—transmitted sciences through the practice of hearing them discourse. Baghdad also became a depository of Shi'i works. Thus, for instance, Abu al-Hasan al-Qazwini al-Qadi first brought parts of the book written by one Muhammad b. Mas'ud al-'Ayyashi, a Shi'i scholar of Samarqand, to Baghdad in 356/966.[39] As a result of the flow of Shi'i books, several Shi'i libraries had come into being. Such was the library of Abu Nasr Sabur b. Ardashir (d. 416/1025–26), the Shi'i vizier of Baha' al-Dawla, the Buyid, which was established by this vizier in the Karkh in 381/991–92 and which had some ten thousand volumes. This library existed until it was set on fire by Tughril Beg, the Seljuq, in 450/1058–59.[40] As is evident from Ibn al-Nadim's *al-Fihrist*, Shi'i books were in wide circulation in Baghdad in those days, and most of these works had been seen by Ibn al-Nadim himself. He recorded their names and contents meticulously, and this information was also used by Tusi to compose his *al-Fihrist*.

The position and influence of the Shi'ites in Baghdad was in part due to the prestige of persons like 'Ali b. Yaqtin (d. 182/798−99). He held a high position in the 'Abbasid caliphate and had an intimate relationship with the caliphs. The Barmakids were also sympathetic to the Shi'ites. Hisham b. al-Hakam was attached to Yahya b. Khalid of the Barmak family. He acted as his deputy, appearing and speaking at the court. Historical sources of this period indicate that many Shi'ites held prominent posts in the 'Abbasid imperial government. The extent to which the Shi'ite forces had prevailed in government affairs is evident from the events surrounding the fates of Mansur al-Hallaj and al-Shalmaghani, who had both posed serious threats to the Imamite doctrine of the Hidden Imam and who had both been executed following their denouncing by the Imamite theologians. The occultation of the twelfth Imam presumably exacerbated the difficulties of the nascent Imamite community, which was in need of a firmly established doctrinal basis to react to the dissidence caused by extremists and undisciplined Imamites like al-Hallaj and al-Shalmaghani, about whom we shall say more in Chapter III. But the prominence of the Shi'i families in the cultural life of Baghdad and the prudent leadership provided by their eminent scholars, in all likelihood, helped the necessary adjustment required with the discontinuance of the Imamate which forms the cardinal point in the Twelver Shi'i ideology. With the rise of the Buyid dynasty, the Shi'i spiritual as well as physical forces which had remained less noticeable and also less ambitious began to be felt overtly.

The Buyids ruled Baghdad for over a century (A.D. 945−1055) and reduced the 'Abbasid caliphs to mere puppets. The Buyid *amirs* had very close ties with the Imamite jurists. Their patronage of the Shi'i doctors gave Shi'ism a new impuetus after the *ghayba*. In general, the Buyid period witnessed open vindication of Shi'i doctrines, and discussions with all the opponents of the Imamites were arranged under state sponsorship. The prominent Imamite theologian al-Mufid was visited by the Amir 'Adud al-Dawla in Baghdad; Ibn Babuya and his brother Husayn b. 'Ali b. Babuya had a good relationship with al-Sahib b. 'Abbad, the learned Buyid vizier in Rayy. Debates and discussions were held between Ibn Babuya and al-Sahib in the presence of Rukn al-Dawla, the son of Adud al-Dawla. Shi'i power had increased so much in Baghdad that the

Karkh region became the scene of conflict and riots between the Shi'ites and the Hanbalites.[41] The atmosphere of Baghdad became full of strife, and not only Shi'ites and Hanbalites were drawn into the conflict; strife occurred even among the different Sunnite Schools.[42]

The 'Abbasid caliphs used to appoint a *naqib* (chieftain) for the Shi'ites, who, it appears, was the *naqib* of the Talibids, the descendants of 'Ali. The renowned family of the Sharifs acted as the *naqib* of the Talibids as well as the leaders of all the Shi'ites in Baghdad. These Sharifs included al-Sharif Ahmad and his two famous sons, al-Sharif al-Radi and al-Sharif al-Murtada, and al-Radi's son al-Sharif Abu Ahmad 'Adnan. This was the most influential Shi'i family of the period, among whom al-Murtada was also disappointed as the leader of the *hajj* by the caliph.

The Culmination of Imamite Learning in the Fifth/Eleventh Century

The movement of epitomizing and systematizing all that was needed for the survival of the Imamite "school" was completed by al-Kulayni in the first quarter of the fourth/tenth century. The subsequent phase of the dogmatic promulgation of the Imamite creed was carried on by the Imamite scholars in Baghdad. The most brilliant among these scholars, and the one with whom should be recognized the culmination of this process, was Tusi, rightly known as Shaykh al-Ta'ifa (the leader of the Imamite community).

Tusi was born apparently in Tus, as his name would suggest, in the year 285/995–96. He entered Baghdad in the year 408/1018, when he was twenty-three years of age. Immediately upon his arrival there he attached himself to the Imamite theologian and jurist al-Mufid. Of all the teachers with whom Tusi had studied, al-Mufid figures most prominently in his writings. Tusi, in his biography of al-Mufid, after listing the latter's works, says: "I heard him discourse on all these books. Some of them were read to him; others I read to him several times while he listened."[43] Al-Mufid was the highest authority in theology and jurisprudence, and according to Ibn al-Nadim's testimony, the leadership of the Imamite *mutakallimum* culminated in him. Al-Khatib al-Baghdadi, the young contemporary of al-Mufid, relates the extent to which al-Mufid's discourses had caused concern among the Sunnites of Baghdad so that when he died, "God relieved people from the spread of deception by him."[44] All biographers are unanimous in according al-Mufid keen insight, quick wit, and the ability to overcome the adversaries of the Imamite school in argument.

In the five years that Tusi spent with al-Mufid, until the latter's death in 413/1022–23, he mastered all the Shi'i sciences that had developed in the milieu of Baghdad, where al-Mufid held discussions with al-Qadi 'Abd al-Jabbar, the Mu'tazllite, and al-Baqillani, the leading Ash'ari. Al-Mufid was a prolific author: some two hundred works have been attributed to him. Most of these were written in refutation of the works of al-Jahiz, al-Sahib b. 'Abbad, 'Ali b. 'Isa al-Rumani, al-Jubba'i, and other prominent theologians, and in vindication of the Imamite doctrines, especially the question of the Imamate. Still other works were written in modification or correction or even refutation of some works written by his Shi'i masters, such as Ibn al-Junayd, Ibn Babuya, and others. Tusi's *Tahdhib al-ahkam*, which is a commentary on al-Mufid's *al-Muqni'a*, a text on jurisprudence, demonstrates Tusi's intellectual development under al-Mufid and the prominence of the Imamites in Baghdad under the Buyids.

Tusi, as a foreign student in Baghdad, was supported financially by al-Sharif al-Murtada. The latter had fixed a scholarship of twelve dinars per month for him. This also gives us an idea of how young students in Baghdad were supported with basic financial aid provided by some prominent teachers, not unlike the modern day arrangement at most Shi'i centers of learning. After having studied under al-Mufid and a few other Imamites, whose names have been recorded in the sources, Tusi had little to learn from al-Sharif al-Murtada as far as the science of transmission and the *hadith* were concerned. This fact is alluded to in his biographical note on al-Murtada where he says: "He (al-Murtada) reported *(hadith)* on the authority of Tala'kibri and al-Husayn b. 'Ali b. Babuya and others among our teachers."[45] It is probably for this reason that in his important collections of *hadith* Tusi does not record anything on the authority of al-Murtada, who himself had remained al-Mufid's student. In his other works on *hadith* besides *al-Tahdhib* and *al-Istibsar* (two of the four canonical compilations of the Shi'i *hadith*) the latter's name occurs rarely. In his *Fihrist* Tusi mentions al-Murtada among those from whom he had heard al-Kulayni's *al-Kafi*.[46] But as for *kalam*, Qur'anic exegesis, lexicography and other literary sciences in general, *fiqh* and principles of the Law, Tusi greatly benefited from al-Murtada, whose opinions are readily recorded. Sometimes even a critique of them is offered in the works written on these subjects. Tusi composed some of his most important works during this period. It is important to note that most of these works were written at the request of some prominent scholars. This in itself indicates first, the pre−eminence of Tusi as a great teacher and author, and second, his ability to react to the serious need for theological exposition of the Imamite creed. In fact, after al-Murtada's death in 436/1044−45, Tusi occupied his place as the leader of the Imamites until 448/1056−57 and was held in great esteem and respect throughout his successful career as Imamite jurist and theologian. He was highly regarded by the Buyids as well as by the 'Abbasid caliphs. His moderate stance on theological issues and his meticulous recording of the opinions of different schools of Law in his work on comparative Law entitled *al-Khilaf fi al-fiqh*, and in his exegesis of the Qur'an, *al-Tibyan*, have prompted some Sunni biographers to affiliate him with the Shafi'i school. However, it can be suggested that the conciliatory nature of Tusi's approach in his writings, in which he took the contemporary reactionary atmosphere of Baghdad into consideration, reflects his efforts to minimize religious strife between various schools in order to encourage a more peaceful co-existence. This factor is also evident in his ardent support of the notion of *taqiyya*, whose sole purpose was to encourage and even require the Shi'ites to accommodate themselves to the Sunni majorities with whom they had to exist. Employing *taqiyya* was needed to minimize enmity that could originate from public statements about the Imamite doctrines that would be subject to misunderstanding. Presumably, this *taqiyya*-motivated life gave rise to Tusi's alleged affiliation with the Shafi'i legal system. Moreover, this *taqiyya* orientation also prevented Shi'ism from becoming generalized among the great body of newly converted Muslims in Iraq, especially following the defeat of the Buyids by the Sunni Seljuqs. This latter change in power brought about the migration of the Shi'i doctors like Tusi to Najaf, near Kufa.

In the last years of his long stay of some forty years in Baghdad, Tusi witnessed much power struggle and political turmoil. Some of the events were directly related to the Shi'ites and their leaders, whose success depended on specific conditions in that sector of the population affected socially or economically by the Sunnite majority. During the Sunni-Shi'i riots of Baghdad in the year 449/1057−58, Tusi's library was set on fire and his house pillaged in the Karkh quarter.[47] According to another report, his books were burned several times in public, and Tusi, out of fear, used to hide in Baghdad.[48] It is significant to note that his writings, in general, do not reflect any disturbances caused by these events and their effect on his mind. Thus even his polemical writings show much sobriety and restraint on his part. It is only in the beginning of his book on the subject of the *ghayba* of the twelfth Imam, which was written in the year 448/1056–57, close to the events in the Karkh and his migration to Najaf, that he writes in explaining his reason for this undertaking, apparently following a request by al-Mufid, "I made a decision to carry out his order and obey his command although time is running short and the mind is unkempt. Times are full of impediment and events are harsh. . . ."[49] This statement indicates the restraint under which Tusi had been placed. Yet his work on *ghayba* is the best written on the subject so far and has remained unsurpassed in subsequent centuries.

With Tusi's migration, the center of the Shi'ite learning in Baghdad disintegrated, and many Imamite doctors remained in hiding or also migrated to places away from the capital. The Seljuqs patronized Sunnism, and Baghdad once again became the abode of Sunni learning, especially after the founding of the Nizamiyya school in 457/1064, which was officially inaugurated in 459/1066. By the time Tusi died in 460/1067, the Imamite school had been theologically promulgated; the legal foundation of the school was firmly laid and needed very little elaboration in the years to follow. The Imamite doctors after the fifth/eleventh century explicitly followed Tusi, whose writings had clearly assimilated not only the opinions of the Shi'i Imams, but also their major disciples up to the year 460/1067.

2. The Twelver Messianic Imam, al-Qa'im al-Mahdi

The Samarra period of the 'Alid Imams, who had by this time acquired official recognition as the leaders of the moderate Shi'ites, the Imamiyya,[1] marked the crucial epoch in the history of Twelver Shi'ism. The dissent within the Shi'ite groups over the question of succession was not a new thing at this time. The followers of Ja'far al-Sadiq, for example, had disagreed on the successor of this Imam when he died in 148/765–66. Al-Sadiq had several sons, and no fewer than four of them, Muhammad, 'Abd Allah, Musa, and Isma'il, were acknowledged by different factions as their Imam.

Hasan al-'Askari died in 260/873–74 in Samarra, apparently having left no son whom people had seen to take his place. Consequently, the most immediate and sensitive problem facing the Shi'ites at this time was to determine the successor of al-'Askari. The Imam, as the Shi'ite sources report, could not openly declare his successor since "the days were difficult [for the Imam and his followers] and the Caliph (al-Mu'tamid [256/869–70]) was relentlessly searching for him (his successor) and wanted to get his hands on him by any means he could. It was also at this time that the story was being circulated that the Shi'ites were awaiting his appearance [to redress their grievances]. This was the reason why [the Imam] did not reveal his son during his lifetime nor did the majority [of his followers] know him."[2] The crumbling of the 'Abbasid power, especially during the Samarra period, under the turmoil of internal revolutions, seemed to portend the long–awaited rise of the messianic Imam. The troubled events that took place during this time confirmed the story that a descendant of the Prophet would rise with a sword (al-qa'im bi'l-sayf) and wipe out injustice on earth. This promise was a consolation to the oppressed who were looking forward to the establishment of God's will on earth. The Shi'ites sought to identify the 'Abbasid caliphate as a symbol of injustice and oppression at this time. The messianic function of the expected Mahdi, retold in numerous apocalyptic traditions, was the main reason for the 'Abbasid endeavors to crush various 'Alid revolts during their caliphate. In describing various descendants of Abu Talib who were killed during the 'Abbasid period, the author of *Maqatil al Talibiyyin* makes a point to the fact that the person killed was proclaimed as al-Mahdi and that his followers expected him to rise against the ruling power.[3] In consequence, the Imam kept secret the child's birth, which, as affirmed by the Twelvers, occurred in the year 255/868–69, and allowed only his trusted close associates to know of the existence of his successor.

A large number of the moderate Shi'ites had upheld the belief that al-'Askari himself was the twelfth and the last Imam with whom God, in his wrath, had discontinued the Imamate. They had adopted the Fathiyya thesis, which maintained that after al-Sadiq, his son 'Abd-Allah (by the surname of *aftah al-ra's* [broad-headed] or *aftah al-rijlayn* [broad-footed]) was the Imam, before Musa al-Kazim was recognized as the Imam. The Fathites admitted the Imamate of two brothers if the elder brother has no son, as happened in the case of Musa al-Kazim, who followed his elder brother 'Abd Allah, who had no heir. The Imamate of the two brothers, according to the Twelvers, was unlawful after al-Hasan and al-Husayn, the two sons of 'Ali.[4] Thus both 'Abd Allah and Kazim could not be acknowledged as the Imam. 'Abd Allah's Imamate was questionable on the other ground, too, namely, that an Imam could not die without seeing his successor.[5] The latter belief seems to have been well-formulated by this time, since the Shi'ites who upheld the Imamate of al-'Askari made this a deciding factor by basing their contentions on it, and disagreement on this issue led to the formation of various subsects of the Imamiyya themselves. Al-Nawbakhti has enumerated as many as fourteen of these factions,[6] while al-Shahrastani limits them to eleven.[7] Al-Mas'udi counts as many as twenty.[8] A careful study of these different factions reveals the general confusion created by the death of al-'Askari over the question of the Imamate and how some individuals took advantage of the situation by supporting one view or another and gathering followers around themselves.

The period which gave rise to all this confusion began with the caliphate of al-Mu'tamid and continued up to the time of al-Muqtadir

(295–320/908–32). During this time the agents *(wukala')* of the dead Imam persisted in upholding the belief that there existed an infant son of al-'Askari in occultation, who would rise when God would command him to do so. The upholders of this belief were under attack from all sides and met with severe opposition. The 'Abbasids were particularly concerned about the messianic successor of al-'Askari in concealment. Al-Mu'tamid, for this reason, ordered the house of the Imam to be investigated, and all the rooms were locked after being searched. Efforts were made to find out if the Imam had left a son, and midwives were appointed in the harem of the Imam in order to detect any pregnancy. One of the slave girls was suspected to be pregnant and isolated in a room in a special house where she was kept under surveillance.[9] On one occasion, al-'Askari's wife (Sayqal,[10] the mother of the infant Imam) was imprisoned on refusing to reveal the whereabouts of her son. According to some Shi'ite sources, in order to stop the officers from searching for the child, she denied that she had borne a son to al-'Askari during the latter's lifetime, and claimed that she was pregnant. Al-Mu'tamid ordered her to be held in his harem under close watch. This situation continued until the year 263/877, when the caliphate was caught in the political disturbances caused by the Zanj and by the provincial leaders in Iran, Egypt, and Syria. Consequently, Sayqal was forgotten, and she escaped from the hands of caliphal authorities.[11]

The 'Abbasids had also supported Ja'far, a brother of al-'Askari and claimant to the office of the Imamate, in order to create a dispute within the Imam's family. Our sources describe Ja'far as a worldly and pleasure-loving man, who in order to become the Imam had used various repressive means in the presence of al-Mu'tamid, and more than once had tried to slander those who upheld the Imamate of the infant son of al-'Askari in concealment. He was also responsible for the imprisonment of Sayqal, because through his instigation the caliph had asked her to reveal the whereabouts of her son. On the matter of the inheritance of al-'Askari, a conflict arose between Hadith, the mother of al-'Askari, and Ja'far, who sought to get his hands on the inheritance. The issue was finally solved seven years later when the caliph ruled the inheritance to be divided between Hadith and Ja'far.[12] After Sayqal's escape from al-Mu'tamid's palace, a great enmity arose between the respective supporters of Sayqal and Ja'far. Caliphal authorities understandably took the side of Ja'far, while Sayqal was supported by the group who upheld the Imamate of her infant son. The dispute flared up to an uncontrollable degree, and Sayqal was given protection by a member of the powerful Shi'ite family of the Nawbakht.[13]

Thus al-'Askari's death, the undecided question of his succession, and the claim to the Imamate made by Ja'far (his brother supported by the 'Abbasids) left the Imamiyya in conflict and divided them into several subsects. The study of these subdivisions will give some idea of the difficulties faced by the agents, the personal representatives of the last Imams in Samarra, in giving the ultimate recognition to succession to al-'Askari in accordance with Twelver belief and providing the astute leadership demanded of them in those unfavorable circumstances.

The Subdivisions of the Imamiyya after al-'Askari

Compared with other Books on Sects (*al-milal*) which discuss these subdivisions of the followers of al-'Askari in 260/873–74, Hasan b. Musa al-Nawbakhti (d. at the beginning of the fourth/tenth century) has preserved the earliest and most detailed information on the positions taken by different groups. Al-Nawbakhti was one of the leading Twelver theologians in the first half of the tenth century, a period which coincides with the early years of the disappearance of the last Imam, the period which lasted up to the year 329/940–41.[14] He has devoted even more space to the important question of the stand taken by the Twelvers. This account of the Imamiyya and their Imams during this period has rendered al-Nawbakhti's *Firaq al-Shi'a* (The Sects of the Shi'a) one of the primary sources for the investigation of the development of the Twelver idea of the messianic Imam al-Mahdi.

Al-Nawbakhti summarizes the central doctrines of each of the fourteen factions after the Imamate of al-'Askari as follows.

Faction (1)

This group believed that Hasan al-'Askari had not died, was alive in occultation, and was al-Qa'im. They argued that an Imam could not die before seeing his offspring who would succeed him, and that there was always the Hujja[15] of God on earth. Since al-'Askari left no successor, they said, it was right to hold that he was not dead and had disappeared in accordance with the report which states that al-Qa'im will have two forms of *ghayba* (occultation) and that this was his first occultation. He

[42]

will return as al-Qa'im[16] and al-Mahdi after his first occultation, and he will be known, after which he will disappear for the second occultation.[17]

It is relevant to note that similar ideas were held about the seventh Twelver Imam, Musa al-Kazim (d. 183/797−800), by the group known as al-Waqifiyya (i.e. those who stopped with the Imamate of al-Kazim). This name will be discussed more fully below with its antithesis the Qat'iyya (i.e. those who maintained the continuance of the Imamate in the person of al-Kazim's son, 'Ali al-Rida [d. 202/817−18]) Whereas in the case of al-Kazim, it was certain that he left a son to succeed him, in the case of al-'Askari, the fact of his having left a son was in dispute. Consequently, in the case of al-Kazim one does not hear of the argument about the necessity for an Imam to see his successor before his own death; rather the emphasis lies on his being al-Qa'im, the messianic Imam, indicating the end of the line of the Imams, the reverse of what was to be stressed in the case of al-'Askari. When al-'Askari died, the controversial issue of the continuance of the Imamate was once again raised, and divided the Imamiyya into the Waqifiyya (i.e. those who stopped with the Imamate of al 'Askari) and the Qat'iyya (i.e. those who held his son al-Qa'im to have succeeded al-'Askari). The argument this time was focused on whether an Imam could die without making a clear designation of his successor. The doctrinal dispute of the Waqifiyya and Qat'iyya also suggests the impatience of the Shi'ites at the delay in the rise of the Qa'im, the former stressing early messianic action, with the latter postponing the revolution to a future time.

Faction (2)

This faction maintained that al-'Aksari had died and would live again after his death as al-Qa'im al-Mahdi, because, they contended, al-Qa'im was a person who rose after death and in consequence had no successor. If al-'Askari had an offspring, then his death would be proved and his return (*ruju'*) would not be necessary, since the Imamate would automatically pass on to his son. As al-'Askari did not appoint anybody as the executor of his will, nor did he leave a will and testament, there is no doubt about his being al-Qa'im, since he died without leaving a successor. But, they added, he was living after death and was hidden because of fear, since like other Shi'ite sects they too believed in the necessity of the *hujja* on earth, whether alive, manifest (*zahir*), or hidden. They quoted 'Ali as having said, "O God, You will not leave the earth devoid of

[43]

a *hujja* of Your own for mankind, whether manifest or hidden, lest Your proofs and Your signs are invalidated." For this reason al-'Askari continued to live after his death.[18]

Faction (3)

This group believed that the Imamate passed on to Ja'far, the brother of al-'Askari, after the latter's death, by his own designation *(nass)*, and that Ja'far had accepted it. They contended that the Imamate was Ja'far's right from the beginning and so it returned to him. When they were told that the Imam was not on good terms with his brother Ja'far at all during his lifetime, and even after his death when Ja'far disputed over the inheritance of the Imam (so how could he designate him as his successor?), they replied that this was only outwardly, and that otherwise Ja'far was obedient to the Imam al-'Askari and followed him. This group argued for the Imamate of Ja'far, resorting to the argument of the Fathiyya, who asserted that Musa al-Kazim became Imam in accordance with the testament of his brother 'Abd Allah, not of his father Ja'far al-Sadiq. They acknowledged the Imamate of 'Abd Allah b. Ja'far, after having rejected it previously, and rendered its acknowledgment incumbent on themselves in order to rectify their beliefs. Their leader and the one who initiated them to this doctrine was a well known Fathite theologian of Kufa by the name of 'Ali b. al-Tahi al-Khazzaz. He strengthened the Imamate of Ja'far and invited people to accept him. In this task he was assisted by the sister of al-Faris b. Hatim b. Mahuya al-Qazwini,[19] who was among the extremist Shi'ites, having been cursed by al-'Askari's father 'Ali al-Hadi.[20] The Fathiyya were numerous, especially in Kufa where they had the leadership of theologians like al-Khazzaz and others among the Banu al-Zubayr and Banu al-Fadal.[21]

Faction (4)

This group maintained that Ja'far was the Imam after al-'Askari not by the designation of his brothers (Muhammad, who had died during his father's lifetime, or al-'Askari, who died without leaving an offspring), but by that of his father al-Hadi. Al-'Askari's claim to the Imamate was rendered invalid because the Imam does not die without appointing a successor or without having a son to succeed him. Al-'Askari did not designate anyone nor did he leave a "visible, well-known, and manifest" descendant behind; hence he was not an Imam, they said. Secondly, the

Imamate could not be vested in two brothers; in support of this, they quoted the tradition on the authority of the sixth Imam, al-Sadiq: "There will be no Imamate vested in two brothers after al-Hasan and al-Husayn."[22] Another addition to the Imamate which should be traced back to Musa al-Kazim is the clause about the Imamate vested in two brothers. The claim of al-Kazim's brother to the Imamate was also discredited on the same ground, that after al-Hasan and al-Husayn there would be no Imamate vested in two brothers. The Imamate of al-Hasan and al-Husayn appears to have been a reserved privilege of the immediate sons of 'Ali and Fatima, who naturally hold a special status in Shi'i piety.[23]

Faction (5)

This faction reverted to the opinion which acknowledged the Imamate of Muhammad b. 'Ali, who had predeceased his father 'Ali al-Hadi (254/868). They discredited the claims of both al-'Askari and his brother Ja'far to the Imamate on the grounds that there was no clear designation of their father al-Hadi, nor did any testamentary document exist to establish their right to the Imamate. Of these two claimants, they further asserted, Ja'far did not deserve to put forward his claim at all since his unrighteous and wicked character was well known. As for al-'Askari, they said, he died without leaving a successor, which was a proof that Muhammad, his elder brother, was the Imam who was rightfully appointed by his father. Al-'Askari left no offspring, contrary to what was required in an Imam, namely, that he should have a successor. Therefore, Muhammad b. 'Ali al-Hadi was the Imam, as he, in every respect, was endowed with those virtues requisite in an Imam and was the Qa'im al-Mahdi.[24]

In discussing the qualities required in an Imam, this group stressed two points: righteousness *('adl)* and posterity *('aqb)*. By the first point Ja'far's claim was discredited, and it was emphasized that immoral behavior in an Imam, even under *taqiyya* (dissimulation), was reprehensible. It appears that Ja'far's supporters might have tried to shield his moral shortcomings by reverting to the principle of dissimulation under which true beliefs were concealed. The second point, namely the need for posterity, was used to discredit al-'Askari's claim to the Imamate in much the same fashion as the Fathiyya and later Waqifiyya had done. The Fathiyya had used the argument to support the Imamate of al'As-

[45]

kari's brother, while the Waqifiyya had, in the absence of al-'Askari's successor, declared the latter to be the messianic Qa'im al-Mahdi.

Faction (6)

This group maintained that al-'Askari left a child by the name of Muhammad, who was born two years before his father died. All those who asserted that al-'Askari had no son to succeed him were thus wrong. It was impossible to believe that al-'Askari left no posterity, especially after his Imamate had been acknowledged by all. On the contrary, his son was the Qa'im. They further asserted that he was in concealment, being afraid of Ja'far and other enemies, and that this was his first occultation. He was the Qa'im known in his father's time and designated by him.[25]

This faction is the Qat'iyya, who, according to al-Mufid's account of the subdivisions, maintained that the Imam after al-'Askari was his son 'Ali and not Muhammad. With this difference in name, the rest of the details concerning *ghayba*, adds al-Mufid, "is word to word the same as maintained by the Qat'iyya."[26] There is also the difference in the year in which the Qa'im was believed to have been born by the official Twelver rendering. In all probability, this confusion over the year of birth continued up to a much later period, just as the true name of the Qa'im was kept as a secret not to be divulged.[27]

Faction (7)

They asserted that a son was born to al-'Askari eight months after his death, and that those who held that a son was born to him in his lifetime were liars and vain because if he had been born, the Imam would not have concealed him, since no one before him had been concealed. But the Imam died without knowing that he had a son. It was improper, they said, to insist stubbornly on this matter and to contradict that which was "evident, logical and commonplace." Moreover, this was known to the government and to other people, and for this reason his inheritance was not divided until the government became certain that the supposition about the Imam having a child was vain. Thus the matter became secret. Eight months after al-'Askari's death a child was born who was named Muhammad, in accordance with the instruction left in his father's will and testament, and who became hidden.[28]

[46]

Faction (8)

This group maintained that al-'Askari had no son at all, because they had sought for him and could not find him. If people insisted in maintaining that al-'Askari had a son in hiding, then such a claim could be put forward for any dead person who left no offspring, such as the Prophet and 'Abd Allah b. Ja'far al-Sadiq. Or a claim could be put forward for more than one son, for instance, in the case of 'Ali al-Rida. But there were reports which affirmed that the Prophet had no son and al-Rida had only one son, Muhammad al-Jawad, just as we have a report that al-'Askari had no son. The fact was, they held, that one of al-'Askari's slave girls was pregnant and would give birth to a male child who would become the Imam. It was impossible that the Imam would die without a descendant, because that would invalidate his Imamate and the earth would remain without a *hujja*. Those who upheld the Imamate of the infant son of the Imam, born during the latter's lifetime, contended that it was impossible and against custom that the pregnancy of a woman should last more than nine months, while many years had passed and the slave girl had not given birth to a child. On the other hand, it was not against reason and quite possible that a person might have a son in concealment and unknown to others. Thus the latter stance was more plausible than theirs.[29]

Faction (9)

This group held the doctrine of the end of the Imamate after al-'Askari. This was possible both rationally and customarily. They argued that since prophethood *(nubuwwa)* could end with Muhammad, so could the Imamate after al-'Askari. They did not doubt the fact of his being dead and, according to them, it was not contrary to common sense that the Imamate could terminate with him. To vindicate their position they cited a tradition on the authority of the two Sadiqs, the fifth and the sixth Imams, to the effect that the earth cannot be void of a *hujja* except when God is enraged by the sins of mankind, at which time He takes away His *hujja* for as long as He deems necessary. This doctrine, they maintained, did not invalidate the Imamate; on the contrary, other events corroborate this belief. For instance, it was known that there was neither a prophet nor a *wasi* (legatee) between Muhammad and Jesus, which proved that there was an interval of time when there was neither a prophet nor the executor of his will. This period was similar to the intermission *(fatra)*[30] when there was no hujja. Imam al-Sadiq called *fatra* that time during which there was neither a prophet nor an Imam. The earth would remain like this until God would send the Qa'im from among the descendants of Muhammad when required, to restore the true faith as he had done before.[31]

The position of this faction was in a sense between the Waqifite and the Qat'ite positions. While they confirmed the death of al-'Askari, they did not maintain his messianism, as the Waqifites would have done; nor did they believe in the Imamate and messianism of his son, as the Qat'ites would have held. Indirectly they had falsified the claim of those who maintained that al-'Askari had left a son. The doctrine of *fatra*, which was used by the Muslim theologians to designate the interval between the two prophets, was extended to include the intermission between the two Imams, since the prophets and Imams together formed the category of the *hujja*. Consequently al-Qa'im could be "sent" anytime when required from among the descendants of the Prophet.

Faction (10)

The group was known as Nafisiyya because when Muhammad b. 'Ali al-Hadi, who was the Imam through his father's will and testament, died, he designated his brother Ja'far as his successor, entrusting his will to the hands of a young slave of his father by the name of Nafis who was in his attendance. Nafis was also entrusted with the books, the secret knowledge, the weapons, and all that was needed by the *umma*, to be handed over to his brother and successor Ja'far, after his father, 'Ali al-Hadi's death. The latter alone knew about this arrangement. But when Muhammad b. 'Ali died during his father's lifetime, those who favored his brother al-'Askari for the Imamate came to know about this and became jealous of Nafis. Nafis, being afraid of their intentions and fearing that the Imamate might be invalidated, called Ja'far and handed over what his master had entrusted to him. Consequently, Ja'far became the Imam and not al-'Askari, who, according to their assertion, was not designated by his father. The Nafisiyya held Ja'far to be al-Qa'im and the best of mankind after the Prophet.[32]

This faction adds one more group of the Imamiyya to those who maintained the Imamate of Ja'far, the Fathiyya. By accepting the Imamate of Muhammad his brother, who had predeceased his father, from whom the symbols of the Imamate (namely, the books and the weapons) passed on to Ja'far, they had upheld the general Fathite thesis concerning the Imamate of two brothers after al-Hasan and al-Husayn, especially when the elder brother had left no posterity.

Faction (11)

This group maintained that the Imam was al-'Askari, but they were not sure who succeeded him, his son or his brothers, although they accepted the doctrine that there could not be a time when the earth could be void of the *hujja* of God. So they put off any statement until the matter became clear for them.[33]

Faction (12)

This is the stand taken by the Imamiyya. Al-Nawbakhti's exposition can be taken as the earliest formulation of the Twelver doctrine of the messianic Imam and thus will be fully quoted here:

The twelfth group, who are the Imamites, maintain that the case is not as all other factions having upheld. There is a *hujja* for God on earth among the descendants of al-Hasan b. 'Ali [al-'Askari]. God's decree is in effect and he is the legatee *(wasi)* of his father in accordance with the method laid down by the previous traditions. Now, there can be no Imamate vested in two brothers, following one another, after al-Hasan and al-Husayn. Therefore, Imamate is not possible except among the descendants of al-Hasan b. 'Ali [al-'Askari]. This will be the case until the creation comes to an end with God's ordinance. Even if there remained two persons on earth, one of them would be the *hujja*; if one of them died then the remaining one would be *hujja*, as long as the commands and interdictions of God remained among the people.

On the other hand, it is not permissible that there be an Imamate among the descendants of the one whose Imamate has not been proved. It is not incumbent on the people to acknowledge as *hujja* the one who died in his father's lifetime, or the descendants of such a person. If this were permissible then the claims of the adherents of Isma'il b. Ja'far [al-Sadiq] and their school would have been sound; and, on the same grounds, the claims of Muhammad b. Ja'far [al-Sadiq] to the Imamate would have established the latter's Imamate; and, as a result, the Imamate of these persons would have been true after Ja'far b. Muhammad's death. All that has been mentioned above is attested by the reports of the two Sadiqs [the fifth and sixth Imams] which no one in the community disputes or doubts the authenticity of, and which have come from authentic sources, strength of links and perfect chains of transmission. The earth cannot be void of a *hujja*. If the Imamate

[49]

disappeared from the world even for a moment, the earth and its inhabitants would perish. It is not proper to uphold the doctrines of any of these factions.

We have conformed to the past tradition and have affirmed the Imamate [of al-Hasan al-'Askari], and accept that he is dead. We concede that he had a successor, who is his own son and the Imam after him until he appears and proclaims his authority, as his ancestors had done before him. God allowed this to happen because the authority belongs to Him and He can do all that He wills and He can command as He wishes concerning his appearance and his concealment. It is just as Amir al-Mu'minin ['Ali] said: "O God, You will not leave the earth devoid of a *hujja* of Your own for mankind, be they manifest and well known, or hidden and protected, lest Your *hujja* and Your signs are annulled." This then is what we have been commanded to do and we have received reliable reports on this subject from the past Imams. It is improper for the slaves [of God] to discuss divine affairs and pass judgement without having knowledge and to seek out that which has been concealed from them.

It is also unlawful to mention his [al-'Askari's successor's] name[34] or ask his whereabouts until such time as God decides. This is so because if he (peace be on him) is protected, fearful, and in concealment, it is by God's protection. It is not up to us to seek for reasons for what God does. Rather, discussion and seeking the answer to this question is prohibited; thus, it is neither lawful nor proper. The reason is that if what is concealed were revealed and made known to us then his and our blood would be shed. Therefore, on this concealment and the silence about it, depends the safety and preservation of our lives. It is also improper for us or for any other believer to choose an Imam by depending on personal opinion and arbitrary choice. Indeed, it is God who chooses him for us. He manifests him, when He wills, because He knows better how to manage the affairs of His creatures, to the best of their interest; and the Imam also knows himself and his time better than we do. Abu 'Abd Allah al-Sadiq, whose state is evident, his place well known, his genealogy undeniable, his birth non-concealable, and his renown spread among the élite as well as the masses, said: "God's curse be on the one who gives me a name." A man among his followers once met him. The Imam turned away from him. It is also reported that another of his Shi'a met him in a street and avoided the Imam, neglecting to salute him. The Imam thanked him for that and praised him, saying to him: "But so and so met me and greeted me, and did not do a good thing (thereby)," and for that reason he reproached him and accused him of a detestable act. Similarly, there are reports about Abu Ibrahim Musa b. Ja'far [al-Kazim] who, too, had prohibited (his followers) to name him in this manner. Abu al-Hasan al-Rida used to say: "If I knew what people want from me, I would destroy myself in my own eyes, in performing that which does not consolidate my religion, such as a game of pigeons, cock-fighting and other similar things (. . . I would have destroyed myself in doing things like playing a game of pigeons, cock-fighting and other similar things, which do not strengthen my religion)." [If this was the situation in the days of the past Imams] how can it be permissible [to name the Imam] in our own days, under severe surveillance and the tyranny of the ruler, and his lack of respect for the rights of persons like them (the Imams), especially after what [al-Hasan al-'Askari] had to go through at the hands of Salih b. Wasif[35] in his prison? How can then one name the Imam about whom the information is not disclosed, nor is his name revealed and whose birth has been kept secret? Many reports have been mentioned that al-Qa'im's birth will be kept secret from the people, and his renown will be brief; he will be unknown; and he will not rise before he becomes manifest and is acknowledged as an Imam, the son of an Imam, and a legatee, son of a legatee; he will not be taken as an example before he rises. In spite of this, it is inevitable that his and his father's reliable associates, even if in small number, would have been informed about his authority. [The Imamate] will not be disrupted from the succession of al-Hasan [al-'Askari] as long as the decree of God, the Exalted and Glorious, will continue. It will neither derive by the relationship of brother, nor is this permissible. The indication of the Imam and the will and testament from the Imam, or for that matter, from any other person, are not valid until they have been attested by at least two witnesses. This is the path of the Imamate, the clear and definite path, on which the Imami Shi'a, the one whose Shi'ism is sound [continues].[36]

The above exposition of the Imamiyya brings out clearly the efforts of their leaders to disprove the contentions of all other groups mentioned above and to maintain that al-'Askari had died leaving his son as his successor, whose name was unlawful to mention and who was the Imam after his father until such time that, by the permission of God, his status became clear and his position became manifest for the people. The main group who, it appears, had posed a severe challenge to the Imamiyya was the Fathiyya, whose doctrines have been refuted above by al-Nawbakhti more thoroughly. The second group, against whom a set of contentions regarding the concealment of the Qa'im and prohibition to name him is directed, is the Waqifiyya, who maintained the completion of the Imamate with al-'Askari and upheld his messianism. There also occurs mild refutation of the Isma'ili as well as the Zaydi positions. The latter had emphasized the Imamate of the descendant of the Prophet who would rise with the sword in support of his claim. Actually, at the time when *Firaq al-shi'a* was composed (completed around A.D. 900) both the Isma'ilis and the Zaydites had gained some political victories,

[51]

and not until the next generation of the Imamite scholars following the Nawbakhtis do we find a severe attack on the Zaydi and Isma'ili positions by the Imamiyya. The importance of the above exposition cannot be overstated, particularly in light of the doctrinal elaboration through which the idea of the messianic Imam in Twelver Shi'ism has passed. It is significant to note that in the above exposition apparently very little attention has been paid to emphasizing the Mahdiism of the successor of al-'Askari. In fact, the word *mahdi* has not been used as a title of the last Imam, while the usual messianic title *al-Qa'im* appears in a casual way. Probably the early theologians of this school were more concerned with establishing the Imamate of al-'Askari's successor, which was, obviously, more crucial to the survival of the Twelver Shi'ism, than the question of his being the Promised Mahdi.

Faction (13)

This group maintained doctrines very similar to those held by the Fathiyya before them. They asserted that al-'Askari, who had succeeded his father as the Imam, had died and Ja'far, his brother, had succeeded him as the Imam, just as had happened in the case of Musa al-Kazim, who became the Imam after 'Abd Allah, his brother, according to the tradition which states that the eldest among the sons of the Imam succeeds his father.[37] They accepted the tradition that two brothers cannot become Imams in succession, after al-Hasan and al-Husayn, but they added that this could be true only when the preceeding Imam had a son to succeed him; otherwise it was inevitable that the Imamate should pass to his brother.

Another significant development in the Imamate doctrine in this group was the acceptance of a tradition which says that only an Imam washes the dead body of the previous Imam. This, they contended, happened in the case of Musa al-Kazim, who washed his father's body by the order of 'Abd Allah, who was then the Imam, while al-Kazim was *al-imam al-samit* (the silent Imam).[38] These are the pure *(al-khalis)* Fathiyya, who consider it lawful for a brother to succeed to the Imamate, if the eldest of the sons of the Imam has no son to succeed him; therefore, the Imamate of Ja'far is valid.[39]

Al-Nawbakhti's account ends with the above-mentioned thirteen factions, although he says in the beginning that there were fourteen subsects after the death of al-'Askari. But al-Mufid, who, in his account of the subdivisions of the Imamiyya, had followed al-Nawbakhti's exposition, has the Faction (13) of the latter as fourteenth in his *Fusul*. Al-Mufid's thirteenth faction maintained as follows:

This group held that the Imam after al-'Askari was his son Muhammad, and he was the awaited *(al-muntazar)* Imam; however, he had died and will become alive and rise with the sword in order to fill the world with equity and justice as it is filled with oppression and wickedness.[40]

It is possible that this sect may have been dropped in the original manuscript of al-Nawbakhti's *Firaq*.[41] However, al-Mufid's account completes al-Nawbakhti's fourteen factions of the Imamiyya. But in those days when the question of the Imamate had become a central issue among the Shi'ites and when any individual with sufficient skill and daring could express opinions on the Imamate, taking advantage of the confusion, and gather around himself a considerable following, gradually the number of the subdivisions of the Imamiyya had also increased beyond fourteen. Thus, in al-Mas'udi's time, these factions were numbered at twenty, and al-Mas'udi had mentioned the beliefs of all these in his two lost works *al-Maqalat fi usul al-diyanat* (Opinions Concerning the Fundamentals of Religious Positions) and *Sirr al-hayat* (The Secret of Life).[42] The dispute over the succession to al-'Askari, it seems, had continued for a much longer period, and if one bears in mind the tendency among the heresiographers to classify sects under particular individuals and their views,[43] then the number of the subdivisions after al-'Askari may well have exceeded the figure of twenty mentioned by al-Mas'udi.

Thus, for instance, al-Shahrastani mentions another sect which, being uncertain as regards the facts, believed that one of the members of the Prophet's family was the Imam, *al-rida min al Muhammad*. This phrase, as the history of sectarian development in Islam shows, was used by some groups if the person for whom the allegiance was being sought was not known, especially among the descendants of 'Ali. Thus al-Hallaj, for example, initially called upon people in behalf of somebody from *al Muhammad* without naming the person.[44] Al-Shahrastani calls this group *al-waqifa*, meaning "uncertain," "hesitant," or "in doubt"; this group among the subdivisions of the Imamiyya remained "in doubt" until God manifested His *hujja* by revealing his face without any miracle to support his claim. Rather, his only miracle would be the following he would have of a people who would obey him without any controversy and without any need to vindicate his Imamate.[45]

In Ibn Hazm's classification of the Shi'ite sects the doctrinal position taken by the Imamite faction, the twelfth faction according to al-Nawbakhti, regarding the twelfth Imam is under the Qitti'iyya or Qat'iyya group of the Imamiyya.[46] To comprehend the use of the word Qat'iyya it is necessary to contrast it with its antithesis, al-Waqifiyya. Outwardly, the problem seemed to surround the reality of the preceding Imam's death and the question of his successor, which obviously depended on it. But, inwardly, it was the struggle between the group which preached direct political action and the one which had adopted political quietism. It is not without reason that one finds the Imamiyya Qat'iyya, the upholders of political quietism, refuting the messianism of the Waqifiyya, who threatened the survival of the former by their chiliasm. The Waqifiyya, those in doubt or uncertain, maintained that the Imamate after Ja'far al-Sadiq (d. 148/765–66) passed on to his son Musa al-Kazim (d. 183/799–800) and that the latter was alive and would continue to live until he ruled the East and West of the earth, filling it with justice and equity. On the other hand, the Qat'iyya were those who definitely affirmed that the death of Musa al-Kazim was real and the Imamate was transferred to his son 'Ali al-Rida (d. 202/817–18), in opposition to the messianism of the Waqifiyya.[47] Al-Shahrastani uses the term *al-waqifiyya* also for the Isma'iliyya, who believed in the return of Isma'il, al-Kazim's brother.[48]

Gradually, these two titles were also used to designate those who believed that the Imamate ended with al-'Askari, who would return as the Mahdi, and those who believed in the reality of al-'Askari's death and transferred the Imamate to his son al-Mahdi, the twelfth Imam, the Waqifiyya and the Qat'iyya, respectively. The followers of this latter belief constitute the bulk of the Shi'ites, and with the spread of the doctrine of the twelve Imams and the extinction of the other Shi'ite factions, the term "Qat'iyya" was used only for those who believed in al-'Askari's death and transferred the Imamate to the Mahdi, as a synonym for a word of a definitely later origin, Ithna'ashariyya—the Twelvers.[49]

The dissension within the Imamiyya concerning the Imamate after al-'Askari seems to have reached such an extent that, even among the prominent theologians of this group, at least in the early days following the year 260/873–74, there was no agreement on the number of the Imams. Al-Mas'udi, for example, in explaining the term *al-qitti'iyya* says: "These are the ones who have affirmed the Imamate of the twelve Imams, and this restriction of the number of Imams is in accordance with what Sulaym b. Qays al-Hilali has mentioned in his book, which has been reported by Aban b. Abi 'Ayyash, that the Prophet, peace be on him, told Amir al-Mu'minin 'Ali b. Abi Talib, 'You and your twelve descendants are the rightful Imams.' " Al-Mas'udi adds, "And no one else besides Sulaym b. Qays has reported this tradition."[50]

Sulaym b. Qays heads the list of the Shi'ite jurists with the name of the books they composed in Ibn al-Nadim's *Fihrist*. According to him, Sulaym was among the companions of the Amir al-Mu'minin, and according to the Imamite sources, the companion of the Imams, 'Ali, al-Hasan, al-Husayn, and 'Ali b. al-Husayn.[51] Perhaps Ibn al-Nadim refers to 'Ali b. al-Husayn as Amir al-Mu'minin and not 'Ali, who alone bears this title in the Shi'ite writings. 'Ali b. al-Husayn lived at the time when al-Hajjaj, the governor of Iraq (694–714), was trying to crush the Shi'ite opposition to the Umayyad caliphate, to which Ibn al-Nadim makes reference in regard to Sulaym, who, as a fugitive from al-Hajjaj, took refuge with Aban b. Abi 'Ayyash. Aban was another close companion of 'Ali b. al-Husayn, who gave shelter to Sulaym.

"When death drew near to him he said to Aban, 'I am indebted to you and now death is present with me. Oh, son of my brother, by order of the Apostle of Allah, may Allah bless him and give him peace, it is thus (as described. in my book).' Then he gave him a book which was the well-known book of Sulaym b. Qays al-Hilali, from which Aban b. Abi 'Ayyash quoted, but which was not quoted by anyone else."[52]

The tradition quoted by al-Mas'udi might well have been in this book of Sulaym, which was in Aban's possession. The tradition quoted above added to the problems already existing concerning the Imamate after al-'Askari, because it makes the number of the Imams thirteen. Relying on this tradition, Hibat Allah b. Muhammad al-Katib, who was among the prominent Shi'ites during this period and a contemporary of Abu al-Qasim al-Husayn b. Ruh (d. 326/920–21), the third agent of the twelfth Imam, had included Zayd b. 'Ali b. al-Husayn, the founder of the Zaydiyya, also among the Imamite Imams.[53]

Besides the thesis about thirteen Imams growing out of Sulaym's *hadith*, still another view was maintained by a person no less prominent than Abu Sahl al-Nawbakhti, a great scholar of the Imamiyya who died around A.D. 923. Abu Sahl had spent some fifty years of his life in the critical years of the Imamite faith after al-'Askari's death, during the deputyship of the second agent Abu Ja'far Muhammad b. 'Uthman al-'Amri (d. 304 or 305/917—18), when he was considered the head of the Imamiyya sect. Having spent most of his time in acquiring religious sciences, more particularly, *kalam* and the art of disputation, he vindicated the Imamite doctrine of the Hidden Imam and systematized it according to the principles of the Imamite faith. Abu Sahl, according to Ibn al-Nadim, had an idea about the Qa'im of the family of Muhammad "which no one had before him. This was what he used to say: 'I tell you that the [rightful] Imam was Muhammad ibn al-Hasan and that, although he died in concealment, there has arisen in the cause during the concealment his son, and so it will be with his son's issue, until God consummates his dominion by causing him to appear.' "[54]

It is hard to accept the attribution of such a belief to the leader of the Imamiyya when all the sources are in agreement about the efforts of Abu Sahl in vindicating the *ghayba* (occultation) of the twelfth Imam and his contribution towards the systematization of the Qat'iyya doctrines, in collaboration with the second and third agents of the twelfth Imam, namely, Abu Ja'far al-'Amri and Abu al-Qasim al-Nawbakhti. But he was not alone in upholding such views, which appear to be the outcome of the delay in the reappearance of the Qa'im. Besides Abu Sahl others maintained that the twelfth Imam had died and would rise again at the end of time, a view which al-Nawbakhti does not have in his exposition of the factions. Only Tusi and before him al-Mufid mention this faction. Furthermore, Tusi refers to still another group which believed in thirteen Imams, assuming that the twelfth had died and the Imamate had passed on to his son.[55] Even al-Hallaj, according to Louis Massignon, used to say that the twelfth Imam had died, there would be no manifest Imam, and the Day of Judgment was at hand.[56]

The Differences between al-Nawbakhti and al-Mufid on the Imamiyya Faction

The treatment of the Imamite faction by these two eminent Twelver scholars shows the development of the Imamite position concerning the twelfth Imam, during the first century after al-'Askari's death. Al-Nawbakhti, who died at the beginning of the fourth/tenth century, although apologetic, has preserved the earliest and the original Imamite viewpoint about the concealment of the last Imam. His exposition of the

Qat'iyya faction does not include any elaboration on the nature of the occultation, nor does it outline the two forms of occultation. Furthermore, the contentions in the exposition support the continuation of the Imamate and the succession of al-'Askari's son to the Imamate, without emphasis on the messianism of the last Imam. After a century or so, when al-Mufid (d. 413/1022) composed his exposition, the question of the succession to al-'Askari was more or less settled among the Imamiyya. Thus al-Mufid dwelt upon other questions, such as the occultation and the Mahdiism of the twelfth Imam, and elaborated on al-Nawbakhti's exposition, which he had before him when writing the section on the subdivisions of the Shi'ites after al-'Askari. The century between the two theologians was the period during which the Imamite religion was consolidated by the astute and prudent leadership of the *wukala'*—agents of the Imam; the scholastic efforts of a number of highly esteemed jurists like al-Kulayni (d. 329/940−41), al-Nu'mani (d. 360/970−71), Ibn Babuya (d. 381/991−92), and others; and the protection and patronage of the Imamite form of Shi'ism afforded by the Shi'i Imami dynasty of the Buyids in Baghdad. The period was marked by the Shi'i ascendancy due to the Fatimid and Buyid pre-eminence in some of the central lands of the Islamic empire. It was a Shi'i century during which Twelver Shi'ism laid its firmest religious and intellectual foundation and produced a number of creative religious writings which became the standard version of the creed for future generations. The Buyids encouraged Shi'i learning, and with their patronage of the theologians of various schools they helped foster a Mu'tazilite form of *kalam* among the Shi'ites. One of the leading *mutakallimun* of this century was al-Mufid, whose intellectual endeavors were able to utilize the developments of the preceding period to give a definitive form to the Imamite doctrines. Al-Mufid's treatment of al-Nawbakhti's exposition concerning the Qat'iyya faction evidently supports the view that al-Mufid was concerned with emphasizing that part of the doctrine which had become important during his time. Consequently, his presentation could be taken as the fully developed and systematized view of the Imamate of the twelfth Imam. In order to see the development of Twelver Shi'ism as far as the belief in the twelfth Imam goes, it is important to quote the full description of the Imamiyya Qat'iyya by al-Mufid, as was done above in the case of al-Nawbakhti's exposition of the twelfth faction. He says:

When Abu Muhammad al-Hasan b. 'Ali Muhammad died, his adherents were divided into fourteen factions, as reported by Abu Muhammad al-Hasan b. Musa [al-Nawbakhti], may God be pleased with him. The majority among them affirm the Imamate of his son al-Qa'im al-Muntazar (the awaited). They assert his birth and attest his designation by his father. They believe that he was someone named after the Prophet and he is the Mahdi of the people *(al-anam)*. They believe that he will have two forms of *ghayba*, one longer than the other. The first *ghayba* will be the shorter *(al-qusra)*, and during it the Imam will have the *nuwwab* (deputies) and the *sufara* (mediators). They relate on the authority of some of their leaders and their trustworthy sources that Abu al-Hasan had made him (his son) known to them, and shown them his person. They disagree, however, on his age after his father's death. Many of them hold he was five years old at the time when his father died in 260 (873–4), and al-Qa'im was born in 255 (868–69). Some of them maintain, however, that he was born in 252 (866–67), thus making his age eight years at the time of his father's death. [Still others] maintain that his father did not die until God had perfected al-Qa'im's intellect, taught him wisdom and unmistakable judgement *(fasl al-khitab)* and distinguished him from the rest of the people. This was so because he is the Seal of the *Hujjas (khatam al-hujaj)*, the legatee of the legatees, and the Qa'im of the Age. They justify such a possibility on rational grounds inasmuch as its impossibility is removed (i.e. if they can prove it is not impossible, it becomes possible), and his being taken under the power (of God). Further evidence lies in what God says in the story about Jesus: "And he shall speak to the people (when) in cradle," [3:45] and in the story of John: "We granted him authority while yet a child" [19:12]. They believe that *Sahib al-amr* (the Master of the Command) is living and has not died, nor will he die even if he remains for a thousand years, until he fills the world with equity and justice as it is filled with tyranny and injustice; and that at the time of his reappearance he will be young and strong in [the frame of] a man of some thirty years. They prove this with reference to his miracles and take these as some proofs and signs [of his existence].[57]

Besides elaborating on the occultation and the role of the twelfth Imam as the Mahdi of the *umma*, al-Mufid seems to be concerned with two other points in his exposition, which might have been occasioned by the criticism of the adversaries of the Imamiyya: first, the possibility for the Imam of becoming the *hujja* of God and possessing the authority while still in infancy; and second, the possiblity of possessing a long life in occultation. Al-Mufid vindicates the former point by quoting the verses about Jesus and John from the Qur'an; the latter point is subjectively defended by what the Mahdi will perform as the messianic Imam, and by what his adherents had witnessed in the form of miracles and signs during his youthful existence. The reference may be to the sections of Ibn Babuya's work on the twelfth Imam in which a list of those whose lives were prolonged by God *(mu'ammarun)* and those who had seen the Imam, always in the form of a youth, are related. These were the "reliable authorities," who had reported the existence and the miracles of the twelfth Imam. The absence of any criticism of the Fathiyya or Waqifiyya positions corroborates the point that by the time al-Mufid composed his work, the Qat'iyya had been consolidated into the only surviving sect of the Imamiyya, who had recognized the twelfth Imam as the *khatam al-hujaj* and the messianic Imam, the Mahdi, who would appear in the near future. Thus, in all probability, from this period onward the term *"imamiyya"* became the synonym for *"qat'iyya"* and *"ithna 'ashariyya."* It was also during the period immediately preceding al-Mufid that al-Qa'im came to be designated as *al-qa'im al-muntazar*—the Awaited Qa'im, the title so distinctly employed by al-Mufid. In the early Imamite sources several titles are used for the twelfth Imam, especially because of the prohibition concerning calling him by his name. Some of these titles have been preferred over others. The frequent occurrence of the following three titles in these sources (to be presently discussed separately) conveys the manner in which the Imamites had comprehended and aspired to see the role of their last Imam, al-Mahdi: al-Qa'im; Sahib al-amr; and al-Hujja. The first two titles have much more of a political emphasis than an eschatological one, which is evidently connoted in the title al-Mahdi; the third indicates essentially what an Imam, as an heir of the prophetic mission, should display. The apparent difference in the emphasis laid on certain doctrinal aspects of the Imamiyya faction in the two expositions of al-Nawbakhti and al-Mufid indicates the difference of stress laid on these more frequently used titles of the Imam. The study of the Imamite sources of this period leads one to assume that, at least at the beginning of the Imamite history, which should be placed at the end of the third/ninth and the beginning of the fourth/tenth century, the twelfth Imam's role was conceived more as al-Qa'im and Sahib al-amr, while no idea about his being al-Mahdi, the eschatological savior of Islam, had yet been accentuated. The title al-Mahdi, with its messianic implications, became a prominent feature of the Shi'ite creed in the period subsequent to the Short Occultation (A.D. 873–945). It is plausible to maintain that the prolonged occultation of the Imam was one of the factors which contributed toward interiorization of al-Mahdi's function, who became *al-*

mahdi al-muntazar (the Awaited) and *mahdi akhir al-zaman* (of the Last Days), especially when under the caliphate the establishment of truly Islamic justice in the foreseeable future had become impossible. This development in the Imamite doctrine of the Hidden Imam was the culmination of the moderating efforts of Ja'far al-Sadiq begun in the mid-eighth century. The hope in the future coming of the Imam thus became the moderating force among the Imamiyya, who postponed any political action pending the appearance of the Awaited Mahdi and Qa'im. The following consideration of the above-mentioned three titles will further corroborate the point that the Imamites during the period of al-Mufid were witnesses to the full development of the Twelver messianism—the politically quietist movement, which aimed at peaceful existence within the Muslim community at large, while retaining its peculiarity regarding the Imamate, especially the Imamate of the Hidden Hujja.

The Title al-Qa'im

The translation of this title rendered by Massignon, "chef redresseur des torts," seems to be very close to the idea connoted in the word itself, an idea which is put forward in the traditions mentioned by the Imamite theologians on the authority of the Imams. For instance, an associate of Ja'far al-Sadiq by the name of Abu Sa'id al-Khurasani asked the Imam, "Why is al-Qa'im known as al-Qa'im?" He answered, "Because he will rise *(qama)* after his death for an important task, and will rise by the command of God."[58] Another tradition, reported on the authority of the fifth Imam al-Baqir, states: "Our task resembles that of a person who is put to death by God for a hundred years and then is raised again."

The resurrection of al-Qa'im after death seems to have been accepted at first, as we saw in the second faction in al-Nawbakhti's exposition above, but was later refuted by the Imamite theologians like Tusi, who, in vindicating the Imamite doctrine of the ever present Imam, says that al-Qa'im is not the one who will rise after having died, for the simple reason that such an assumption would necessitate the earth's being void of a *hujja* until his return.[59] Much later, in the tenth/sixteenth century, Muhammad Baqir Majlisi defended the Imamite viewpoint by offering an interpretation of the above-mentioned traditions. He said that in such traditions, the death of al-Qa'im should be taken figuratively; in other words, al-Qa'im's memory would die in the minds of people to such an extent that they would assume that his bones had decomposed, and then, just as God did in the case of 'Uzayr (Ezra) the prophet, who was brought to life after a real death of a hundred years, al-Qa'im would also be made to reappear hundreds of years after his occultation *(ghayba)*. The other argument used by Majlisi in this vindication is a most common one among Muslim traditionists, namely, that such traditions being *wahid* (rare), cannot be taken as reliable, unless their authenticity is established. "Rare" traditions are not successively reported, and in order to attain the required certainty one has to make sure that the person relating it is thoroughly reliable.[60]

Al-Nu'mani, who is a primary source on the question of *al-ghayba,* lived during the Short Occultation of the twelfth Imam. He prefers the title al-Qa'im to al-Mahdi in his work on this subject; if he does mention both together, al-Qa'im al-Mahdi seems to be the order used by him. This further indicates that al-Qa'im is the main title and al-Mahdi the secondary one. In addition, there exists a tradition which clearly shows that the early Shi'ites must have been confused by the additional title al-Mahdi given to their Imam. It is reported on the authority of Abu Basir, a companion of Ja'far al-Sadiq, that when the Imam was asked, "Are al-Mahdi and al-Qa'im one (and the same person)?" the Imam said, "Yes." So he was asked, "Why was he named Mahdi?" He answered, "Because he guides to the secret things; and he is named Qa'im because he will rise after death. He will rise for an important task."[61] Another tradition with a similar theme is related by al-Nu'mani. The tradition reports that al-Baqir said:

> When al-Qa'im from the family of the Prophet will rise he will distribute equally among the people and will establish justice among his subjects. Thus those who obey him will obey God and those who defy him will defy God; but he will be called al-Mahdi, the one who will guide, since he will guide to the secret matters *(amr al-khafi)* and will bring out the Torah and other books of God from a cave in Antioch and will rule the people of the Torah according to the Torah, and the people of the Gospel according to the Gospel, and the people of the Qur'an according to the Qur'an.[62]

This tradition throws further light on the importance of the title *al-Qa'im* in the early Imamite sources, where the use of *al-Mahdi* seems to be only an attribute. All Imams are Qa'im. The fifth Imam al-Baqir was once asked about al-Qa'im. He struck the sixth Imam al-Sadiq with his hand and declared, "By God, he is the Qa'im of the family of the Prophet." When al-Baqir passed away (113/731–32), the one who had heard this from the deceased Imam came to the sixth Imam and informed him about it. The Imam said, "The report by Jabir (i.e. the transmitter) is right." Then he added, "Maybe you believe that not every Imam is al-Qa'im, following the Imam who was before him."[63]

The Function of al-Qa'im

In some traditions the function of the last Qa'im is given special emphasis, as the following report shows: All Imams are Qa'im, ". . . but that Qa'im who is going to inherit the Prophet's banner, Joseph's shirt, Moses' rod and Solomon's ring is the one who will once again unfold the banner of the Prophet which was last spread by 'Ali at the Battle of the Camel."[64]

Majlisi, in his commentary on *al-Kafi* of al-Kulayni, explains that al-Qa'im in the Shi'i tradition refers to the person who will rise with the sword, and this applies to all the Imams, especially the last Imam. But sometimes the Imams used to explain it as *al-qa'im bi'l-imama,* meaning the one who carries out the duty of the Imamate, when it applied to all Imams; and *al-qa'im bi'l-jihad,* the one who carries out the duty of the holy war, when it applied to the last Imam. This was the way, adds Majlisi, the Imams had chosen not to disappoint those Shi'ites who were expecting their Imams to rise against the unbearable existing circumstances. So the twelfth Imam is al-Qa'im whose rise against injustice is awaited.[65] Hence he will be the one who will take revenge on those who killed al-Husayn in Karbala' and even their descendants, adds another report. A tradition is related on the authority of al-Sadiq, who said that when al-Husayn was killed, angels raised a hue and cry to God and said, "O our Lord, did they treat al-Husayn, Your best friend *(safiy)*, in this manner?" He said, "God will raise for them (the enemies of al-Husayn) the cry of al-Qa'im," and he added, "by this He will take vengeance against those who wronged him."[66] The Qa'im will call people to Islam as did the Prophet of God. The redressing of the wrongs committed by the *umma* against the family of the Prophet is al-Qa'im's main political function. This political emphasis in al-Qa'im's function is so great that the Imamites maintain that he replaces what they regard as the tyrannical caliphate of the Umayyads and the 'Abbasids, whose swords had not

Further on Colors

Sacked:

① p.22   Red + white Jafr

② tradition from Mufaddal
   161-166
      161   yellow turban
      162   black turbans

r outspread hands.

in a thirsty land.

our life-denying pursuit of life,
w what it means to be your children.

ur outspread hands.

in a thirsty land.

spared the Family. This is the main implication of the oft-quoted Shi'i phrase "the establishment of justice and equity on earth." It was the *jihad* aspect of al-Qa'im's role which the Imams, from al-Sadiq on, were trying to neutralize in order to appease their adherents' expectation of a more just social order. But the revolutionary aspect of al-Qa'im's function continued to be emphasized in the literature on the twelfth Imam; and much later, when the Safavids opened a new chapter in the Imamite history by proclaiming the Imamiyya form of Shi'ism as the state religion of their dominions, the traditions about al-Qa'im's temporal role were interpreted in order to accommodate the achievement of this phase of al-Qa'im's function by the Safavid Shah Isma'il I (967–68/1501). One such tradition is cited by Sayyid Mir Lawhi, a contemporary of the Safavid theologian Majlisi, in criticism of the latter's interpretive translation into Persian of the following tradition about al-Qa'im. The tradition is related on the authority of al-Sadiq, who said:

> When al-Qa'im will rise in Khurasan, he will proceed to Kufa and thence to Multan, passing through the *jazira* of Banu Kawan; but al-Qa'im among us will rise in Jilan among the people of Daylam and there will appear for my son the Turkish flags. . . .

This tradition, according to Sayyid Mir Lawhi, was rendered into Persian by Majlisi as follows:

> When a king rises from Khurasan and conquers Kufa and Multan and passes through the *jazira* of Banu Kawan, which is in the vicinity of Basra, at that time a king will rise among us in Jilan who will be supported and assisted by the people of Barka, which is in the vicinity of Astarabad. . . .

Then Majlisi adds:

> It is clear that the one rising in Khurasan indicates the Amir of the Turks, Chinghiz Khan . . . and the one rising in Jilan indicates the King, the protector of the Religion, Shah Isma'il Safavi, may God associate him [on the Day of Resurrection] with the Pure Imams; that is the reason why the sixth Imam refers to him as "my son" [in the tradition].[67]

There is no doubt that this tradition must be taken as a later fabrication. But the important point to remember is that Majlisi could successfully identify Shah Isma'il Safavi, whose political success in establishing the

Imamite religion as an official state religion is the main purpose of Majlisi's interpretation, with al-Qa'im of the family of the Prophet.

Our primary sources indicate that in all probability the political success of al-Qa'im was expected in the near future, after the disappearance of the twelfth Imam, and not at the End of Time, an expectation which must be attributed to the later doctrine of the occultation. The other title used for the twelfth Imam, namely, Sahib al-amr (the Master of the Authority), is further evidence for our argument.

The Title Sahib al-amr: "The Master of the Authority or Command"

This is another title of the twelfth Imam which appears side by side with *al-Qa'im*. The Imam Ja'far al-Sadiq was once asked if he was the Master of the Authority to which all the Shi'ites were looking forward. The Imam replied that neither he nor his son nor the son of his son was the Sahib al-amr, because Sahib al-amr was the one who would fill the earth with justice as it is filled with wickedness. There existed, the Imam added, a period of intermission between the Imams just as there was before the Apostle of God emerged.[68] Another report is related by al-Kulayni in which 'Abd Allah b. 'Ata, a close associate of the fifth Imam al-Baqir, once urged the Imam to rise because of the large following he had in Iraq and because of his unique status in the family of the Prophet. The Imam replied to him, saying that he was not the Sahib al-amr, and that Sahib al-amr would be the one whose birth would be concealed from the people. "He is your Master. For sure, there is none among us who is well-known among the people and on their lips can escape an unjust death," added al-Baqir.[69]

The Sahib al-amr is supposed to arise with the sword and fight those who have wronged the *ahl al-bayt*. In consequence, he becomes the *sahib al-sayf*—the Master of the Sword.[70] More significant is the precise time when the Master of the Sword will appear. As one would expect, several traditions mention that the day will be the day of 'Ashura' (the tenth of Muharram)—the day on which al-Husayn was killed at Karbala', the day when the family of the Prophet was wronged by the Umayyads.[71] The day of 'Ashura in the pious literature of the Shi'ites stands as a symbol of the afflictions suffered by the Family, and it has been used to dramatize the claims of the *ahl al-bayt* as those most rightful and deserving to be the successors of the Prophet. All this leads us to confirm that the early Shi'ites expected that not only their twelfth Imam, but also other Imams before him, would rise against the existing state of affairs and redress their grievances against the caliphal authority. Al-Kulayni has preserved an important tradition which shows that the Shi'ites, more than anything else, expected their Imams to assume full control of the political scene, in order to set things right, whereas the Imams, who were fully aware of the futility of any direct political action, encouraged their adherents to look forward to the fulfillment of their expectation in the future when the Qa'im, the Sahib al-amr, would emerge from the *ghayba* to establish the just rule. A close associate of the eighth Imam, 'Ali al-Rida, told the Imam, it seems, after his being appointed as heir apparent to the caliphate by al-Ma'mun, that he hoped the Imam was the Sahib al-amr and that God would bestow on him the Imamate openly without need of the sword, "since people have paid allegiance to you and coins have been struck in your name." The Imam said that there was no Imam among them who, after having attained fame, having been referred to regarding religious questions, and having openly received taxes due to him, would not die of poison; this situation would continue until "God chooses a child from among us as an Imam, whose birth and upbringing is concealed and whose descent is well known."[72]

So far we have discussed at length two of the most frequently used titles of the twelfth Imam in the early Shi'i traditions and their immediate connotation; both titles denote authority of a more temporal and political nature than is implied by the messianic figure al-Mahdi, due to appear at the End of Time. The eschatological significance of al-Mahdi seems to be a later concept, because even the word *mahdi*, as we have seen above, conveyed a different idea in the beginning, where it was used to show a special mark of the Shi'i Imam who was endowed with a knowledge of secret matters and of the revealed scriptures of God. This meaning should be contrasted with the much later one of the word *mahdi*, which has become the meaning accepted even today by Imamite writers:

> The twelfth Imam is known as the Mahdi because he himself has found the way, and has been entrusted with the task of guiding mankind. Those who will live under his rule will all be Muslims and the followers of the Qur'an by the favor of his guidance.[73]

This explanation of the word *mahdi* fits what is implied in the title al-Qa'im, as used in the early sources. The title Mahdi seems to have become synonymous with al-Qa'im, or, more likely, it supplemented the function of al-Qa'im by embodying within itself an eschatological emphasis during the absence of the twelfth Imam. The delay in the establishment of justice and equity "in the near future" was an important factor in the accentuation of al-Mahdi's function as the Islamic messiah, besides his being the Qa'im of the family of the Prophet, and the *hujja* of God, a title to be discussed below. The latter is the most popular title of the twelfth Imam in Imamite literature. Perhaps this is the only title which is indicative of the religious role of the twelfth Imam and, when used with *al-Qa'im* or *Sahib al-amr,* carries within itself the full implication of the doctrine of the Imamate as taught by the Imamiyya.

The Title al-Hujja

We have seen above that all the Shi'i Imams are the Hujja (the Proof) of God, and as such they are endowed with special qualities which entitle them to bear witness against those who refuse to accept the authority of God and follow his injunctions. They are the only persons who stand as proofs of His existence and the existence of His revelation on earth. In other words, as *hujja*, the Imams are the competent religious authorities, who, because of their peculiar responsibility as the Proofs of God, are appointed by Him among mankind to enable them to acquire the knowledge of the Creator and to give them the example of saintliness. This is the force of the phrase "the Proof of God." 'Ali b. Abi Talib, in one of his most widely cited speeches, is reported to have prayed to God to appoint His *hujaj* (proofs) on earth, who should follow one another in sequence for mankind in order to guide them to His religion, and inform them about Him, so that those who have believed in Him do not get scattered and overwhelmed, "Be they (the *hujaj*) manifest and not obeyed, or hidden and being looked forward to with a view to their appearance."[74]

The *hujaj* of God are thus the ones who guide mankind to God's religion and inform them about Him. This makes it necessary for the *hujja* to be an authority on religious matters who can be relied upon because of his competence in those sciences. Another tradition which stresses the religious role of the *hujja* is reported on the authority of Ja'far al-Sadiq, who said that there continued to be on earth a *hujja* from God who knew the lawful and the unlawful and invited people to the way of God.[75]

The twelfth Imam, in this sense, is referred to as the *hujja* of God. Although, the sources say, he has a name, "it is unlawful to call him by his name" or "to reveal his name." The tenth Imam, 'Ali al-Hadi (to whom only a small number of traditions are credited) is reported to have said:

> My successor is al-Hasan [al-'Askari], how would you (my followers) react to his successor? The person asked, "What do you mean, o son of the Prophet?" The Imam said, "Because you will not see his face, nor will it be lawful for you to mention his name." "Then how should we style him?" the person asked. "Say, the *hujja* from the family of the Prophet," said the Imam.[76]

Thus the twelfth Imam came to be styled al-Hujja b. al-Hasan al-'Askari. As a consequence this Imam possessed the title al-Hujja also as his name. In one of his discussions with his companions the sixth Imam, al-Sadiq, already explains the necessity of the *hujja* for the existence and well-being of the world. According to al-Sadiq, anyone who does not receive a revelation should look for a prophet to whom obedience is obligatory. The Prophet was the *hujja* from God for His creatures, and when he passed away it was 'Ali who was the *hujja* in his place. The Qur'an, which was considered by some Muslims to be the *hujja*, could not be so because the Book of God needed a custodian who could say that which was true, and who could not be defeated by groups such as the Murji'ites, the Qadarites, and even the Zindiqs, who did not believe in it and yet quoted verses from it and defeated the great scholars of the Qur'an. The custodian of the Qur'an had to be someone who knew the entire Qur'an. That person after the Prophet was 'Ali, who was custodian of the Qur'an, and obedience to him was obligatory, since what he said about the Qur'an was right.[77] In this sense, then, 'Ali or any other Imam was that person through whom the inaccessible inner meanings of the Qur'an and the knowledge of God become accessible; such a person serves as the proof among mankind of His will, as interpreted by these competent authorities. Thus the Prophet and the Imam both stand as the *hujja* of God on an equal footing, or rather, the later *hujja* (i.e. the Imam) is even more important because the true interpretation of the revelation depends entirely on him, since it would otherwise fall into the hands of those who are incompetent in performing this crucial duty. In Imamite theological works the term *hujja*, then, designates the category formed by prophets and Imams together, in that either of them must always exist as the guide to God's will. As explained by al-Sadiq, only such a *hujja* can solve the religious problems which arise because of the misinterpretation of the Qur'an. They are the authorized interpreters of the Word of God, and the present such authority, according to the Imamiyya, is the twelfth Imam—al-Hujja, the son of al-'Askari.

The Mu'tazilites, as Ibn Babuya (d. 381/991–92) tells us, used to criticize the views of the Imamiyya about *al-hujjat al-gha'ib*—the Hidden Hujja. How could such a person, they said, be considered as the Hujja when the people had not even seen him or known him? To this, Ibn Babuya relplies that the Hidden Hujja is like the heart in the body, which, although hidden, plays the most vital role of guiding the various parts of the body into the best path.[78]

The title al-Hujja, in contrast to the other titles which are often used to designate the twelfth Imam, emphasizes the religious and spiritual aspects of his function, whereas *al-Qa'im* or *Sahib al-amr* conveys his role as the ideal ruler of Islam who will restore Islamic justice in the world.

The Twelfth Imam as the *Mahdi al-Anam* (the Mahdi of the People):

The idea of a future restorer was in circulation among the Islamic peoples much earlier than the tenth century. The notion of the messianic Imam, with his special divine knowledge and his destiny of bringing true Islamic justice to the oppressed, seized the imaginations of many during the last decades of the Umayyad rule. Thus, when the Imamites were occupied with disentangling the question of the successor to al-'Askari, the idea of the messianic role of the Imam formed the cornerstone of all the sub-divisions of the Imamiyya. The title al-Mahdi, which appeared sometimes along with the title al-Qa'im was, in the beginning, merely a designation for the ideal Islamic ruler. But with the delay in the great social transformation under al-Mahdi's command, the title took on eschatological tones in Imami Shi'ism. The Imamate of the twelfth Imam was unique in the sense that in him merged the two prominent ideas of Shi'ite messianism: the occultation and the return of the future restorer of justice. The emphasis laid on his being the only true Mahdi, promised in the traditions of the Prophet, whose basic function was not very different from that visualized for al-Qa'im or Sahib al-amr except for the time factor, it seems, was presumably for two reasons. First, the prolongation of the *ghayba* had shaken the belief of many followers in their Imam, and they had to be reassured that the delay in the Imam's rise was due to the fact that he was the foreordained Mahdi, promised by the Prophet, who was waiting for the divine command and succor to appear when it would be needed. In the meantime the adherents of the Imam had to remain on the alert and prepare for the Mahdi's coming. Ibn Babuya, who wrote a book on the twelfth Imam, entitled *Kamal al-din wa tamam al-ni'ma* (The Perfection of Religion and the Fulness of Blessing), explains the reason for his undertaking in the introduction of that work:

> That which moved me to write this book is that when I finished performing the pilgrimage *(ziyara)* [to the tomb of] my master Abu al-Hasan al-Rida, I returned to Nishabur where I stayed for some time. During this sojourn I found many of the Shi'ites who used to come and visit me were baffled about the *ghayba* [of the twelfth Imam] and were in doubt about the Qa'im and had gone astray.[79]

The above citation shows the critical situation in which the Imamite theologians were placed from within.

Second, the title al-Mahdi, with its eschatological connotation, had much wider recognition than the other titles used for the messianic Imam such as al-Qa'im or al-Hujja. By the early tenth century the Mahdi tradition had gained acceptance even among the Sunnites, especially the idea that the ideal ruler of the Muslims would be among the descendants of Muhammad through his daughter Fatima and son-in-law 'Ali, the latter being the one to whom the Prophet had transmitted a secret teaching. Indeed, the early elucidation of the term *mahdi* did emphasize the latter aspect of the twelfth Imam. But the accentuation of his eschatological role was meant to vindicate the Imamate of the Hidden Imam against the objection raised by the adversaries of the Imamiyya. Hence, the Mahdiism of the twelfth Imam became the prominent feature of the Twelver Shi'ism and supplemented the immediate implication of al-Qa'im, the sole legitimate ruler capable of maintaining the true faith and the world free from oppressors, at the End of Time. It also helped the

Imamites, who were growing impatient at the delay in the *qiyam* (rise) of the Imam then, and who had to endure the unjust government of the caliphs until the Imam appeared as the Awaited Mahdi, because there was always in existence a true Imam, whether or not he was at the moment ruling or even making an attempt to gain rule. In the meantime, they were able to guide their own lives, since they could refer to the deputies of the Imam, who were custodians of his rulings and who were available at all times during the occultation. The deputies had also been greatly responsible, as we shall see, for collecting and compiling all the information needed to keep hope in the true Imam alive and to remind the Shi'ites that there was no greater meritorious act than to acknowledge one's Imam, because "the one who acknowledges his Imam and dies before the rising of the Sahib al-amr will have the status of the one who will be fighting in the army of the Imam, under his banner."[80] In the following pages we will examine the pious literature on the twelfth Imam which discusses the characteristics of the Twelver Mahdi in the Imamite religion.

The Miraculous Birth of the Imamite Mahdi

In general, the birth of an Imam holds a special significance in Shi'ite hagiography, because none of the historical sources has what the pious Imamite literature has preserved for us; moreover, if the historical works like that of al-Mufid ever begin to describe the supernatural events surrounding the birth of an Imam, those passages become hagiographical. In the biographies of the Imams written by the Shi'ites themselves, it is hard to draw a line between these two types of works, because the accounts are usually dominated by stories similar to those found in the Sufi accounts of their saints. In studying the lives of the Shi'ite Imams, especially that of the twelfth Imam, we are relying on sources which cannot be characterized as completely historical or completely hagiographical. Nevertheless, these are the very sources which can make an essential contribution to an understanding of the period in which the idea of the eschatological figure of al-Mahdi became prominent in the Imamite religion. This literature has not been considered worthy of attention by many scholars, who undertake to interpret the Imamite idea of the Mahdi by relying almost exclusively on non-Imamite writings. The Imamite writings on this subject are invaluable keys to an understanding of the forces which culminated in the conviction that sooner or later the world would be filled with justice by the twelfth Imam as it is now filled with injustice; hence they deserve thorough analysis and serious discussion.

The importance given to the births of the Imams may be clearly discerned in the many traditions recounting the manner of their creation and their essential substance. Unlike other men, the Imams were shaped not out of the dust of the earth, but first created as forms of light singing the praises of God long before the material world came into being. In a long tradition the Prophet, addressing his daughter Fatima, is reported to have said:

> Oh daughter, God (praised and exalted be He!) cast a glance on the inhabitants of the earth and chose your father and made him a prophet. He cast a second glance and chose your husband 'Ali, and made a brother and legatee for me. He cast a third glance and chose you and your mother and made you two mistresses of the women of the worlds. He cast then a fourth glance and chose your two sons and made them two masters of the youths of paradise. . . .[81]

In creating the Imams, then, God, so to speak, turned his face toward the world, and His glance generated the *ahl al-bayt,* who are regarded as the true source of divine mercy. Thus on the night in which the Imam is born, not a child is born but that he is a believer, and if polytheism *(shirk)* is born on that night, God transforms it into belief *(iman)* in honor of the newly born Imam.[82] The birth of the twelfth Imam, who is the Mahdi, and who has been declared as the most excellent *(afdal)*[83] of all the Imams, is as miraculous as the birth of Moses or Jesus, and even more significant.[84]

The story of the birth of the twelfth Imam is told in full detail by Ibn Babuya[85] and Tusi. But al-Mufid avoids the account of the miraculous birth of the twelfth Imam in his work on the biographies of the Imams, *al-Irshad.* Of all the early Imamite theologians, al-Mufid impresses one by the sobriety and apparent objectivity of his writings. It may plausibly be suggested that he found it unnecessary to follow Ibn Babuya, who had a different purpose in composing his work on the twelfth Imam, namely, to reassure the perplexed Shi'ites about the existence of their Imam. As we shall see, al-Mufid did not accept Ibn Babuya's writings uncritically, even on matters pertaining to the fundamentals of religion.

[71]

Tusi, who had studied under al-Mufid, also had a purpose behind writing his work on the *Ghayba* and consequently, although following al-Mufid's footsteps, chose to include material which would be beneficial to the spiritual lives of those who were loyal to the belief in the Imamate of the twelfth Imam.[86]

The most notable point in this story of the nativity of the Imamite Mahdi concerns the mother of the Imam, whom we saw earlier in our discussion of al-'Askari's death. According to the tradition, she was a slave girl by the name of Narjis, from Byzantium. Here again, al-Mufid does not speak of her being a slave girl or from Byzantium. Another Shi'i writer, probably his contemporary, Shaykh Husayn b. 'Abd al-Wahhab, accepts that she was a slave girl and adds that he had seen many authentic reports that Narjis was a slave girl belonging to Hakima, daughter of Muhammad al-Jawad (the ninth Imam) and paternal aunt of the eleventh Imam al-'Askari, in whose house she was born and brought up; one day, 'Ali al-Hadi, the tenth Imam, saw her and declared that to her would be born one peculiarly graced by God.[87]

The other point worthy of attention is the frequent comparison between the birth of the Imamite Mahdi and the birth of Moses, and the similarity of the circumstances which both Narjis and the mother of Moses had to face. The Imamites report that both Moses and the Mahdi were in fear of being killed by the rulers of their time, because the rulers were aware that the emergence of these two would bring an end to their rule. As a result, God, who has foreknowledge of events to come, made special provision in the case of their mothers, that neither, although having conceived the child, should have any visible signs of conception up to the time the child was born. The story of the Twelver Mahdi is beautifully told in the Imamite hagiography. The report varies a little in our sources, but I have taken the earliest account, which is preserved by Ibn Babuya. The following citation will give the reader the feel of the pious material on the twelfth Imam and the way the Imamiyya had come to visualize their last Imam, the only legitimate claimant to the Imamate after al-'Askari, and the only person through whom truth and justice would once again become a triumphant cause. Furthermore, the account reveals the privileged position of the Imam endowed with miraculous powers from childhood, which enabled him to perceive the true destiny of the *umma* and become the leader of the final restoration. It is difficult to appreciate the purpose behind the preservation of such pious narratives without comprehending the Imamite teachings about the Imams being the Qa'im and the Mahdi—the only hope for the end to oppression and suffering in this world.

Ibn Babuya relates the account on the authority of Hakima, who holds a very decisive place as the one who has reported on the birth of the twelfth Imam. The sources show that she was highly respected by the tenth and eleventh Imams and was often entrusted with esoteric knowledge. She is also described as "the one who possessed the secret knowledge of the Imams and was among the agents and *abwab*—the gates (the means by which one communicates with the Hidden Imam) of the twelfth Imam after the death of the eleventh Imam, al-'Askari."[88] She says:

In the year 255 [A.H.] on the fifteenth night of Sha'ban [29th July, 870] Abu Muhammad [the eleventh Imam] sent for me with the message, "O aunt, tonight is the fifteenth night of Sha'ban.[89] Break your fast with us. Verily, God the Exalted, in the near future, will make His *Hujja* manifest and he will be His *Hujja* on earth and successor [to the Imamate]." I was overjoyed to hear this tiding and, putting on my clothes, went out immediately until I came to Abu Muhammad. He was sitting in his courtyard. I asked him who the mother of the child was. He said, "Narjis." I said, "May God make me a sacrifice for you, there is no sign of conception in her." The Imam said, "This is the reason why I have told you [only]." So I went in and greeting them I took my seat. Narjis came forward and removed my shoes and said, "O my lady and the lady of my family, how are you tonight?" I replied, "You are my lady and the lady of the family." She did not understand what I said and asked, "What are you saying, O aunt?" I said to her, "O my daughter, God the Exalted will give you a son tonight who will be the Master in this world and the next." She blushed with abashment. When I finished the evening prayers I broke fast and then laid down to sleep. At midnight I got up and offered prayers. I finished praying while she was asleep and I found nothing had happened to her. Then I sat down reading the supererogatory (*mu'qaba*) prayers, after which I lay down again. I woke up dismayed but she was still asleep. After a while she woke up, performed her prayers and went to sleep again. I began to doubt [what Abu Muhammad had predicted] and just then Abu Muhammad called out from where he was sitting, "O aunt, do not be in a hurry. The moment is approaching *(al-amr qad qariba)*." So I sat down and recited the *Sura* of *Sajda* and *Yasin*.[90] It was during this time that she woke up alarmed and I rushed to her and said, "The name of God be on you *(bismillah 'alayki)*! Do you feel anything?" She said, "Yes, O aunt." "Gather yourself and procure peace in your heart," I said to her. At that time I was taken over by weakness, as was she. Then I woke up sensing the voice of my Master and when I raised the covering on

her I saw him (peace be on him) in prostration and the parts of his body
[which should touch the ground in this position][91] were on the ground. I
took him up to my bosom and saw him pure and clean.[92] Abu Muhammad
called out to me and said, "Bring my son to me, O aunt." So I took him to
Abu Muhammad. He took him by putting his hands under his back and
buttocks and his feet resting on his chest. Then he put his tongue in his
mouth and gently stroked his hands on his eyes, ears and joints. Then he
said, "I bear witness that there is no god but God; He is unique and has no
partner and Muhammad is the prophet of God." He continued sending his
greetings to 'Ali, the *Amir* of the faithful and on the Imams, one after
another until he reached his father's name. Then he paused and forbore
from saying it. Abu Muhammad said, "O aunt, take him to his mother, so
that he may greet her, and then bring him back to me." I took him to his
mother. He greeted her and I took him back to the Imam and left him
there. The Imam said, "O aunt, come to visit us on the seventh day."

The next morning I went there and greeted Abu Muhammad and raised
the curtain to see my Master. But I did not see him. I asked [Abu Muham-
mad], "May God make me a sacrifice for you, what happened to my Master?" He said, "O aunt, I have entrusted him to the One to whom the
mother of Moses had entrusted her son." I came back on the seventh day
and greeted the Imam and took my seat. He said, "Bring my son to me." I
brought my Master to him. He was wrapped in a piece of cloth and the
Imam repeated what he had done the first day. . . .[93]

The other frequent comparison is between the ability of the twelfth
Imam to speak while just a child, with that of Jesus, as reported in the
Qur'an (19:30); since both were the *hujja* of God, they spoke with the
authority of grown men. A tradition is recounted that a very close associate of al-'Askari, by the name of Ahmad b. Ishaq, asked the Imam,
after the birth of the twelfth Imam, how he could be assured that the
child was the Imam after him or, as he puts it, "What is the sign to set my
mind at peace?" At that, the boy began to utter, "I am *Baqiyyat Allah* (the
Last one from God) on earth and His avenger against His enemies."[94] So
just as Jesus was to perform signs, proving through miracles his prophetic mission, the Mahdi of the Twelvers also gave the proof of his Imamate
in the same manner. Both being the *hujja*, the Imamites contend, they
were endowed with similar powers of performing miracles.

The Miraculous Appearance of the Mahdi at the *Hajj*:

This is another feature of the Imamite Mahdi. Mecca is not only the
place where his *qiyam* (rise) will commence at the End of Time, but also

(as many Shi'ites believe) his residence. A rare tradition narrates that the Sahib al-zaman (the Master of the Age) has a special home named *bayt al-hamd* (the house of laudation) in which a brilliant lamp has been burning from his birth until the day he will rise with the sword.[95] Another tradition makes his home somewhere in the mountains between Mecca and Ta'if.[96] Wherever his home may be, the Shi'ites assert that he comes for the pilgrimage to Mecca every year. Tusi relates a tradition in which a person by the name of 'Ali b. Ibrahim al-Fadaki was performing the *tawaf* (circumambulation) of the Ka'ba when he saw a young man with a bright countenance surrounded by a group of people. The young man was speaking eloquently to them. Al-Fadaki asked a person standing there who that person was. The man said, "The son of the Apostle of God, who appears one day in the year for his special followers, to converse with them and they with him."[97]

The Imamite sources on the twelfth Imam are full of such traditions which emphasize one thing, that every year the *hajj* is being attended by the one closely related to the Prophet, who is also the promised one to appear in the future. Most of these traditions have a uniform ending, that is, the narrative ends with the young man (the Imam) asking the person (in most cases the transmitter of the tradition) if he recognized the one to whom he was speaking. The person would reply in the negative and the young man would continue with a declaration: "I am the Qa'im of the Age; I am the one who will fill the earth with justice and equity. Indeed, the earth is not void of the *hujja*, nor can people remain in any interval of time without him."

The significance of Mecca as the most revered sanctuary of the Muslim world is clear, and its choice as the place of his residence or regular visit (particularly during the *hajj* season) is discernible, especially when his re-emergence as the Mahdi also would commence from Mecca. We saw above the traditions recounting the twelfth Imam's appearance on the day of 'Ashura, and one would have expected the place of his residence or reappearance to be either Kufa or Karbala'—places which are mentioned by some traditions, I assume, of very late origin. But that would have limited the role of the twelfth Imam as the 'Alid Qa'im only, while the emphasis on Mecca appears to have had a wider implication, particularly when one notes the usual insistence in the Imamite writings that the only true Mahdi, who will appear before the Day of Judgment, as promised by the Prophet, can be no one else but the descendant of al-Husayn, the son of 'Ali. Most probably, excluding the other sons of 'Ali and confining Mahdiism to the descendants of al-Husayn, the son of Fatima, was the way to prove the claim to the Mahdiism of the twelfth Imam, although many other descendants of al-Husayn were proclaimed Mahdis by different Shi'ite groups during the period between Muhammad b. al-Hanafiyya (the first official Mahdi) and the twelfth Imam. The Imamites maintained that since al-Husayn had suffered at the hands of the *umma*, God rewarded him by selecting his descendant as the Sultan who would be the *hujja* for the people[98] — the whole *umma* and not just the Shi'ites. According to another tradition, a person who had met the twelfth Imam in Mecca asked him about the time when he would appear. The Imam replied that the sign of his appearance would be total turmoil and chaos in the world. At that time he would come to Mecca and would be in the Ka'ba, when the people would be demanding that an Imam be appointed for them. A discussion would follow until a person would get up among this group and would look at the Imam, and then would say, "O people, this is the Mahdi, look at him," and they would take his hand and place it between the Rukn and Maqam, two spots in the sanctuary of the Ka'ba, and would pay allegiance to the Imam, though until then they had been on the point of despair.[99]

The death of al-'Askari marked a crucial period in the history of the Imamite Shi'ism. The question of the succession to this Imam not only divided the Imamiyya into several subdivisions, but it also gave rise to several issues in the doctrine of the Imamate itself. The ultimate survival of the Qat'iyya among the Imamiyya factions was in large measure due to their recognition of the authority of the agents of the Hidden Imam who were greatly responsible for uniting the Imamiyya and providing leadership during the formative period of Twelver Shi'ism. During this time the role of the twelfth Imam was defined in terms of his being al-Qa'im, Sahib al-amr, al-Hujja, and above all, al-Mahdi of the *umma*. The prolonged occultation of the twelfth Imam had given rise to the most critical period in the lives of his deputies, who were confronted with criticisms from within as well as without. The accentuation of the Mahdiism of the twelfth Imam, besides his being al-Qa'im, was to justify his delay in *qiyam* and to enhance his universal role as the savior of mankind. But for how long and how effectively the Imamite theologians could vindicate the Imamate of the Hidden Hujja was a problem that required both traditional and rational deliberation, and to which solutions were offered throughout the medieval period of Imamite Shi'ism. The justification for the *ghayba* of the twelfth Imam was going to occupy the intellectual efforts of the Imamites during the years following the Imam's disappearance.

3. The Occultation
of the Imamite Mahdi

The occultation or *ghayba* of the messianic Imam was the central belief in the doctrine of the Mahdi. It was, as a matter of fact, a direct corollary of the belief in the end of the line of the Husaynid Imams with the twelfth Imam al-Qa'im, which necessitated upholding the tenet that the last Imam was alive, since mankind cannot remain without the *hujja* from God. But his life was in danger, and, therefore, for his own protection he had to remain in concealment. The delay in the establishment of "justice and equity" by the Qa'im al-Mahdi had greatly enhanced the evolution of the already known idea of the *ghayba*. There is little reason to discredit the Imamite thesis about the intolerable 'Abbasid persecutions of the 'Alid Imams during the Samarra period, which had compelled the last Imam to go into occultation. But, in addition to this thesis, one might detect the underlying factor which contributed to the development of the idea of *ghayba* from the early days of the Shi'ite history, namely, that when the situation was beyond the control of those who were demanding the Islamic rule of justice, as was the case during and following the Samarra period of the 'Abbasid caliphate, the belief in the *ghayba* of the Imam and his eventual return *(raj'a)* at a favorable time helped the Shi'ites to endure under difficult circumstances and to hope for reform pending the return of the Mahdi. By the end of the reign of al-Mu'tamid (256−79/870−92), the futility of gaining ascendancy by radical means had become clear to the Shi'ites. In consequence, the belief in the *ghayba* of al-Qa'im held obvious attraction for those who now looked forward to the happening of the promised events accompanying the emergence of the hidden Imam, which would adjust the present unbearable historical circumstances in favor of the oppressed who remained loyal to the

Imam. Such messianic expectation, consequently, did not require the Shi'ites to oppose the establishment actively; rather they were required to remain on the alert at all times and pave the way for the Mahdi's coming by constantly re-evaluating contemporary historical life, on the basis of the apocalyptic traditions which related the signs regarding the Imam's reappearance.

In studying the evolution of the doctrine of the *ghayba*, I have found it expedient to trace the trends evident in the early Imamite sources in respect to the doctrinal systematization of the *ghayba* as represented on the one hand by the traditionists *(muhaddithun)* and on the other by the theologians *(mutakallimun)*. Although these two trends are not well defined in the sources, it appears that the early Imamite jurists before al-Mufid (336−414/947−1023) depend greatly on the prophetic traditions and the interpretation of the Qur'anic verses related on the authority of the Imams, in order to vindicate the Imamate of the twelfth Hidden Imam. This does not mean that the Imamites before this period paid no attention to the art of *kalam* as such, because according to al-Kulayni (d. 329/940−41), the Shi'i *kalam* was much developed during the lifetime of the two Sadiqs and used in theological controversies by some of their prominent disciples like Hisham b. al-Hakam, who is reported to have had discussions in his youth on the necessity of the Imamate with one of the earliest Mu'tazilites, 'Amr b. 'Ubayd (d. 145/762), in Basra.[1] Also under this disciple of al-Sadiq, the theory of Imamate as maintained by the Imamites was given a definitive form in the middle of the second/ eighth century.[2] On the other hand, the doctrine of the *ghayba* could not have been formulated and linked with the central doctrine of the Imamate at that early stage, when the *ghayba* must have been taken as a temporary phenomenon at the most. Among the Imamite jurists who may be taken as a representative of the traditionist approach to the problem of the *ghayba* are al-Nu'mani (d. 360/970−71), the author of *Kitab al-ghayba*, and Ibn Babuya (d. 381/991−92), whose *Kamal al-din wa tamam al-ni'ma* remains the comprehensive work on the subject of the twelfth Imam and his *ghayba*.

The period which marked the end of *al-ghaybat al-qasira* (the Short Occultation), to use Tusi's terminology, and the beginning of *al-ghaybat al-tamma* (the Complete Occultation)[3] was a decisive one in the history of the Imamite religion because it forced great changes in the approach of its doctors. The vindication of the Imamate of the Hidden Hujja, which was under severe attack from both the non-Imami Shi'i groups and the Sunnis, needed more formidable methods than mere reliance on arguments from the Qur'an or traditions. This consideration, it seems, forced the Imamite scholars to adopt *kalam,* in Mu'tazili form, to substantiate their contentions about the necessity of the Imamate and the existence of the twelfth Imam in occultation. The list of the great early names in Imamite theology is headed by al-Mufid and his erudite student al-Sharif al-Murtada (d. 436/1044−45), who both are believed to have attended the lectures of the Mu'tazilite, al-Qadi 'Abd al-Jabbar al-Asadabadi (d. 415/1024−25).[4] Ibn al-Nadim, the contemporary of al-Mufid, remembers the latter as one of the greatest *mutakallimun* of the Imamites with whom "culminates leadership among his associates of the Imamiyya [sect] of the Shi'a in Law, theology. . . ." Al-Mufid's correction of Ibn Babuya's *Creed* is the classic example of the transition in the approach of the Imamite scholars of this period, who stand out as thoroughly trained in *kalam* disputation. The various titles of al-Mufid's works, such as *al-Idah fi al-imama* (The Elucidation Concerning the Imamate), *al-Radd 'ala al-Jahiz al-'uthmaniyya* (The Refutation of al-Jahiz the 'Uthmani), and so on, cited by his two other students al-Najashi (d. 450/1058−59) and Tusi,[5] indicate the difference of approach between him and his predecessor, Ibn Babuya, demanded by their respective periods.

Al-Sharif al-Murtada composed one of the chief works on the Imamate entitled *al-Shafi fi al-imama* (The Unequivocal Answer Concerning the Imamate) in reply to the refutation of the Imamite stand on the question of the necessity of the Imamate, discussed in the sections dealing with the Imamate in *al-Mughni fi abwab al-tawhid wa al-'adl*[6] by 'Abd al-Jabbar. The work is purely *kalam*, and in the course of justifying the doctrine of the Imamate it also vindicates the *ghayba*.

The use of *kalam* and the open vindication of the Imamate of the Hidden Hujja was to some extent the result of the favorable relationship of the Imamite theologians like al-Mufid and al-Sharif al-Murtada with the 'Abbasid caliphs and the Buyid Amirs.[7] The Imamites following the *ghayba* of the twelfth Imam were able to recognize and even cooperate with the Buyids, without sacrificing their loyalty to the Imam. On the other hand, the Buyids had, at least politically, preferred Imami Shi'ism, in particular that part of the doctrinal structure of the *ghayba* which accepted the rule of the "oppressor' (the caliph, as seen by the Imamites), without making the twelfth Imam responsible for his removal and without requiring the *umma* to pay allegiance to him as an Imam until his reappearance. Ibn Babuya reports that 'Ali al-Rida (d. 202/817–18) said once,

> "I see the Shi'ites [in future] who will become like cattle looking for a pasture and will not find one. [This will occur] when the third among my descendants (i.e. al-'Askari) will have died." Somebody asked the Imam, "Why, O Son of the Prophet?" He replied, "So that when he rises with the sword he will not be responsible for the allegiance paid by anybody to him (lit. he will have nobody's *bay'a* on his neck.)"[8]

This is interpreted to mean that during the *ghayba* there will be no obligations on the *umma* to bind to him who will be the theocratic ruler in future, when God commands him to appear. This appears to be a prudent accommodation of the Imamite theologians of this period with rulers like the Buyids who, having professed Imamite Shi'ism, were bound to the obedience of the Imam; but because the twelfth Imam was in *ghayba* and this particular clause existed in this doctrine, they could continue to be Imamites and still let the caliph be selected from the 'Abbasids and not the 'Alids.

Although a number of great Imamite scholars wrote their theological expositions of the doctrine of *ghayba* during the years between the end of the Short Occultation (940) and the Seljuq occupation of Baghdad (1055), it is difficult to determine precisely under which Imamite theologians the doctrine in question found its complete systematization. Both the *muhaddithun* and the *mutakallimun* have vindicated the Imamite position, but it is actually Tusi whose endeavors in the systematization and vindication of this particular doctrine have proved to be most fruitful. The main characteristic of his approach to this problem is the *blending* of the traditionist and theological defenses of the *ghayba*.

Tusi composed his work when the Imamites were once again in disfavor with the 'Abbasids. The shortcomings of the previous works, it appears, must have been discerned by al-Mufid, who urged Tusi to compose a book on "the *ghayba* of *sahib al-zaman*, the reason for his *ghayba*, the cause for which his *ghayba* is prolonged and his concealment has continued, even though he is very much needed since wickedness is spreading. . . ."[9] Hence Tusi undertook to vindicate the doctrine on both traditional and theological lines. He subjected the existing sources to such thorough study that no Imamite scholar after him has been able to

[*81*]

add anything new to the subject of *ghayba*. In this chapter we will be concerned with the approach of the Imamite traditionists to the doctrine of the *ghayba*; the theological exposition of the *ghayba* will be discussed in the following chapter.

The Traditionist view of the *Ghayba*

The early Imamite sources assert that the twelfth Imam went into occultation from the year 260/873–74, the year his father al-'Askari died.[10] But Tusi[11] and before him al-Mufid[12] hold a different opinion, namely, that the occultation began from the early days of al-Qa'im's birth—either the third or seventh day, as the report goes. Tusi reports that when Hakima, the aunt of al-'Askari, came to see the child on the third day, the Imam told her:

> The child is under the protection of God, and in his custody; He had concealed him *(satarahu)* and hidden him *(ghayyabahu)* until he permits him [to reappear]. So when God hides my face and takes me away and when you find my followers *(shi'ati)* in dispute [about him] then inform those reliable among them [of what you have witnessed]. But keep this to yourself, and they too should keep the matter secret. Indeed God will hide His friend *(wali)* from the people and conceal him from his slaves, and no one shall see him until Gabriel brings forward his horse for him [to rise and ride], "for God will enact a matter which is destined to take place." (8:42)

This account or the one which reports that Hakima came on the seventh day, according to Tusi,[13] indicates that al-Qa'im went into occultation much before 260/873–74.

The earliest elucidation of the term *ghayba* appears in Ibn Babuya's *Kamal al-din*. Earlier than Ibn Babuya, one would have expected al-Kulayni to throw light on the sense in which the term *ghayba* is to be construed; but his *al-Kafi* is silent on this matter. It appears that Ibn Babuya's interpretation of *ghayba* became the official explanation of the later Imamite writers, because no significant changes have been introduced in this elucidation throughout Imamite history. Ibn Babuya says:

> The occultation *(ghayba)* does not mean non-existence *('adam)*. Sometimes a person goes into occultation from a city where he is well-known and whose inhabitants were used to seeing him; [at the same time] he is in occultation in respect to some other city [where he is not known or seen]. Sometimes a

person is in occultation from one community while he is present for another, or, he is hiding from his enemies and not from his friends, but still he is said to be in occultation and in concealment. In this case, by "occultation" is meant "occultation" from his enemies and those unreliable friends who cannot be trusted with his secret. As a result, his situation is unlike his predecessors who used to live openly among both friends and enemies. In spite of this [occultation] his friends report his existence and convey his commands and interdictions to us. Such reports by these [friends] are reliable and proof [of his existence] against those who are trying to find excuses.[14]

The above-mentioned interpretation cannot be dated earlier than the year in which al-Kulayni died, and when, significantly, the so-called *ghaybat al-qasira* came to an end. Even more important to note is that the report could not have been written before the elucidation of the *ghayba* into two forms. It is al-Nu'mani who, for the first time, undertook to spell out the two forms of *ghayba* in his *Kitab al-ghayba*, which was composed around 342/953, some thirteen years after the beginning of the Complete Occultation. Al-Nu'mani's interpretation was accepted as the official one and came to be included in the Imamite creed. Perhaps it is in the prolongation of the occultation that the reason for the two forms of *ghayba* for the twelfth Imam must be sought.

The two forms of the *ghayba* of the Twelfth Imam:

The two forms of the *ghayba* are based on the traditions, undoubtedly of later origin. Al-Kulayni's section on the *ghayba* of the twelfth Imam has several traditions, of which the majority report only one form of the *ghayba* for the Imam before he rises with the sowrd. Zurara b. A'yan, one of the eminent disciples of al-Sadiq and author of several important Shi'ite works, reports that he heard al-Sadiq say, "There will be occultation for that child before he rises." The same report goes on to give the reason for the child's occultation, which is, "he is afraid," and the Imam pointed to his stomach "meaning afraid of being killed." The Imam then continues to recount the condition of the Shi'ites to Zurara, which resembles al-Nawbakhti's exposition of the Imamite factions after al-'Askari's death. For instance, the Imam says that he is the one regarding whose birth people will dispute. Some will say his father died without leaving a successor; others will say he was still in his mother's womb when his father died; still others will hold that he was born two years after his father's death. This tradition is almost certainly fabricated, because the period of its circulation may be placed during the first part of the occultation of the Imam when al-Nawbakhti composed his *Firaq al-shi'a*, as the contents indicate. The point to remember in the report is the mention of one form of *ghayba* before the *qiyam* (rising). Those traditions which mention two forms of *ghayba* imply quite a different meaning of the two occultations than what was later interpreted as the Short and the Complete Occultation. Al-Kulayni mentions the following tradition about two forms of *ghayba*, reported on the authority of the sixth Imam, al-Sadiq:

> For the Qa'im there are two forms of *ghayba*; in one of them he will be present during the Hajj. He will see the people but they will not see him.[15]

The two occultations in this tradition do not state the length of time. This suggests another fact, namely, that until the days of al-Kulayni, who died at the end of the so-called Short Occultation (329/940−41), the two forms of *ghayba* were not divided into *sughra* (Lesser) and *kubra* (Greater), as was the case much later. None of the early sources uses these two terms *sughra* and *kubra* for the two occultations. Al-Kulayni in another tradition on this subject uses the terms *qasir* (short) and *tawil* (long) for the two occultations. This tradition states that the Qa'im will have two occultations; one will be short *(qasir)* and the other long *(tawil)*. During the first occultation no one will know his whereabouts except his special *Shi'a*; during the second one, only his special slaves will know his place.[16] The terms *qasir* and *tawil* as used above do not connote the meaning of *sughra* and *kubra*, which most probably originated in the writings of the Imamites during the Safavid period. The occultation was already considered as *tawil* when Ibn Babuya composed his *Kamal al-din*. In one place he relates his meeting with a man in Baghdad who complained to him that the *ghayba* had become prolonged and the unbearable confusion had caused many Shi'ites to turn away from the Imamate of the twelfth Imam because of the long occultation.[17]

A study of the above-mentioned traditions reveals another important point in regard to the explanation of the two forms of *ghayba*. According to the first of these traditions, in one of the occultations the Imam will not be seen by his followers. The *ghayba* here is not specified in terms of "short" or "long." In the second tradition, the first *ghayba* is perhaps as it was later interpreted, the period of the agents of the Imam, and the second *ghayba* is after the period of the *abwab* (the "gates," i.e. the agents, through whom the Imam could be communicated with). In both cases the later elucidation of the occultations, which will be discussed below, is absent. The discrepancy between the description of the two forms of the *ghayba* leads one to assume that, at least in the beginning, it was not quite clear which of the two would last longer; later on the Imamite jurists established that the second form of *ghayba* will also be the longer one, since during this *ghayba* it will be said that the Imam has perished.[18] That the occultation was considered to be a temporary arrangement is evident from most of the sources of this period.[19]

While the reasons for the division of the *ghayba* into two forms may never become known, it is necessary to discover who represented the hidden Imam during the Short Occultation and to find out the reason for the discontinuation for an indefinite period of this deputyship to the Imam.

The Short Occultation: *al-ghaybat al-qasira*

Al-Nu'mani, the contemporary of Ibn Babuya, in his *Kitab al-ghayba*, after relating a number of traditions on the two forms of *ghayba*, including the two above-mentioned traditions reported by his teacher al-Kulayni, makes a digression to explain the meaning of the *qasira* occultation which, it appears, was more or less formulated during his time. This is the first work where one finds this elucidation of the Short Occultation, an elucidation which must have been accepted as it stands by later authorities. The absence of this interpretation of the Short Occultation in the earlier important compilation of al-Kulayni, whose death occurred in the same year as that of the last agent of the twelfth Imam, 'Ali b. Muhammad al-Samarri (d. 329/940−41), is further evidence that the explanation offered by al-Nu'mani is of later origin than the year 329/940−41. Al-Nu'mani explained the Short Occultation as follows:

> As for the first *ghayba*, it is that occultation in which there were the mediators *(al-sufara')* between the Imam and the people, carrying out *(qiyamm)* [the duties of the Imam], having been designated [by him], living among the people. These were the eminent persons and leaders from whose hands emanated cures derived from the knowledge and the recondite wisdom which they possessed, and the answers to all the questions

which were put to them about the problems and difficulties [of religion]. This is the Short Occultation *(al-ghaybat al-qasira)*, the days of which have come to an end and whose time has gone by.[20]

Among the eminent persons who served as mediators between the Imam and the people, four hold a prominent position. In fact, later sources identify the Short Occultation with the period of these Four Agents, who (as they claimed) were designated by the Imam. These Four Agents were:

1. 'Uthman b. Sa'id al-'Amri[21] (260/874–75)
2. Muhammad b. 'Uthman al-'Amri (d. 304/916–17)
3. al-Husayn b. Ruh al-Nawbakhti (d. 326/937–38)
4. 'Ali b. Muhammad al-Samarri (d. 329/940–41)

The Four Agents and the Ghayba

In the early sources like *al-Kafi* of al-Kulayni, al-Nu'mani's *Ghayba*, and Ibn Babuya's *Kamal al-din*, there is no separate section devoted to the Four Agents. In fact, the agents are not confined to four in any of these works. Tusi mentions several *wukala* (agents) of the Imam in his *Rijal*.[22] Ibn Babuya, in a long section of his book dealing with the persons who had seen the twelfth Imam or had witnessed his miracle, mentions a list of the *wukala'* and the places where they were engaged in performing the duties of the deputyship of the Imam. Thus, according to him, in Baghdad there were 'Uthman al-'Amri, his son Abu Ja'far, Abu Tahir al-Bilali, and al-'Attar; in Kufa, al-'Usayni; in Ahwaz, Muhammad b. Ibrahim b. Mahziyar; in Qumm, Ahmad b. Ishaq; and so on.[23] In the same section he mentions the name of the second agent, Abu Ja'far al-'Amri, three times without qualifying him in any way as the special agent *(al-na'ib al-khass)* of the Imam. The first agent 'Uthman al-'Amri is mentioned as al-Samman (seller of cooking fat), the foremost of the Shi'a, who was present at the time when Ja'far, al-'Askari's brother, wanted to perform funeral prayers over his brother's dead body and was stopped by a boy who came out from behind the curtain saying, "O uncle, I have more right to perform prayers over my father."[24]

In a section dealing with the birth of al-Qa'im, Ibn Babuya relates a tradition about the birth which, according to this report, took place on Friday, the eighth of Sha'ban, 256 A.H.; also that the mother of al-Qa'im was known as Rayhana or Narjis or Sayqal or Sawsan; and that the Qa'im's *wakils* were 'Uthman al-'Amri, who designated his son Abu Ja'far; while the latter designated Abu al-Qasim al-Nawbakhti, who in turn designated al-Samarri. The latter did not designate anyone since the Imam had entered the Complete Occultation.[25] This is the only *hadith* which mentions the four agents in sequence; but the occurrence of the citation in this section is evidently casual, because the main purpose of the tradition is to give a variant in the birth date of the twelfth Imam, which is not accepted as authentic by the Imamites. At still another place in a section dealing with *tawqi'at* (written or signed answers or notes) received from the twelfth Imam, Ibn Babuya mentions the last three agents who had received such notes from the Imam commanding them to designate their successors, but he does not mention a sequence of three agents nor the fact that the sequence ended with al-Samarri. In another place he relates an account which appears to show that, whether appointed by the Imam to do so or not, the second and third agents used to receive the *khums* tax[26] due from Shi'ites on behalf of the Imam. The report states that a man by the name of Muhammad b. 'Ali al-Aswad used to carry the goods *(amwal)* which were endowments in the name of the Imam to Abu Ja'far Muhammad b. 'Uthman al-'Amri, who used to give him a receipt for them. One day, two or three years before Abu Ja'far died, he brought some of the goods to him. Abu Ja'far ordered him to hand them to Abu al-Qasim al-Ruhi al-Nawbakhti, which he did and asked for the receipt from him. Abu al-Qasim apparently did not like it, and he complained to Abu Ja'far, who told al-Aswad not to ask for receipts from Abu al-Qasim and added, "Whatever reaches the hands of Abu al-Qasim has reached me. So from now on take the goods to him and do not ask for receipts."[27]

From the several reports in these early sources two points become evident. First, the deputyship of the Imam was not confined to the Four Agents in this period. The stress laid on the Four seems to be because of the influence they exerted on the Imamites of this period. Second, in all probability, the institution of the deputyship *(niyaba)* was a later explanation to solve the meaning of *al-ghaybat al-qasira*, as interpreted by al-Nu'mani. It was, in fact, al-Nu'mani who for the first time elucidated the Short Occultation in the terms seen above. Al-Mufid does not embark on the question of the two forms of *ghayba* in his account of the twelfth Imam in *al-Irshad,* and hence does not treat the subject of the Four Agents during this first *ghayba.* But in some places he mentions "our companions characterized by the *sifara* (mediatorship)," when he re-counts the story of a man who had come from Egypt to Mecca after al-'Askari's death and heard the dispute over the latter's succession.[28] At still another place he mentions the *sifara* of Hajiz b. Yazid and the doubt people had as to whether he was appointed by the Imam or not. The doubt arose when a man by the name of al-Hasan b. 'Abd al-Hamid wanted to pay to the agent of the Imam the *khums* which had accumu-lated with him. His doubt was removed by a note received from the Imam confirming the trustworthiness of Hajiz, who acted on his be-half.[29] Another person by the name of Muhammad b. Ahmad al-Iskafi, we are told by al-Mufid, "in those days was the *safir*," who had goods belonging to the Sahib (i.e. the twelfth Imam).[30] All this tends to estab-lish the fact that besides the Four Agents there were many others who were known to hold the *sifara* of the Imam and were entrusted to collect *khums* tax.

It is Tusi who for the first time devotes a special section to these agents of the Imams (including the Four) as "the praiseworthy agents" who, according to him, were approved by the eleventh and twelfth Imams themselves.

The First Agent, Abu 'Amr, 'Uthman b. Sa'id al-'Amri

Tusi in his *Rijal* mentions him as the close associate of the tenth (d. 254/888) and eleventh Imams and their thoroughly reliable agent.[31] He began his career at the early age of eleven as the agent of the tenth Imam, 'Ali al-Hadi.[32] Nothing is known about the date of his brith or death. He was appointed as the agent of the eleventh Imam, al-'Askari, around 256/869–70 after the death of al-Hadi in 254/868. A group of the Shi'ites who had come from Qumm to visit al-Hadi asked him about the person whom they could consult and entrust with the taxes in his absence. The Imam said, "There is Abu 'Amr, the trustworthy. What-ever he says to you is from me and whatever he gives to you is from me." The same group related that after al-Hadi's death, one day they came to see his son al-'Askari and asked him the same thing they had asked his father. The Imam pointed to Abu 'Amr and said, "He was the trusted person of the preceding Imam and remains the same during my lifetime and after my death."[33]

The circumstances under which the first agent lived are well known. Abu 'Amr plied the trade of a seller of cooking fat and consequently acquired the nickname of al-Samman. This, as Tusi reports, was the way to hide his true identity as the agent of the Imam. The Shi'ites used to bring their dues for the Imam to Abu 'Amr, who used to hide them in the cooking fat containers and take them to al-'Askari under *taqiyya* and apprehension.[34] There is enough evidence to assume that the primary function of all the agents, including Abu 'Amr, was to handle the *khums* tax which was due to the Imams from their followers. As the personal representatives of the last Imams in Samarra, who for most of their lives were kept under close watch by the 'Abbasids, the *wukala'* had taken over the administration of the central structure of the Imamiyya. After the disappearance of the last Imam, they were the virtual leaders of the Shi'ites, looking after their religious as well as their financial affairs. One day a group of Yamanite Shi'ites came to visit al-'Askari in Samarra. The Imam sent for Abu 'Amr, who arrived within a short period. The Imam told him to collect what the group from Yaman had brought, "since you are the agent *(wakil)* and the trusted person in the matter of the wealth of God." The Yamanites confirmed the agency of Abu 'Amr by repeating what the Imam said. Then the Imam added, "Yes, and bear witness that 'Uthman b. Sa'id is my agent and his son Muhammad is the agent of my son, your Mahdi."[35]

The funeral rites of the eleventh Imam were performed by Abu 'Amr,[36] and this honor, says Tusi, could not have been given to him except by the direct order of the Imam. His office of the deputyship was confirmed by the twelfth Imam by sending him notes in reply to his questions "in the same handwriting which was seen during al-'Askari's time."[37] As pointed out above, nothing is known about the time of his death, but his *wikala* toward the twelfth Imam must have been of short duration because most of the sources give more importance to his son, Abu Ja'far Muhammad, whose *wikala* was confirmed with that of his father by al-'Askari.

The Second Agent: Abu Ja'far Muhammad b. 'Uthman al-'Amri (d. 304 or 305/916 or 917)

He served as the agent of the twelfth Imam at the most critical period of the Imamite history, namely, the period following the death of the eleventh Imam, al-'Askari. The ultimate recognition of the Imamite thesis concerning the succession to the Imamate after al-'Askari was achieved under the leadership of Abu Ja'far, who was assisted in this decisive task by Abu Sahl al-Nawbakhti, the great Imamite theologian of this period. Abu Sahl's favorable relationship with the Shi'ite vizierate family of the Banu al-Furat and other 'Abbasid officials greatly enhanced the recognition of the Imamite theory of the twelve Imams, even among other Muslims. The uncertainty over the successor of al-'Askari had caused much confusion among the rank and file of the Imamites, and up to the death of the first agent in 260/873–74, there does not seem to have been any agreement upon the existence of the son of al-'Askari. Consequently, the Imamiyya, as was seen above,[38] had been divided into at least fourteen sub-divisions, of which the Fathiyya, who had upheld the Imamate of Ja'far, al-'Askari's brother, had attracted numerous Imamites. Under Abu Ja'far al-'Amri and his associates, who served as his agents in other Shi'ite centers like Kufa, Ahwaz, Rayy, Azarbayjan, Nishapur, and other cities,[39] the unification of the Imamiyya as a single school recognizing the infant son of al-'Askari as the twelfth Imam in concealment was achieved. This process of uniting the Shi'ites under the Imamate of the twelfth Imam must have engaged the energies of Abu Ja'far for a considerable time, and his role as the leader of the Imamiyya must have commenced at a later date than the year 260, when he must have been acknowledged as the agent of the twelfth Imam by the majority of Shi'ites.

According to Tusi, Abu Ja'far served as the agent of the Imam for as long as fifty years, the longest among all the agents, and he was confirmed in this position by both al-'Askari and the learned Imamites, including his father.[40] They had all recognized his reliability and that of his father. At one time his father was asked to take an oath to the effect that he had seen the twelfth Imam, and he did so; Abu Ja'far reported the well-known tradition, after taking an oath, "The Sahib al-Amr is present during the *hajj* every year, and he sees the people and knows them, although they fail to see him or know him,"[41] and that he (Abu Ja'far) had seen him holding the drapes of the Ka'ba and praying, "O God, avenge me against my enemies."[42]

Tusi, in his account of the second agent, concedes the fact that it was mainly due to the efforts of this agent that the Imamites were able to obtain necessary information about their Imam, and that he was so highly esteemed even by the Imam that he was endowed with superhuman powers through the Imam. The questions which were put to him by the Sunnites were answered in writing by the Imam, and the "handwriting was similar to that seen during the lifetime of 'Uthman, his father."[43] There are also indications that the name of al-'Askari's successor had been kept secret up to the time of the *wikala* of Abu Ja'far. The latter had related to the Imamites that during the *hajj* of that year, when he saw al-Qa'im praying near the Ka'ba, the Imam had commanded him to tell those who were asking his name that they should either keep quiet and go to Paradise or talk about the subject of his name and accept the Fire, since if they came to know the name of the Imam, they would publicize it, and if they knew his whereabouts, they would lead the people there and put his life in danger.[44]

The ascription to the special agents of the Imam of peculiar foreknowledge of events to come and other such attributes, which previously had been held to belong to the Imams only, presumably began with Abu Ja'far, because he had acted as the personal representative of the Imam for a much longer period than did other agents. Furthermore, Abu Ja'far's position was greatly strengthened with his being recognized as the leader of the unified Imamite school towards the end of the third/ninth century. Al-Nu'mani r ade reference to this in his description of these prominent figures who acted as mediators between the Shi'ites and the Imam. Abu Ja'far had prepared for himself a tablet to be installed on his grave, and on it were engraved the verses of the Qur'an and the names of the Imams.[45] He was also believed to have studied under the twelfth Imam and his father, who had transmitted his knowledge from al-Hadi and al-'Askari. Among the books he wrote was a work entitled *Kitab al-ashriba* (Book on Beverages) which, according to the report of his daughter Umm Kulthum, was handed down to al-Husayn b. Ruh al-Nawbakhti and then to the fourth agent, al-Samarri. Abu Ja'far died in the year 304 or 305/917−18.

[*91*]

The Third Agent: Abu al-Qasim al-Husayn b. Ruh al-Nawbakhti (d. 326/937−38)

Abu al-Qasim was among the close associates of the second agent and had shared the responsibility of the Imamite leadership by assisting him. The preceding two agents had led a life of almost political quietism, but Abu al-Qasim was a well known and highly respected personage at the 'Abbasid court because of his close relationship with Abu Sahl, the leader of the influential Nawbakhti family, to whom he was related on his mother's side, and with Abu 'Abd Allah al-Husayn b. 'Ali, the vizier of Muhammad b. Ra'iq (d. 330/942),[46] and also because he was held in high favor by the Shi'ite vizier family of Banu al-Furat.[47] He was appointed as the agent of the Imam by Abu Ja'far in the presence of a group of prominent Imamites such as Muhammad b. Humam al-Iskafi (d. 332/944),[48] a contemporary of Abu Sahl Isma'il b. 'Ali al-Nawbakhti (d. 310/922−23), who was also present with other leaders. Abu Ja'far, as it appears from the source, did not mention anything about his having been ordered by the Imam to appoint Abu al-Qasim as the deputy. There is no evidence of this, at least, in the earlier days of this appointment. The documentary evidence which corroborates this is in Tusi's account of Abu al-Qasim.

A man by the name of Ja'far b. Muhammad al-Mada'ini used to bring his *khums* tax to the second agent. Before handing over the tax he used to ask a question which, as he claimed, no one before him had asked. The question was, "Does this money, which amounts to so much, belong to the Imam?" The agent used to affirm that it did, whereupon al-Mada'ini would once again ask the same question and wait for the reply. Only after this would he hand over the money to the agent. The last time he went to see him he had four hundred dinars to give him. Abu Ja'far directed him to give the amount to Abu al-Qasim. Al-Mada'ini, the reporter, thought Abu Ja'far must have been displeased with him and had therefore directed him to Abu al-Qasim. So he returned to obtain confirmation of his statement. The agent grew angry and said, "Get up. May God give you peace! I have appointed Abu al-Qasim in my place and at present he holds my status [as the agent]." Al-Mada'ini asked if he had appointed him as his successor by the command of the Imam. The agent replied, "Get up. May God give you peace! It is just as I have said." Al-Mada'ini had no choice but to obey him.[49]

The above account brings out two facts, of which one, as pointed out previously, is that the early agents were both the treasurers of the Imam, collecting *khums* due on the followers of his Imam, and his *bab*, through whom the Imam could be communicated with. Second, the Shi'ites expected the agents to be appointed by the Imam, whereas for the agents it was prudent to designate a person acceptable to all the Imamites. Many Shi'ites were expecting another person, by the name of Ja'far b. Ahmad b. Matyal, who was also one of the close associates and advisors of the second agent, to be appointed as an agent. The choice of Abu al-Qasim was not only what the times required but also must have been influenced by another eminent member of the Nawbakhti family, namely Abu Sahl. He was one of those leading Imamites present in the last days of the second agent who bore witness to the designation of Abu al-Qasim as the agent. In fact, he was also considered as a possible candidate to succeed Abu Ja'far. After Abu al-Qasim's designation he was asked the reason for his not being appointed rather than Abu al-Qasim, as the agent of the Imam. He replied that his Imam knew better about the person who could be appointed as his mediator. The position, he added, required a person who would not reveal the whereabouts of the Imam, whereas he was a person who was engaged in discussing and vindicating the doctrines of the Imamiyya which were being attacked by their adversaries. "If I had known what Abu al-Qasim knows about the Imam of the Age, perhaps in the course of my discussion, when I was slow in bringing forward strong reasons to prove my contentions, I would have revealed the whereabouts of the Imam. But Abu al-Qasim, for instance, had the Imam hidden under his garments, and even if he were being cut to pieces, he would still not reveal his presence to his enemies."[50]

The second agent was asked by some prominent Imamites about his successor, and he informed them that al-Husayn b. Ruh Abu Bahr al-Nawbakhti was to be his successor and the mediator between him and the Sahib al-Amr. To strengthen his decision, it seems, he added that he had been commanded to announce the designation of Abu al-Qasim and had done so. Later on, although the sources do not discuss it openly, it seems that some people must have had second thoughts about accepting Abu al-Qasim as the agent. The reason was that there were quite a few other prominent persons among the Imamites who were assisting the second agent in performing his task and who possessed an even more privileged position than that of Abu al-Qasim. One such person was Abu Sahl, who, as seen above, was asked the reason for his not being appointed as the agent. Among those who in the beginning opposed Abu al-Qasim's appointment was a person by the name of al-Husayn b. 'Ali al-Wajna' al-Nasibi, who was also present at the meeting of the Shi'ite leaders in the presence of the second agent. This matter was ultimately resolved in the year 307/919–20 in the presence of Abu al-Qasim in Baghdad, when al-Nasibi accepted the validity of the *wikala* of the third agent.[51]

That Abu al-Qasim's choice was well calculated and extremely prudent on the part of Abu Ja'far, there seems to be little doubt, more particularly when seen in the light of those formative years of the Imamite creed during the Short Occultation. Abu al-Qasim was especially known for his shrewdness, and even admired, as it appears, for his use of *taqiyya*,[52] which the Shi'ites deemed particularly necessary to practice during this period. Ibn Babuya quotes several traditions in support of this practice, which was criticized by other sects.[53] Financially, too, this agent seems to have prospered better than his predecessors, mainly because of the rich endowments made by the Shi'ite viziers and other officials of the court.[54] His intimiate relationship with Abu Ja'far, the second agent, as reported by the latter's daughter, Umm Kulthum, also increased his respect among the Shi'ites. According to Umm Kulthum, Abu Ja'far had during his lifetime declared him to be thoroughly reliable and entrusted him with secret messages to be conveyed to the Imamite leaders.[55]

Immediately after his deputyship, his position was confirmed by a note received from the Imam on the seventh night of Shawwal, 304 (23rd November, 917). This event was another indication that there must have been some disagreement regarding his being accepted as the agent of the Imam and that the dispute had been solved, most likely, by the issuing of this note.[56]

The early years of Abu al-Qasim's deputyship were favorable for the Imamites, who had little difficulty in communicating with the agent in Baghdad. They brought the goods belonging to the Imam to his agent without undergoing any hardship at the hands of the 'Abbasid officials. The *dar al-niyaba* had become the frequenting place of the 'Abbasid officials, noblemen, and viziers, especially the Banu al-Furat, who were considered to be the followers of the Imamiyya religion and who looked on Abu al-Qasim with high esteem. But this period of respite did not last very long. Following the downfall of the Banu al-Furat in 306/918 and their replacement by Hamid b. 'Abbas and his partisans, Abu al-Qasim's career as the agent met with misfortunes. During this time Abu al-Qasim was forced to go into hiding because of some disagreement which occurred between him and the new vizier. Also during these years Abu al-Qasim appointed Muhammad b. 'Ali, known as al-Shalmaghani (from Shalmaghan, a town in Wasil) as mediator between him and the Shi'ites. Al-Shalmaghani was a highly esteemed Imamite scholar and author. He was among the close associates of Abu al-Qasim. So eminent was his position that on the same day that Abu al-Qasim took over the deputyship officially in the presence of other prominent personages, when, it seems, al-Shalmaghani was absent, the agent followed by other Imamite leaders went to the latter's residence,[57] presumably to inform him of the succession to Abu Ja'far al-'Amri.

In 312/924–25 Abu al-Qasim was imprisoned by the Caliph al-Muqtadir (908–32) because of his failure to give the court the money it was asking. It was probably during this period that al-Shalmaghani, having become jealous of Abu al-Qasim's position,[58] claimed not only the position of the agent of the Imam but also of the twelfth Imam himself.[59] The date of al-Shalmaghani's apostasy is not clear. But, according to some events, it can be maintained that this deviation of al-Shalmaghani from the Imamite religion must have begun before Abu al-Qasim's imprisonment, since Ibn al-Athir mentions this incident of his apostasy in the beginning of Hamid b. 'Abbas' vizierate, which he held between the years 306–11/918–23; it was Abu al-Qasim who revealed his apostasy,[60] when still in prison. Al-Shalmaghani seems to have contested the deputyship very strongly before making claims to prophecy and divinity, judging by the way he described it to a person by the name of Abu 'Ali b. al-Junayd, saying that Abu al-Qasim and he were involved in the matter of claiming the deputyship and that they both knew what they were doing. "We were wrangling over this matter just as dogs would do over a corpse."[61]

Al-Shalmaghani, who at one time was highly esteemed by the Imamites and whose writings remained reference works for later Imamite scholars, greatly endangered the institution of the *niyaba* (deputyship) of the Imam, and it may be plausibly argued that the reason this institution was terminated shortly after Abu al-Qasim's shrewd leadership was concern that the *na'ib* might subsequently lay claim to the Imamate itself. At times, persons like al-Shalmaghani were instigated by patrons at the 'Abbasid court.[62] Fortunately for the Imamites, Abu al-Qasim's influence and authority were so great that those who were already attracted by al-Shalmaghani's claims gave up their allegiance to him, as Tusi says, when Abu al-Qasim issued a statement cursing al-Shalmaghani, and another ruling was issued from the Imam himself through his agent.[63] Tusi reports that the ruling from the Imam had been issued through Abu al-Qasim in 312/924–25, when the latter was in the prison located in the palace of the 'Abbasid al-Muqtadir. He had sent it to one of his trusted companions in Baghdad to be circulated among the Shi'ites.[64]

Abu al-Qasim died in 326/937 and was succeeded by 'Ali b. Muhammad al-Samarri.

The Fourth Agent, Abu al-Hasan 'Ali b. Muhammad al-Samarri (d. 329/940–41)

Nothing is known about his early life, but it seems he too belonged to the close associates of al-'Askari. His deputyship was too short lived to have caused any changes in the institution of the *niyaba*. He died in 329/940–41. Before he died the Shi'ites came and asked him about his successor, and he said, "The matter is in the hands of God, and He will bring it to accomplishment." Here Tusi adds his comment that therefore "the complete *ghayba* is the one which occurred after the death of al-Samarri, God be pleased with him."[65]

A few days before his death a note came from the Imam which read as follows:

In the name of God. O 'Ali b. Muhammad al-Samarri, may God reward your brethren in your death, which is going to take place in six days' time. So take care of your affairs and do not appoint anyone in your place, since the complete occultation has taken place. I will not appear until God permits me to do so (may His name be exalted) and that will be after a long time and after the hearts become hard and the earth is filled with wickedness. In the near future there will be those among my followers who will claim to have seen me. Beware, those who claim this before the rise of al-Sufyani and the [hearing of the] voice from the sky are liars. . . .[66]

The Implications of the Period of the Four Agents

The study of this period between 260–329/873–941, which is, according to the later Imamite sources, the period of *al-ghaybat al-qasira*, or the period of *al-nuwwab al-arba'* (the Four Agents), brings us to the consideration of the following conclusions.

First, the inclusion of the list of the eminent personages, among whom the Four stand in high esteem, in the discussion on the *ghayba*, however out of place it may seem, was required in order to prove the existence of the twelfth Imam. Tusi makes this point clear as he says that the accounts of the *sufara'* (mediators) and *abwab* (gates) during the period of the *ghayba* were mentioned because the validity of the *ghayba* depended on the proof of the Imamate of the twelfth Imam and on the proof of the deputyship of his agent. The appearance of miracles, adds Tusi, at the hands of these persons is a clear proof of the Imamate of the Master of the Age. The benefit of including their account in the book which treats the question of *ghayba*, contends Tusi, is the nullification of the objection raised by the enemies of the Imamiyya against the Imamate of the Hidden Imam.

Second, the agents were more than four during this period, the four being prominent in Baghdad, which had by then become heavily populated by the Shi'ites. The prominence of the four seems to have been in their shaping of the attitude of the Imamites in respect to the *ghayba* of the last Imam. It should be borne in mind that nowhere does Tusi, whose *Kitab al-ghayba* had been our main source of information on the lives of these agents, mention the four, whom the later sources designate as *al-nuwwab al-arba'*. The center of Imamite activity during this period, as pointed out above, was Baghdad whence the agents appointed by these eminent ones went to act as treasurers and jurisconsults who could be referred to, in matters pertaining to religion, in other major Shi'ite centers such as Qumm and Rayy.

Third, the claim of the agents that they were designated by the Imam himself was always in dispute, more so during the term of the third agent Abu al-Qasim al-Nawbakhti. Tusi, in his account of those who became "apostates" during this period of the Short Occultation and for whom a rescript cursing them was received from the Imam, mentions a person by the name of Ahmad b. Hilal al-Karkhi, a disciple of al-'Askari. Al-Karkhi had refused to acknowledge the deputyship of Abu Ja'far Muhammad b. 'Uthman al-'Amri, who had been accepted as the agent of the Imam through his designation by al-'Askari. After the latter's death the Shi'ites asked al-Karkhi why he did not accept the deputyship of Abu Ja'far al-'Amri, and why he did not refer to him in matters pertaining to religion even after the Imam, who should be obeyed, had designated him. In reply he said that he had not heard the Imam designate him.

[97]

"But I do not refuse the deputyship of his father, 'Uthman b. Sa'id. If I had been sure that Abu Ja'far was the agent of Sahib al-zaman, I would not have dared to oppose him." A rescript cursing him, adds Tusi, was received by Abu al-Qasim al-Nawbakhti, the third agent.[67]

The dispute over the question of the deputyship of the Imam had become so acute that not only had different persons claimed the prerogative, but they also had formulated new doctrines which, as the Imamite theologians assert, had all the potential of destroying the foundations of Imamite Shi'ism in its formative stage at this time. Al-Shalmaghani's claims to this position were mentioned above, and had it not been for the astute leadership of Abu al-Qasim, the newly developing doctrine of the Imamate of the Hidden Hujja would have been uprooted. Al-Shalmaghani's influence can be measured by the following report concerning his various valuable writings on different subjects, which were in use even after his execution in 322/933–34. Abu al-Qasim was asked, after al-Shalmaghani's apostasy, about the latter's books which had filled the homes of the Imamites. The agent replied that a similar question was put to al-'Askari concerning the books written by the Banu Fadal who had become Fathites by accepting the Imamate of Muhammad b. 'Ali al-Hadi, the brother of al-'Askari; to this question the Imam said, "Practise what they have reported [on our authority] and leave that in which they have included their personal opinions."[68]

Besides al-Shalmaghani, a number of other persons made similar claims, most of them during the deputyship of the third agent, Abu al-Qasim al-Nawbakhti. The reason for this situation was, most probably, that the generation of the close associates of the Imams, who had been in direct contact with al-Hadi and al-'Askari, was declining as the days went by, and the hope in the rise of the twelfth Imam by this time was greatly frustrated. Thus any ambitious person like al-Shalmaghani or al-Hallaj who came forward first with the claim to be the *bab* and then with pretensions to be the Imam himself found adherents among the Imamites. The Imamites, it seems, no longer found the belief in the Imam al-Qa'im, who was at the same time *al-gha'ib* (hidden), adequate to redress their grievances in the growing political turmoil of the period. Abu al-Qasim al-Nawbakhti's competent leadership, his good relationship with the Sunnite Caliphate and the viziers, assisted in making his *niyaba* a strong and respected institution for a short time. But the temporary nature of the *niyaba* itself was the main factor in its discontinuance in the year 329/940—41 after al-Samarri's death. An additional factor seems to have been that the Imamites, after al-Samarri, had no eminent personage to take over the *niyaba*. The "leaving of the matter in the hands of God" in the note received by the last agent is an indirect indication of the absence of those close associates who could be entrusted with the task of acting as *al-bab* between the Imam and his followers. If perhaps the later Imamite theologians like al-Sharif al-Murtada or Tusi had lived earlier, one of them might have followed al-Samarri, and the *niyaba* would have continued beyond the year 329/940—41, but as an Imamite would put it, "This was the will of God."

The Complete Occultation: *al-ghaybat al-tamma*

The concern of the Imamite theologians at this time was to justify the delay in the rise of the twelfth Imam as the Qa'im of the family of the Prophet. The deputyship of the Four Agents had more or less decided the course of Imamite history. By the end of 329/940—41, with the appearance of al-Kulayni's *Usul al-kafi,* it is evident that the doctrinal development of the Imamite school had reached its culmination. But the question of the prolonged *ghayba*, beyond the life-span of an ordinary person, had perplexed the rank and file of the Imamites. The absence of any discussion on the *ghayba* in al-Kulayni's monumental work indicates that up to the year 329/940—41, the Imamite theologians were not faced with resistance, either internal or external, to the doctrine of the occultation of the Imam. The period following the death of al-Samarri marked the critical situation of internal resistance to the belief in *ghayba*, about which al-Nu'mani complained in the introduction of his work on *ghayba*. Al-Nu'mani's critical remarks about the Shi'is of his generation, who doubted the disappearance of the Imam, corroborate the contention that up to the year 329, the Shi'is must have hoped for the return of the Imam; following that year, which marked the age of the Imam as some seventy-five years, the situation was regarded as inconceivable. The explanation that the Imam had no mediators during the second occultation indicates the uneasiness felt by the Shi'ite leaders in their attempt to advance a longer than normal life-span for the Imam, who could not communicate with his followers through his personal representatives. In explaining the second *ghayba* al-Nu'mani says that it is the one in which "the agents and mediators were removed in accordance with God's will

[99]

and planning which he exercises in the creation. It also marks the period in which will occur, through testing and examination, the trial, sifting and purification of those who will be called upon to acknowledge the *ghayba* of the twelfth Imam."[69] Thus the Complete Occultation was the period of hardship for the Shi'ites, who were being tested and sifted and purified, until the matter became clear for them; this will apparently occur with the emergence of the Imam. The accentuation on the twelfth Imam's role as the promised Mahdi, the eschatological leader of the Islamic peoples, must be dated from this period when it had become clear to the Imamites that the Qa'im's appearance "in the near future" was uncertain. By emphasizing the Mahdiism of the twelfth Imam, the Imamite leaders were not only justifying the prolonged *ghayba* of the Imam before he appeared to establish justice and equity on earth but also turning the perplexed Shi'ites toward belief in the eschatological role of their last Imam. Thus Ibn Babuya, who wrote his work on the *ghayba* during this period, reports in the opening section of the book that the doubts of the Shi'ites concerning the *ghayba* of the twelfth Imam spurred him on to compose a work in which the subject of the *ghayba* would be treated in full. The vacuum created by the end of the special deputyship *(al-niyabat al-khassa)* of the Imam, which was discussed above, was somehow filled by the Imamiate jurists, who remained the sole leaders of the Shi'ites during the Complete Occultation.

The important question that must be raised at this point is, where and when does the much later interpretation of the delegation, albeit indirect, of this prerogative of the *niyaba* to the Imamite jurists *(mujtahidun)* begin? The only tradition cited by the later Imamite scholars in support of the indirect *niyaba* of the Imamite jurists during the second occultation is contained in a letter from the twelfth Imam received by a person named Ishaq b. Ya'qub in reply to his enquiries about some religious questions. One of these seems to have related to the question: Who should be referred to in the future in case of difficulty in the matters pertaining to religion? The questions, not included in the text preserved by Tusi, were actually submitted to the second agent, Abu Ja'far Muhammad b. 'Uthman al-'Amri, to be presented to the Imam. So the period in which the tradition appears was that of the "special" agents of the Imam in the Short Occultation and not in the Complete Occultation, when, as the source says, the matter rested in "the hands of God." The tradition under consideration is as follows:

[*100*]

As for the events which may occur [in future when you may need guidance in religious matters] refer to the transmitters *(ruwat)* of our sayings *(hadith)* who are my *hujja* to you and I am the Hujja of God to you all.[70]

The text of the *hadith* as cited above seems to have been tampered with during the later period when tremendous importance must have been attached to this tradition. The text preserved by Tusi has the last part of the sentence as follows: ". . . and I am the *hujja* to you all *('alaykum)*." On the other hand, Majlisi's text reads: ". . . and I am the *hujja* to them (the transmitters) *('alayhim)*." By this latter reading only the transmitters would become directly answerable to the Imam and not all the Shi'ites, who would have to follow the rulings of one of these *ruwat*, in case of difficulty. This would necessarily add to their power in deciding matters pertaining not only to religion but also to social and political problems. In all probability, the early Imamite jurists, it appears, had not even thought of claiming such authority, perhaps because there was no Imamite temporal authority as yet, like that of the Safavids at a later period, to rival them in claiming the *niyaba* of the Hidden Imam during the Complete Occultation.

The "transmitters" in this report, as the translator of Majlisi's volume XIII of *Bihar al-anwar* comments, are limited to the jurisprudents *(al-fuqaha')*, the *mujtahids,* and those who are *marja' al-taqlid* (a competent authority to which a person refers in matters of religion) of the Shi'ites "after the *ghayba* (the Short), since they have, by *ijtihad* and scholarly study of the sources of the Islamic law, mastered the religious sciences and are able to grasp the religious rulings better than anyone else."[71] The absence of such an interpretation in Majlisi's text itself suggests that this interpretation of the *ruwat* as the *mujtahids* belongs to the Qajar period of Iranian history when the power of the *mujtahids* increased tremendously, in the absence of any claim by the Qajar rulers to be the lineal descendants of the family of the Prophet. In all probability, this rise of the power of the *mujtahids* began in the Safavid period when persons like Majlisi rose to eminence.

Another example of this kind of reinterpretation of the early tradition relates to the Imamite Mahdi's not requiring anybody's *bay'a* (allegiance) to him until his reappearance. This tradition, as we have seen above, accommodated the Muslim rulers during the early period of the occultation, but was reinterpreted during the Qajar period, when a struggle for power began between the *mujtahids* and the Shi'ite rulers of Iran, who professed the Imamite religion as had the Buyids during the early years of the occultation. As seen above, the Imamite jurists accommodated the rule of the Buyids by interpreting the tradition about the Qa'im's not requiring anybody's allegiance paid to him since he was in occultation. The absence of this requirement of the *bay'a* meant the absence of *ita'a*—obedience to the Imam—which was probably the reason why the Buyids preferred the Imamite form of Shi'ism to any other. But the later jurists, who were challenging the Qajar kings on the question of religious supremacy, reinterpreted the *hadith*, saying that any ruler in a state which recognizes the Imamate of the twelfth Imam must recognize the *hujja* of the Imam, that is the *mujtahid*, as the sole custodian of the religion.[72] The early sources written during the occultation do not specifically treat the question of the illegitimacy of any state or the unrighteousness of the government, even an Imamite one, pending the return of the twelfth Imam.[73] The Imam was regarded by the Shi'ites as the leader of the community and as such he had sole right to establish the temporal authority. Consequently, it was obvious to the Imamite doctors that the establishment of any temporal authority other than the Imam's was a "usurpation" of the constitutional right of the Imam. But, since the *ghayba* had occurred, mainly because of the threat to the Imam's life, and since the period of the *ghayba* was also the period of *taqiyya* (dissimulation), the entire question about the legitimate authority was postponed with the postponement of the *bay'a* to the Imam. Thus the debate about the legitimacy or illegitimacy of the temporal authority in the Imamite state belongs to this later development in the rise of the power of the *mujtahids* and their challenge to the Imamite temporal authority.

Ibn Babuya's Vindication of the Imamate of the Hidden Imam

Earlier it was mentioned that the Imamite traditionists, in attempting to prove the validity of the doctrine of the Hidden Imam, relied greatly on the prophetic traditions and on interpretations of the verses of the Qur'an, related on authority of the Imams. This is demonstrated in Ibn Babuya's exposition of the *ghayba* of the twelfth Imam. He says:

> Our enemies are questioning us in respect of this subject [of the *ghayba* and the Imamate of the twelfth Imam]. They should know that the belief in the *ghayba* of *Sahib al-zaman* rests on the belief in the Imamate of his forefathers,

(peace be on them); and the belief in the Imamate of his forefathers rests on the verification of the Prophet about his and his forefathers' Imamate. This is so, because this subject concerns the Shari'a and cannot be established by reason alone. The religious injunctions are based on the Book and the *Sunna*, as God says in the Qur'an: ". . . and if ye quarrel about anything [which concerns religion] then refer it to God and the Apostle." [4:59] Thus when the Book, the *Sunna* and the rational proof *(hujjat al-'aql)* bear witness for us, what we say is praiseworthy. We say that all the groups—Zaydites and Imamites—agree that the Prophet said, "Verily I am leaving among you two objects of high estimation and of care *(thaqalayn)*:[74] the Book of God and my near kindred, my family. They are my vicegerents after me, and they will not part from each other until they return at the Pool *(hawd)*[75] [on the Day of Judgment]." They are informed about this tradition and do accept it. Hence, it is necessary [to maintain] that there should be one among the descendants [of the Prophet], all the time with the Qur'an, who has the knowledge about the reveleation and knows its interpretation; and who should inform [people] of the will of God just as the Prophet did, [that is,] with certainty. The knowledge of the interpretation of the Book by such a person should be based neither on contrivance nor on deduction, since the knowledge of the Prophet was not of this genre; that is to say, he did not obtain knowledge by deduction, derivation or reasoning. It is not permitted for such a peron to indulge in philological or lexical explanation of the Qur'an; rather, he should inform people about the purpose of God and explain it from God so that his explanation be the proof for the people. Similarly, it is necessary that the knowledge of the descendants of the Prophet about the Book should be based on certainty, enlightenment and intuition. God, the Exalted, in praising the Prophet has said, "Say, this is my way, I invite [ye all] unto God; with clear sight, [which] I and he who followeth me [possess]." [12:108] Thus those who "follow" him are from among his family and his kindred, who inform people about the purpose of God, as it appears in the Book and as He wishes [it to be explained] through certainty, knowledge and insight. Since the purpose of God is manifest and uncovered, it is necessary for us to maintain that the Book is not left without the informer *(al mukhbir)* from the progeny of the Prophet who knows the interpretation *(ta'wil)* to the revelation of the Book. This is what one should comprehend from the *hadith* of al-Thaqalayn (the two objects of high estimation and of care, i.e. the Book and the Family).[76]

The Reasons for the *ghayba* of the Twelfth Imam

According to the Imamite traditionists the main reason for the *ghayba* of the twelfth Imam was *al-khawf*, i.e. fear of being killed. The Imam found himself in grave danger from his many enemies. Zurara,[77] the famous companion of the sixth Imam al-Sadiq, is reported to have asked the Imam about the reason for *ghayba*. The Imam, pointing to his stomach said, "He is afraid of being killed."[78] This fear was peculiar to the twelfth Imam because, as the tradition asserts, his forefathers were not required to rise with the sword and declare *jihad* against their enemies. They were strictly practising *taqiyya* and did not openly call on the people to follow them. Thus the rulers felt safe from that direction. On the other hand, the twelfth was believed to be *al-Qa'im bi'l-jihad* and consequently was believed to wipe out injustice on earth. Therefore, the rulers were looking for him in order to kill him.[79]

To these traditional reasons al-Nu'mani adds two other reasons. The *ghayba*, he says, was meant as a test for followers of the Imam, to see who remained steadfast in acknowledging the Imamate of the Hidden Imam. The other reason for the *ghayba* was to save the Imam from accepting *bay'a* from oppressive rulers and to postpone the whole question of obedience to the Imam until his reappearance. This Imam, unlike his predecessors, will not practise *taqiyya* and will manifest the truth by overthrowing the unjust rule of the enemies of God.[80]

But all these reasons were insufficient to satisfy those Shi'ites who were uncertain of the identity of the last Imam or had doubts concerning his *ghayba*, it seems; a tradition was reported saying that it was impossible to comprehend the reason behind the *ghayba* until the Imam appeared, as had happened in the story of al-Khidr and Moses. This is the story, narrated in the Qur'an (18:60–82), in which al-Khidr finally tells Moses the interpretation of his strange behavior. The story is used as a symbol of the delay in knowing the true reason behind the *ghayba*, the reason for which will be known only when the Imam appears as was the case in the story. It is reported that the sixth Imam was asked the reason for the *ghayba* of the Imam. In reply he said that the Imams were not permitted to disclose the reason behind the *ghayba*. But, the Imam added, the philosophy behind the *ghayba* of the twelfth Imam was similar to that of the *hujaj* of God who preceded him. The reason in all these cases was not revealed until after the appearance of the *hujja* in question, as had happened in the case of al-Khidr. "This matter is from God, the Exalted; it is one of the close secrets of God. He is wise; this is what we accept, and all his actions have reasons behind them, although they may not be comprehensible to us."[81]

The question of the twelfth Imam's *ghayba* because of the fear of being killed was challenged when the conditions were favorable to the Imamites. Thus Ibn Babuya was asked why the Imam continued to be in *ghayba* when the conditions of his Shiʻa had changed drastically under the pro-Shiʻi rule of the Buyids; the Shiʻites were now more numerous and had more freedom to practise their religion openly. To this Ibn Babuya replied that the true situation would remain unknown until the Imam reappeared. But, he continues, the fact that the Shiʻites were in great numbers did not guarantee the safety of the Imam if he appeared, since not all the Shiʻites could be trusted. Ibn Babuya cites the example of Hisham b. al-Hakam, who once discussed the necessity of the Imamate with a Syrian in the presence of the sixth Imam. At one point the Syrian asked Hisham, who was the Imam to whom he was making reference, and Hisham, without considering any danger which might befall the Imam, revealed him. Therefore, Ibn Babuya concludes that the same thing might happen in the case of the twelfth Imam, who was being sought to be killed and whose identity might be revealed by his followers in their discussion with their enemies.[82]

The existence of the *hujja* from God, argues Ibn Babuya, was necessary because the non-existence of the Imam himself on earth would have meant the disappearance of the *hujja* from earth and the end of the religious injunctions, because the latter would have no protector. But if he, in fear of being killed, went into occultation by the command of God, and if he had the known means of mediation, then the *hujja* continued on earth, because both he and the means of mediation were present. Thus the state of *ghayba* did not invalidate the presence of the *hujja*, since this also happened with the *hujaj* before him, as, says Ibn Babuya, in the case of the Prophet himself, who concealed himself for a long period in the valley of Abu Talib.[83] Jabir, the well-known companion of the Prophet, is reported to have asked the Prophet about the benefit of having the Imam in *ghayba*, to which he replied that the Shiʻites would obtain light with the help of the light of the Imam and would benefit by the means of his love *(walaya)* during his occultation "just as the people benefit from the sun while it is covered by clouds. . . ."[84]

The above arguments indicate the extent of attack on the Imamite doctrine of the Hidden Imam by their adversaries and also, it seems, the extent of doubts raised by the lukewarm Shiʻism of the followers of the school. The Shiʻites themselves asked Ibn Babuya about the benefit of having an Imam in *ghayba* "for full thirty years." This appears to be the first thirty years of the Complete Occultation, when the *Kamal al-din* must have been composed (around 360/970–71). Would it not be better to say that there was no Imam on earth at all, rather than saying that it was permissible that the Imam remain in *ghayba* for as long as God deemed it necessary? This crucial question, above all, the Imamite theologians undertook to answer in their numerous works on the *ghayba* of the twelfth Imam. This was the period during which the Mu'tazilite *kalam* was at its peak, and Ibn Babuya was not slow in recognizing the effectiveness of using the *kalam* method in the vindication of the Imamate of the twelfth Imam. The transition from the tradionist vindication of the Imamate and the *ghayba* of the twelfth Imam to the highly theological one was marked by Ibn Babuya himself, who on many occasions found it expedient to quote the *mutakallimun* of the Imamites, such as Abu Sahl al-Nawbakhti, in his vindication of the Imamite stand. But the *kalam* cited therein does not include any of the themes which will be discussed in the next chapter. There is, however, mention of one such theme, that is the *'isma* (infallibility) of the Imam, which in Ibn Babuya's exposition is simply a requirement for the Imam if he is to be followed as the one true Imam. *'Isma,* according to Ibn Babuya, is not something having an outward existence which can be either seen or witnessed. If one accepts an Imam but rejects his being infallible, one cannot be said to have a sound belief.[85]

The use of *'isma* here as an unseen quality of the Imam, its compulsory acceptance as a condition of the Imamate, and its comparison with the acceptance of the Imamate of the Hidden Imam, are entirely new developments in the Imamite writing of this period as compared with al-Nu'mani's earlier statement about *'isma* or the Imam being *ma'sum,* which says that the Imam is "infallible, confirmed, divinely aided, firm; he is protected from imperfection *(khalal),* error *(zalal),* obstinate persistence in disobedience *('inad)* and idle talk *(khatal).* He has been endowed with these because he is His *Hujja* to His slaves, and His witness to His creatures and this is the grace *(fadl)* of God."[86]

The Implications of the Complete Occultation

The Complete Occultation, according to the Imamite writers, began with the end of the special *niyaba* of the Four Agents of the twelfth Imam. During the second occultation no deputy was to be appointed by the Imam, and the "matter is in the hands of God" until the Imam reappears. The mediatorship between the Imam and his followers was indirectly assumed by the *ruwat*, who performed the duties of the special agents of the Imam, without holding the office of the deputyship. The interpretation of the *ruwat* as the *mujtahids*, and the development of their authority as sole interpreters of the will of the Imam, are doubtless of much later origin. The question of the illegitimacy of the Islamic state, especially one with professing Imamite rulers, also belongs to approximately the same era, when the religious classes interpreted the *hadith* of the *ruwat* in order to accommodate the view of their being the *hujja* to the people in the absence of the Imam, who was in turn *hujja* to them.

In later Imamite sources there has been much discussion about the extent of the powers of the *ruwat*, as the general deputies of the twelfth Imam. The reason for such a debate was that the deputyship of the jurists during the later phase of the Complete Occultation gave rise to the question about the legality of assuming functions with political implications, which were in theory confined to the Imam alone. In the event of the prolongation of the *ghayba*, there had evolved an opinion among some prominent Imamite jurists that functions of a constitutional nature, such as forming the government, declaring *jihad* on certain occasions, or convening and leading the Friday service, could not be performed by anyone except the Imam or the one appointed by him directly. Since the *fuqaha'* during the Complete Occultation were not directly appointed by the twelfth Imam, such responsibilities could not be assumed by them. In his lengthy discussion of the question of the legality and incumbency or prohibition of convening Friday prayers during the occultation, Shaykh Muhammad Hasan al-Najafi (d. 1266/1848–49), the Imamite doctor during the Qajar period, explicitly points out that the jurists who had declared the observance of the Friday service to be incumbent even during the *ghayba*, without requiring the believers to take any precautionary measure in performing the regular noon prayer, were the same persons who had declared it otherwise in their previously-held opinion on this issue. This change of their opinion, says al-Najafi, was because of "the love for leadership *(ri'asa)* and power *(saltana)* . . . in Iran *(bilad al-'ajam)*."[87] While the development of such powers of the Imamite jurists could not have created problems in a Sunni milieu, under a Sunni government, in the Shi'ite state it resulted into a struggle of power between the Shi'i monarch and the *mujtahids* — the

[*107*]

ruwat—both, somehow, claiming and implying the *niyaba* of the twelfth Imam in all spheres of the Imam's responsibilities, juridicial as well as constitutional. It is instructive to note that while the early Imamite sources are silent on the question of the illegitimacy of political regimes during the *ghayba*, the latter development clearly demonstrates a common discrepancy between theory and practice.

The whole question of this rivalry between the religious and temporal authority in the later Safavid and the Qajar period has been dealt with by scholars like A.K.S. Lambton, N. Keddie, and H. Algar. But these scholars have not considered the early formative period of the systematization of the Imamite doctrines, especially the doctrine of the Mahdi, although a study of the early period is essential in order to provide the full picture of the development of this phase in Iranian history.

The two forms of *ghayba* (the Short and the Complete) were the result of the evolution of the doctrine of the Hidden Imam from his being essentially *al-Qa'im* (the redresser of wrongs), who would appear in the near future, to his being *al-Mahdi* (the eschatological figure), who would appear at the end of time. There was also a corresponding institutional development from the *niyaba* of the special agents of the Imam during the first *ghayba* to the indirect mediators of the Imam—the *ruwat* during the second *ghayba*. The latter development, therefore, assumes great importance. The prolonged disappearance of the Imam, on the one hand, gave tremendous powers to the jurists and offered them complete freedom of action as far as religious systematization of Imamite Shi'ism was concerned. In consequence, major Shi'i works were compiled and composed during this period. On the other hand, the jurists were confronted with the delicate problem of establishing the authority of the Hidden Imam: only through acknowledgement of this could they endorse their actions as the direct or indirect mediators between the Imam and his Shi'a.

4. The Imamate of the Hidden Imam

The period of the Short Occultation (874–941) was the formative period of the doctrine of the *ghayba* of the twelfth Imam, which has been dealt with in the previous chapter. In the course of time, with the development of *kalam*, the whole question of the Imamate and the Imamate of the Hidden Imam in particular was examined with the aid of the sophisticated technique employed by the practitioners of this art. Initially, the Imamite *mutakallimun* devoted themselves to simple vindication of the doctrine of the necessity of the Imamate and the *ghayba* of the twelfth Imam, based on the interpretation of the verses of the Qur'an, with the prophetic traditions in agreement with this interpretation, including those uttered by the Shi'i Imams. The transition to the theological defense of these doctrines, by subordinating them to the more central dogma of the Justice (*'adl*) of God and the necessity of the Prophecy (*nubuwwa*), was marked by al-Mufid's predecessor Ibn Babuya (d. 991–92), whose view of *ghayba* has been discussed above.[1] Ibn Babuya, the Imamite traditionist, ventured to demonstrate the Imamate of the Hidden Imam by relying mainly on *al-dalil al-sam'i*, the so-called scriptural and traditional proof, proving every statement with the appropriate Qur'anic quotations, ignoring in the process, at times, the context in which the verse appeared, and not giving any consideration to the historical circumstances under which it may have been revealed. Often these quotations were supplemented by the traditions attributed to the Prophet and the Imams. The prolonged *ghayba* of the twelfth Imam, who, as the early sources show, was expected to reappear in the near future, seems to have put pressure on scholars who followed Ibn Babuya to meet the challenge of the more profound criticisms made by the

Mu'tazilites and Ash'arites. These criticisms related to the subject of the necessity of the Imamate; the *'isma* (infallibility) of the Imam; whether the Imam was *lutf* (the grace) of God; the relationship between the Imam and the *taklif* (religious duties imposed upon a believer); and, finally, the rationale of having an Imam in occultation. All these themes were supposed to constitute *al-dalil al-'aqli*—the rational argument (the form of demonstration favored by the speculative theologians, *mutakallimun*) in support of the obligation to appoint the Imam—supplementing the earlier *al-dalil al-sam'i*.

Beginning with al-Mufid (d. 1022), the Imamite theologians deemed it essential to employ *al-dalil al-'aqli* in their exposition of the Imamate of the Hidden Imam. Al-Mufid wrote several works on the Imamate and *ghayba* along dialectical lines, that is, using the formula "if they say this . . . we say. . . ." His work on *ghayba* is entitled *al-Fusul al-'ashara fi al-ghayba*. In ten concise chapters al-Mufid has presented all the important issues connected with the necessity of *ghayba,* the reason behind the *ghayba* of the Imamite Imam, the benefits gained from the Imam during the *ghayba*, and so on. Tusi in his *al-Fihrist*[2] mentions several other titles on this topic by al-Mufid which have apparently not been preserved. Also at this time Imamite scholars began to question the reliability of that part of *al-dalil al-sam'i* which was based on the traditions, because apparently fabricated traditions and unauthentic *isnads* (chains of transmission) were coming to light, although the facts of the fabrication of traditions in certain cases and the defects of their *isnads* were not always admitted (even by those who were concerned), at least in the early days. But Tusi (d. 1067), who worked out a delicate compromise blending the two *dalils* of al-sam and al-'aql and vindicated the *ghayba* by studying the vast number of traditions and giving them the theological complexities of a doctrine, did not fail to observe the discrepancies and spurious origins of some parts of *al-dalil al-sam'i*. At one point in his *Kitab al-ghayba* he openly declared that not only had the transmitters not reported the whole truth about what the Prophet had said, but they had tampered with the facts, changing them according to their personal likes and dislikes.[3] What then was the reliable way to reach the truth *(al-haqq)*, if *al-sam'* could be distorted? It was partly this problem which doubtless impelled the Imamite theologians from al-Mufid onward to embark on *al-dalil al-'aqli*, since it would not only substantiate the necessity of the Imamate but would also defend the Imamate of the Hidden Imam.

In the discussion of the necessity of the Imamate in *kalam,* the two dominant themes of *al-lutf* and *al-taklif,* which form two major pillars supporting the doctrine of the Imamate, bring to light an important dichotomy in the method of establishing what Tusi terms as *al-haqq* (the truth), namely, whether the *asala* (fundamentality) of *'aql* is superior to the *asala* of *sam'* or not. Al-Mufid, in vindication of the Imamite doctrine of the Hidden Imam, which, according to the criticisms of the non-Imamite theologians, was paradoxical, asserts that there were two groups who maintained the necessity of the Imamate: the first group, which included the Mu'tazilites of Baghdad and a large number of Mur-ji'ites, maintained the necessity of the Imamate *'aql*an *wa samc*an , on rational as well as revealed grounds; the second group, which included the Mu'tazilites of Basra, a segment of Ash'arites, and a majority of the Zaydites, held the establishment of an Imam to be incumbent on the ground of *al-sam'* only and refused to accept the *asala* of *al-'aql* in proving the necessity of the Imamate. Both groups, according to al-Mufid, whether they disagreed with the Imamites in their doctrine concerning the designation of each Imam individually, or with each other on the manner of the establishment of an Imam through election *(ikhtiyar)* or by rising *(khuruj)* with the sword and calling people to fight against the illegitimate rulers, concurred that the investiture of an Imam was for the benefit of mankind. The Mu'tazilites of Baghdad in particular asserted that the establishment of an Imam was *aslah* (most salutary) for man's religious and worldly benefit and that both the eventuation of election and the proof of the Imamate were in the public interest of the community *(maslahat al-'amma).* But if this goal was unattainable due to the obstacles raised by the oppressors, then it was permissible for the elders of the community to leave the matter of appointing the Imam unresolved. Such an action would be more salutary, and God has made it lawful for them to apply *taqiyya* (dissimulation) to deviate from the performance of this duty. This opinion of the Baghdad Mu'tazilites, argues al-Mufid, was not different from that held by the Imamites regarding their Imam in occultation, who will appear in the future. It was equally permissible for the Shi'ites, says al-Mufid, who were living under unfavorable conditions, to uphold the Imamate of the Hidden Imam and leave the matter of his establishment until the time when God would command the Imam to reappear.[4] Thus the Imamites, who were preaching the *maslahat al-'amma* in support of the necessity of the Imamate, made sure that a condition was attached to the fulfillment of this *maslaha*. This condition was that any threat from the oppressors to the safety of the Imam should be removed in order to enable him to carry out his function as an Imam. This was to vindicate the *ghayba* of the twelfth Imam, who was unable to stand by his duty to the *maslahat al-'amma* because of the threat to his life. Probably for this reason, from al-Mufid (d. 413/1022−23) onwards the Imamites seem to contribute to the fundamentality of the reason *(asalat al-'aql)* in establishing the truth about the Imamate during the occultation; the only way, asserts Tusi, to prove the existence of the Hidden Imam is by the means of *al-dalil al-'aqli*, of which *al-lutf* is the main example, which makes it inevitable that the Imam should exist at all times.[5]

The Imamite *kalam* considers the doctrine of the Imamate as one of the basic principles of the faith *(usul al-din)*; since it is based on matters concerning reason *(umur 'aqliyya)* in which there is no room for probability, and since the reason for *ghayba* is obscure and difficult to comprehend, the discussion on the Imamate of the twelfth Imam has the preponderance over the discussion on the reason for his *ghayba*. Moreover, the doctrine of the *ghayba* of the Imam is a derivative *(far')* of the principles of the Imamate, which require that "there should be a leader at all times, that this leader should be infallible and that he is such that the community is secure against his committing any bad deed."[6] Thus the theologians commenced their exposition with one of the *umur 'aqliyya*, namely, *taklif*.

The Principle of *taklif* and the Imamate

The word *taklif* is derived from the root *KLF*, the second form of which has the meaning of "imposing upon a person a task of doing a thing" (which is difficult, troublesome, or inconvenient to him). As a theological term it means to apprise a person that there is benefit or harm in doing or not doing certain acts, and that following such an apprisal would inflict hardship upon him, but would not reach a degree of compulsion *(ilja')*. The apprisal *(al-i'lam)*, the certainty of hardship, and the denial of compulsion constitute the basis of *al-taklif*. The apprisal is in the sense that God, who is the *Mukallif*, informs the *mukallaf* (upon whom the *taklif* is imposed) about the nature of the acts which make up the *taklif*, such as the obligation of performing those acts classified as incumbent *(wajib)* and refraining from those classified as prohibited *(muharramat)*. This apprisal can come about in two ways: first, by creating the necessary knowledge *(al-'ilm al-daruri)*[7] in man so as to enable him to grasp those injunctions which can be known by the aid of this type of knowledge, such as the general ethical axioms, good and evil, which are rational categories and can be established by unaided reason; second, by setting up a rational and traditional guidance by means of which man can reflect and obtain information on the nature of the acts to be performed by him. This second form includes the revelation of God through the Prophet, which is the principle source of the traditional guidance.

Al-Hilli, commenting on Nasir al-Din Tusi's definition of *taklif*, says that it is the will of somebody to whom obedience is incumbent, with the condition that his will should not have been preceded by any other will, and that this will should have been made known. The will referred to here is the revelation of God to His *hujja* (proof) for the guidance of mankind, and this will is the first will, that is, not preceded by any other will. Hence, adds al-Hilli, a father, who is one of those to whom obedience is incumbent (others being God, the Prophet, the Imam, the *sayyid* [master in contrast to slave], and the benefactor), cannot be said to have imposed the duty of praying on his son, because his will was preceded by the will of God, who initially imposed this duty on him. After this elucidation of *taklif* al-Hilli explains the goodness *(husn)* of *al-taklif* as follows. *Taklif*, says al-Hilli, is good because God does it, and He does not do evil. The reason for its being good is that it comprises an advantage which is not attainable without it, namely, "exposure" *(ta'rid)* to great benefits which cannot be attained by any other means except *taklif*. This is so by virtue of the following argument: if *taklif* is not for a purpose, then it is vain, which is impossible. If it is for some purpose, then this purpose can either revert to God or to someone besides Him. It cannot revert to Him, since He is perfect and does not need to do something in order to fulfill a purpose. In that case it reverts to someone besides Him, who is the *mukallaf*. Now, contends al-Hilli, if that purpose were possible to attain without *taklif*, then its imposition would become futile action *(al-'abath)*, which cannot be attributed to God; and if it were not possible, then the benefit for which the *taklif* was imposed would become invalidated in the case of a person whose rejection of faith is known. Hence, the purpose of *taklif* is only for the "exposure" to the great benefit, namely *al-thawab*,

[*113*]

which comprises great, pure, and permanent benefits accruing to the *mukallaf* together with respect and praise. That which establishes the definition of *taklif* as "exposure to the great benefits" as logical is the fact that God creates the *mukallaf* with the attributes which enable him to attain the *thawab*, He has incited him to reach the goal, and He knows that he can attain the *thawab* if he performs the duties of *taklif*.

Three objections to the above definition as raised by the non-Imamite theologians are noted by al-Hilli. First, if *taklif* is imposed for some benefit, then it resembles something which wounds a person and then treats him by demanding a remedy; since this is evil, so is *taklif*. Second, if *taklif* is imposed in order to attain some benefit, then it serves as a commutative contract al-mu'awadat), a common practice in commercial transactions in which there is undoubtedly a need for both parties concerned to consent, inasmuch as one who engages in commutation without the owner's permission commits an evil deed. *Taklif*, as maintained by the Imamites, does not specify the prerequisite concerning the consent of the *mukallaf* on whom the duty of *taklif* is imposed. Third, why could not *taklif* be considered as the expression of gratitude for favors received in the past?

Al-Hilli goes on to vindicate the Imamite definition by replying to all three objections. First, there is a difference between a wound and *taklif*. While the former is in itself harmful, *taklif* is not so. The hardship *(mashaqqa)* which is associated with *taklif* is actually in the performance of the acts that comprise *taklif* and not in *taklif* itself. Moreover, in *taklif* there are lasting benefits as compared with the wound which is cured. The cure is nothing more than a relief from a particular harm, after which a person returns to his normal condition. Cupping *(al-ihtijam)* is closer to *taklif* in its effect, because it is carried out to protect a soul from destruction.[8] The goal of *taklif* is the attainment of *al-thawab*.

Second, the precondition about consent which has been mentioned in connection with the commutative contract is because of the different intentions of the people in their business dealings, whereas in *taklif* no commercial exchange is involved. The benefit accruing from the performance of the *taklif* is so enormous that any rational being would be willing to go through the hardship in order to attain it.

Third, in expressing gratitude there is no need to go through the hardship. God has the power to remove hardship from the acts imposed under *taklif*, and consequently, if *taklif* were the expression of gratitude, then the attribute of hardship would necessarily imply futility. Requiring the performance of some difficult task in return for the favor would render the favor anything but favor.

The Imamites have also used the Muslim philosophers' contention in support of the goodness of *taklif*. This contention is a point of departure for most of the Greek ethical and social thinkers. Man, say Imamites, cannot live by hismelf, because he has been created in such a way that he is in need of the aid of others in regard to his own sustenance, clothing, dwelling place, and such other things. This mutual aid cannot materialize except by men's coming together. Living together would necessarily give rise to disputes and quarrels, since every one would be working for his own benefit and would become exasperated with anyone who would get in his way. Consequently, there would be a need for settling disputes and directing the community life. This can be achieved by a Religious Law-giver *(shari‘)* who is distinguished from others by the ability to perform miracles so that all the people may follow him; such a person is referred to as a prophet. However, since the prophet does not remain forever, there is a need for justice to continue by putting into practice the beneficial tradition taught by him in the following matters:

(a) For the contentment of the soul, in order to protect it from the desire of the attainment of bodily appetites *(al-shahawat)* and to prevent it from succumbing to the irascible faculty *(al-quwwat al-ghadabiyya)*, which together form the two "wings" of corruption.

(b) In order that man may continue to contemplate lofty matters, such as the creation of the world and the Hereafter, and to reflect on the attributes of God and the wonders of His creation, all of which lead to the increase of cognition and the broadening of one's vision, so that one may be able to perceive that which lies beyond the world of matter.

(c) In order that mankind may remember the admonitions in the Religious Law, so as to execute justice in the world and increase the recompense and reward in the Hereafter.[9]

Thus it can be affirmed that the purpose of appointing prophets is to guide mankind towards the attainment of great reward in this life and the next. God, whose actions are not without purpose, has imposed *taklif* on mankind to expose them to great benefit which can be attained only through *taklif*. It is largely because of this purpose of *taklif* that *taklif* is good. But it is also *wajib* (incumbent) to impose *taklif* because it suppresses evil. The Mu‘tazilites, according to al-Hilli, agree on this point, but the Ash‘arites reject the incumbency of the imposition of *taklif*. The reason for its incumbency, according to al-Hilli, is that if God does not impose *taklif* on a person in whom all the prerequisites of *taklif*, such as the attainment of the necessary age of maturity or the possession of the rational faculty, are accomplished, then He is enticing him to do evil. Since this is not possible, therefore, it is incumbent upon Him to impose *taklif*. The contention that supports this conclusion is that if God creates allurement for man to commit evil deeds and gratify his bodily appetites by running away from good deeds after having perfected his intellect, and if He does not elucidate for man's rational faculty the acts which are obligatory, as well as the evil aspects of the deeds that are prohibited and the punishment accruing from committing them, then men will certainly persist in doing evil, which is wicked. Hence only through *taklif* can man cease to do evil.

The circumstances that make *taklif* good are those related to *taklif* itself; others related to the act imposed as a duty; some related to the *Mukallif* (i.e. God); and still others concerning the *mukallaf* on whom *taklif* is imposed.

The circumstances that concern *taklif* itself are two: (1) Absence of any cause of corruption *(mafsada)* in *taklif*, in such a way that there should be no occasion of evil in the performance of the duty for either the *mukallaf* himself or for any other person who might be affected adversely by carrying out the obligation imposed. (2) The *mukallaf* should have the power to perform the duty prior to its imposition, in order to think over the matter and perform the *taklif* at the required time.

The circumstances that concern the act also are two: (1) the existence of the act must be possible, and (2) the act to be performed should possess the quality of being more than mere good *(husn)*; that is, the act to be performed should either be incumbent or recommended, while the act to be omitted should be evil, or, at least, its omission should be preferable to its performance. The circumstances that concern God, the *Mukallif*, are that He should know the attributes of an act, whether good or bad, and that He should know the worth of each of them so as to reward the *mukallaf* according to his performance or omission of them respectively.

The circumstance that concerns the *mukallaf* is that he should be capable of performing the act imposed as a duty, and he should possess the knowledge about it, or obtaining that knowledge should be possible for him. Moreover, he should possess the means to perform the act, or, at least, attaining the means should be possible, if performance of a particular duty is dependent on the means *(ala)*.

Knowledge about the circumstances of *taklif* can be *'ilm* (theoretical), *zann* (suppositive), or *'amal* (practical). *'Ilm* can be purely rational *('aqliyy*[an] *mahd*[an] *)*, such as the knowledge of the Creator, His being All-powerful, All-knowing, and so on, which are His attributes and on which depend the validity of *al-sam'* (revelation). This is so because before acknowledging the Prophecy one has to have certainty about the existence of God who can send the Prophet with revelation. *'Ilm* can also be *sam'i*, derived from revelation, such as the duties imposed by the Religious Law, which do not depend on reason. As for *zann*, many rulings of the Religious Law are derived from supposition, such as the *zann* about the direction of the prayer *(qibla)* when a person is in doubt about the right direction. *'Amal* also is either *'aqli* (derived from the reason independent of revelation), such as the returning of a trust to its owner, gratitude to the benefactor, kindness to one's parents, and so on, or *sam'i*, such as prayer *(salat)*, fasting, and so on. These latter acts can be categorized as incumbent, recommended, reprehensible, and prohibited.

Taklif, according to the consensus of the Imamite theologians, has been terminated in order to enable a *mukallaf* to attain the *thawab*. The rational argument that supports this consensus is that if *taklif* were permanent, then attainment of the *thawab* for the obedient *mukallaf* would have become impossible, because *taklif* is conditional on hardship, whereas *thawab* is dependent on being relieved of hardship and trouble. Moreover, *taklif* cannot continue forever, at least not in Paradise.[10] Hence *taklif* and *thawab* cannot be combined; otherwise coercion will become necessary.

Taklif is good for all, asserts al-Hilli, including non-believers, because the purpose of *taklif* is to expose all mankind to the great benefit, *al-thawab*. Several objections are raised to this general character of *taklif*. First, to impose *taklif* on a non-believer is total harm without any benefit in it for him. The reason is that *taklif* is hardship during this life-time; anybody failing to perform it can be punished, which is even greater harm. Thus the benefit accruing from *taklif* is omitted when the person does not receive it, which is evil indeed. Al-Hilli replies that there is no harm in *taklif* itself, nor does it necessitate harm because of its being *taklif*; otherwise such harm would have reached even a believer. Rather, harm lies in the ill-choice of the non-believer himself. The second objection is that one of the conditions of *taklif* is the absence of any cause of corruption for the *mukallaf* or any other person, whereas this *taklif* necessitates harm for the *mukallaf* and may cause harm to the other; thus it is evil. To this al-Hilli replies that the harm which is the cause of corruption is present because of the choice of the *mukallaf* and not because of *taklif* itself. Third, what is the benefit of imposing *taklif* on a non-believer? If *taklif* is imposed to make a person attain the *thawab*, then for a non-believer there is actually no reward; and, as a result, imposing *taklif* on him would be futile. Al-Hilli replies that *taklif* is imposed in order to "expose" man to the *thawab* and not to attain. Consequently, the benefit of "exposure" is available to all alike.

Taklif, on the basis of its apprisal, is divided into two kinds: *al-taklif al-'aqli* (what is known by reason) and *al-taklif al-sam'i* (what is known by revelation or something dependent on it in one way or another, such as *hadith*, *ijma'*, and *qiyas*—the sources of Law). The goodness of *al-taklif al-'aqli* is self evident, since under this kind of *taklif* man can know by reason, independently of revelation, his primary obligations. The goodness of *al-taklif al-sam'i* lies in its being instrumental in disposing man to perform his primary obligations. Thus *al-taklif al-sam'i* is explained as being *lutf* conferred in order to perform *al-taklif al-'aqli*. The fact that demonstrates this is that when a person is assiduous in the matter of religion as prescribed by *al-sam'*, such as praying, fasting, and other prescribed forms of devotion, he will doubtless be more prepared to pursue the primary obligations which are known by reason independently, such as acquisition of knowledge, paying debts, and showing gratitude for benevolence toward him. Thus *al-taklif al-sam'i* is *lutf* for *al-taklif al-'aqli* in the sense that the former facilitates the performance of the latter by providing the incentive to perform that which reason dictates as obligatory. Therefore, imposition of *al-taklif al-sam'i* is incumbent upon God; otherwise negligence of reason and the rational principles would become inevitable, thereby defeating the purpose of creating man.[11]

The foundation of *al-taklif al-sam'i* is the Prophethood and the Imamate, which together constitute the institution of the guidance of mankind. This kind of guidance is the *lutf* of God bestowed on His creatures, and it is incumbent on God to send prophets *(al-bi'tha)* for the purpose of elucidating *al-taklif al-sam'i*, which can be accomplished only by this institution. The Mu'tazilites, according to al-Hilli, maintained that *al-bi'tha* (sending of the prophets) was incumbent upon God. But the Ash'arites did not hold the *bi'tha* to be obligatory. The Mu'tazilites, like the Imamites, considered *al-taklif al-sam'i* to be *lutf* for the performance of *al-taklif al-'aqli* and used a similar argument, as stated above, in support of their contention.[12] The Imamites considered the Imamate to be equally important for the institution of guidance of the Muslim community and argued that the presence of the Imam also implicated *lutf* in *al-taklif al-'aqli*. It is therefore incumbent upon God to appoint an Imam in order to procure the purpose of creation, which is the attainment of *al-thawab*. We have seen al-Mufid's discussion on the Imamate and the difference of opinion regarding the incumbency of the Imam's investiture.[13] It is, however, important to reiterate here that Imamites view the Imamate as the continuation of the Prophethood, and thus the Prophet and the Imams together form the foundation of *al-taklif al-sam'i*. Through these *hujaj*, the Prophet and the Imams, God makes His will known to mankind and exposes them to the attainment of *al-thawab*. Thus the Imamites maintained that as long as there remained *taklif* there remained a need for the *hujja* from God,[14] to act as an intermediary who could elucidate *taklif*. He is the *lutf* of God whose presence makes it easier for a *mukallaf* to draw near to obedience and refrain from disobedience. Thus he must exist at all times to expose mankind toward the attainment of *al-thawab*.

During the *ghayba* of the twelfth Imam the situation of *taklif* changes. In the state of *ghayba*, Tusi says, which is the result of the continuous threat to the Imam's life, *taklif* is removed from that person who is unable to follow certain injunctions because they cannot be elucidated, and certain other people should be blamed because they are threatening the safety of the Imam; such people should be held responsible for the removal of *taklif* in certain cases and not the Imam, who is the *lutf* of God, but has been compelled to remain in occultation.[15]

The relationship between *taklif* and *lutf* is so intimate in the Imamite *kalam* that they seem to form the foundation on which the whole dogma of religious leadership, that is, *al-nubuwwa* and *al-imama*, is constructed. Mainly for this reason, it seems, in *al-dalil al-'aqli* (rational proof) virtually the whole stress was laid on these two principles. Both *lutf* and *taklif* have the same goal of advancing man toward obedience to God and assisting him in refraining from disobedience. Since God has human wel-

[*119*]

fare at heart, both the Imamites and the Mu'tazilites saw it as incumbent upon God to bestow *lutf* on mankind. There is, however, according to al-Mufid, an essential difference: the Imamites made *lutf* incumbent on God because of the liberality *(al-jud)* and the generosity *(al-karam)* by which God is distinguished, and which make it necessary for Him to do the thing most salutary *(aslah)* for the *mukallafun* as long as *taklif* remains in force; the Mu'tazilites, on the other hand, made *lutf* incumbent upon God because of His justice, and if He failed to bestow that, He would be an oppressor. Moreover, they maintained, justice did not require God to do more than what is salutary *(salah)* and beneficial *(nafi')* for His creatures.[16]

The Principle of *lutf*

In the Shi'i *kalam*, as well as in the *kalam* of the Mu'tazilites, discussion of *lutf* logically follows that of *taklif*—which, as defined above, is the will of God revealed in the interest of mankind. God is wise and exercises appropriate planning in His creation. Hence no futile action can be attributed to Him. *Taklif* is one of the things which reveal the wisdom of God and His purpose in creation. It exposes a person to great benefits which cannot be attained by any other means except *taklif*. But it cannot be forced on a person, as it would negate the sense of "exposure" *(ta'rid)*, which is the main characteristic of *taklif*. In this sense a person is shown to have a totally free hand in the choice of his actions, contrary to what the Ash'arites maintained about man's actions, namely, that they are created by God. The freedom of man in choosing his actions gives rise to a crucial question concerning God's purpose: How can God procure His purpose in human affairs when man intrinsically inclines towards disobedience, and how can *taklif*, which is part of His purpose in creation, be fulfilled if it can do no more than expose a person to obedience?

At this point, it seems, the principle of *lutf* must have been introduced. The following tradition in al-Kulayni's compilation may well in large measure have served to provide the earliest outline of this principle. This is, however, the only tradition in *al-Kafi* which tells us something about the principle of *lutf*, in its crude form. The tradition referred to is as follows:

A person asked Imam Ja'far al-Sadiq, "Does God force man to sin?" He replied, "No." The person went on to ask, "Does God leave him free to do what he pleases?" He again said, "No." The person then asked, "Then how does he act?" The Imam replied, "The *lutf* of your Lord is between the two [extremes]."[17]

The *Mukallif* (God) imposes *taklif* on the *mukallaf*, but without using compulsion, because compulsion nullifies *taklif*. *Lutf*, according to al-Hilli, is that thing through which the *mukallaf*, by drawing closer to obedience and refraining from disobedience, attains *al-thawab*. There is no place for *lutf* in enablement (*al-tamkin*), nor does it reach a degree of compulsion. The explanation of this point is that *lutf* is not an instrument by which a person is enabled to achieve a purpose, since if there were a share for an instrument in the enablement of a purpose, then it would not be *lutf*. At the same time it cannot reach a degree of compulsion, because compulsion nullifies *taklif*. This is known as *al-lutf al-muqarrib*, meaning the *lutf* that "causes a person to draw nearer" to obedience. There also exists *al-lutf al-muhassil*, which causes the *mukallaf* to perform the act of obedience without compulsion. Had it not been for this latter kind of *lutf*, a person would not have obeyed. However, both kinds of *lutf* induce a person to perform *taklif* without the use of coercion and allow the person to choose his course of action by his own free will. This is contrary to *taklif*, through the imposition of which a person obeys; since *lutf* is something additional (*za'id*) to *taklif*, it is possible without *lutf* and with *taklif* alone to obey or disobey. *Taklif* in this respect is unlike *lutf*, because once it is imposed, a person is in a position to obey; without it one is incapable of obeying or disobeying. If there is no *taklif*, the question of obedience or disobedience does not arise. Thus it is not necessary that the *taklif* which makes a person obey should be identical with *lutf*; rather, *lutf* is in addition to it. It is clear that obedience is the result of exposure to *lutf*: had it not been for lutf, a person, although empowered to choose of his free will between obedience and disobedience, would not have chosen to obey God. Thus the Imamites contend that it is incumbent upon God to bestow *lutf*, because if God knows that the *mukallaf* will not obey except by means of *lutf*, and if He imposes *taklif* without it, then the purpose of creation would be invalidated. The situation resembles someone who has invited a person for a meal, when he knows that the person will not accept the invitation unless some kind of courteousness is demonstrated, and still does not do so; then he has certainly invalidated his purpose in inviting him. *Taklif*, in other words, resembles legislation, while *lutf* guarantees the execution of the law.

This was the manner in which the Imamites and the Mu'tazilites, who contributed to the belief that man's actions were his own responsibility and not God's, made sure that God would procure His purpose in human affairs. Thus the "*lutf* of your Lord" in the above-cited tradition suggests the underlying principle of *lutf* between the uses of the reply "No" by the Imam Ja'far al-Sadiq. In other words, man was not to be left free in his actions nor were his actions to be predestined, but there was to be a middle way between these two extremes regulated by the principle of *lutf*, through which the purpose of God would be procured.

The Principle of *lutf* and the Imamate

The Imamites have adopted an essentially Mu'tazilite theological doctrine, and, this being the case, it is relevant to set forth the Mu'tazilite view, which seems to throw light on the doctrine held by the Imamites.

The majority of the Mu'tazilites, according to al-Ash'ari, maintained that there was not, among the objects within God's power to enact (*maqdur*), a *lutf* which, if He had exercises it towards anyone who did not believe, would make that person believe. God has no such *lutf* by means of which, if He were to act, it could be said that He determines or does not determine a man's faith. God acts toward none of His servants in any way other than what is most salutary for him in his religion and urges all of them to act according to what He has commanded them. He does not withhold from any of His servants what he needs in order to discharge his obligations to Him. In return for God's concern, man renders Him obedience, which entitles him to the *thawab* which was promised to him. This means that man is free to choose his actions.[18]

When the Mu'tazilites were asked whether it is in God's power to do that which is better for His creatures than what He actually does, they replied that there was no termination (*la nihaya*) to the good things which God could do. It was inconceivable, said the Mu'tazilites, that, if doing the best for man was the objective, God would not do His utmost to aid man. Therefore they objected to the very question, which suggested that God had the power to do something even better for His creatures and had omitted to do it—even though He knew that they had need of the best in order to discharge that which had been imposed upon them as *taklif*. In other words, they said, God will do that which is most salutary for all His creatures in their religion. Thus *lutf* was incumbent on God.

But there were other Mu'tazilites, such as Bishr b. al-Mu'tamir (d. 210/825−26), who believed that God has *lutf*, and if He bestows it on anyone who He knows does not believe, then he comes to believe; but it is not incumbent on God to do this. If God exercises this *lutf* and men believe by virtue of it, then they are entitled to the same reward for the belief exercised by its presence as they would be entitled to if they had believed without it. It is implied that even those people who were not exposed to revelation could guide their lives by natural human endowment and attain the same reward. Bishr also maintained that it was not incumbent upon God to do everything that was most salutary for His creatures. This was impossible since there was no limit to what He could do in this way. But it was incumbent on Him to do what was most salutary for men in the discharge of religious obligation and to remove any obstacles which might stand in the way of their performing that which was made *taklif* on them.[19]

Ja'far b. Harb (d. 236/850−51), another Mu'tazilite, was also a believer in *lutf*. He seems to have refuted Bishr's view of *lutf*, which appeared to override the doctrine of the freedom of man and made him a believer without having a choice. Ja'far b. Harb, according to al-Ash'ari, made it clear that the one upon whom the *lutf* of God was bestowed became a believer voluntarily *(ikhtiyar*[an]*)*. Nonetheless, it did not entitle him to as much *thawab* as he would have had if he had believed without the *lutf*. His view of the most salutary *(aslah)* is that this could be described as what God does for mankind, because He does not expose His creatures except to the highest and noblest of stations and to the best and most abundant reward. Ja'far b. Harb is said to have reverted from this view to that of the majority of the Mu'tazilites.

Al-Jubba'i (d. 300/915−16), says al-Ash'ari, held that God does not have *lutf* which could be described as the power *(al-qudra)* to cause someone to believe who He knows does not believe. Indeed God does what is most salutary for His creatures in their religion. But if there is something which He knows would cause them to believe or prosper by it and He does not do it, then it must be that He intends their corruption. It is not that He has no power to do that for His creatures which, if He did it, would increase their obedience and augment their reward. But al-Jubba'i adds that such an act is not incumbent upon Him, and if He omitted to do such a thing, He could not be charged with acting futilely in summoning man to the faith.[20]

The above Mu'tazilite views show clearly that their view on *lutf* was greatly dependent on their attitude toward human freedom and the doctrine of the Justice of God. The problem of *maslaha* had its origin in the debate regarding the belief that if God is wise He must act wisely. If He is wise, said the Mu'tazilites, then He will do that which is best for His creatures. Hence, if men will increase in their obedience through God's exercise of *lutf*, then He will bestow it. The concept of *lutf* seems to have been an outcome of endeavors to establish some sort of connection between the complete freedom of action in man, as maintained by the Mu'tazilites, and the divine providence, which they termed *lutf*. This was a new term, different from that used in the Qur'anic teaching. In the Qur'an the term *lutf* does not appear. God is described as *latif* toward His creatures in the Qur'an, but the term used for *lutf*—grace—in the Qur'anic passages is *fadl*.[21]

The basic points on which the Mu'tazilites have focused in their exposition of *lutf* appear to be the following:

(a) Good and evil are rational categories which can be known through reason, independently of revelation. God created man's intellect in such a way that it is capable of perceiving good and evil objectively. At this point God made it incumbent upon Himself to bestow that which would draw man close to good and keep him away from evil: this is *lutf*.

(b) Their views on *taklif* and the Justice of God necessarily include a discussion of *lutf*. They maintain that as long as God has imposed *taklif* on man, He should make it possible for him to discharge his obligations. In other words, He should remove any obstacles which might prevent him from carrying out an injunction. This "enabling" would cause man to draw close to the act leading to obedience. This is one kind of *lutf* which enables a person to perform that which is obligatory for him.

(c) All God's actions are based on wisdom; thus it is inconceivable that God would act futilely. This necessitates that in all His actions ther must be benefit (*al-salah*), because a wise person does not act in vain, and God is the Wise (*al-hakim*). Thus God, for instance, does not impose on anyone beyond his capacity; nor does He impose a duty except when a person has attained intellectual maturity and has the power to perform that particular task. Therefore, *taklif* is beneficial to the person who performs *taklif*, and the notion of *al-thawab* (reward) is edifying, because it will

[*124*]

increase obedience in man and prevent him from being disobedient. Consequently, no action of God is void of *salah* and *lutf*.

Lutf then, in the terminology of the *mutakallimun* of the Mu'tazila, is the act which draws man to do what is obligatory for him and to refrain from doing evil. In other words, *lutf* is that by which a *mukallaf* draws closer to obedience and refrains from disobedience in the sense that he is not forced into submission, which is compulsion.[22] Al-Qadi 'Abd al-Jabbar in his exposition of *lutf* says that sometimes *lutf* is described as *tawfiq* (divine aid) and sometimes *'isma* (safe-guarding). But he differentiates between these terms in relation to the *lutf*. The term *tawfiq* is used to indicate the grace to choose obedience but not that which is evil or *mubah* (actions which are classified as "indifferent," i.e. for which neither reward nor punishment is to be expected, but which are permissible). It is *al-lutf al-muqarrib*, that which causes a person to draw closer to obedience. Thus if the *lutf* does not act as *muqarrib* to obedience, it cannot be termed *tawfiq*. The term *'isma* is technically used to connote that *lutf* which prevents the committing of evil. Hence, when *lutf* is bestowed and if it does not prevent committing of the evil, it is not described as *'isma*. In other words, *lutf* in this case is not described as inspiring with the motivation of withholding. Just as in the case of *tawfiq*, *lutf* is "calling" a person to choose obligatory and recommended deeds; in the case of *'isma*, it is "refraining" from doing evil, but not in not committing it.[23]

The Imamites, as seen above, defined *lutf* as that divine act by which a *mukallaf* advances toward a deed leading to obedience and refrains from disobedience; in the attainment of this, enabling by means of an instrument plays no part, since if the instrument had any part in the enablement, it is not *lutf*. *Lutf* exposes a *mukallaf* to the obedience of God by his own free will. It is the result attained at the moment of obedience rendered to God voluntarily; had it not been for this *lutf*, a person would not have obeyed, although it was in his power to obey or disobey. Thus *lutf* is something additional to *taklif*, and it is this *lutf* which is incumbent upon God to bestow. This basic explanation of *lutf* is vital for understanding its relationship to the Imamate.

The Governing Principles *(al-ahkam)* of *Lutf*:

These, according to al-Hilli, are five:[24]

(1) There must be affinity *(munasaba)* between *lutf* and the object on

which *lutf* is bestowed *(al-maltuf fihi)*, in the sense that the occurrence of *lutf* is a necessary cause for the attainment of the status of a particular *maltuf* on which the *lutf* was bestowed. For instance, the obligation of prayer is *lutf* in relation to the act of prayer alone, which becomes *al-maltuf*. The same occurrence of *lutf* does not extend, for instance, to the giving of alms. If this affinity between *lutf* and the object on which *lutf* is conferred had not been made a governing principle of *lutf*, then *lutf* would not have been able to expose a *mukallaf* to the attainment of the particular act on which *lutf* is bestowed. Moreover, the performance of an act on which *lutf* is bestowed would not have been more fitting than the one without *lutf*. The lack of affinity would also necessitate preference of an act by a *mukallaf* without its being preponderant. In other words, in such an act which lacks the required affinity, its being *lutf* is not more fitting than those acts on which *lutf* has not been conferred, since this also would imply a preference of an act without its being preponderant. Therefore, there has to be an affinity between *lutf* and the act on which *lutf* is bestowed; otherwise a *mukallaf* would prefer the performance of an act without its carrying greater weight.

(2) *Lutf* must not reach a degree of compulsion. In other words, in calling a person toward *al-maltuf* (e.g. prayer) *lutf* must not become compulsion, because *lutf* does not force but rather exposes toward obedience. An action done under coercion has one thing in common with *lutf*, in that they both call a person to an action, but the theologians do not term the former *lutf*.

(3) The person must have knowledge of the occurrence of *lutf*; it does not matter whether this knowledge he has is summary *(ijmal)* or detailed *(bi'l-tafsil)*. Without such knowledge of the thing on which *lutf* is bestowed and the affinity between them, *lutf* cannot call a person to a deed on which *lutf* has been bestowed. As for the knowledge of *al-maltuf*, if it is sufficient to call the *mukallaf* to a deed with brief knowledge, then it is not incumbent to have detailed knowledge. For instance, it is sufficient to know in brief that the pain that reaches an animal, in order for it to become food, is *lutf* toward the *mukallaf*. But if *lutf* is dependent on attaining detailed knowledge about an act, then it is necessary to attain it. Brief knowledge about the affinity between *lutf* and *al-maltuf fihi* is enough.

(4) *Lutf* should include an attribute which is higher than mere good-ness *(husn)*, such as the religious obligations classified as incumbent, like ritual prayers, fasting, and so on, or recommended acts which constitute works of supererogation *(nawafil)*. These are among the acts performed by the *mukallafun*. The Act through which God bestows *lutf* is classified as incumbent, because of the wisdom that necessitates its bestowal.

(5) *Lutf* is subject to choice in the sense that it is not necessary that it should be specific; rather it is permissible to choose between two acts which can substitute for each other, for the sake of the desired benefit. For instance, in the case of acts performed by the *mukallaf*, such choice is incorporated in the expiation *(kaffara)* for neglected religious duties. Thus the books on jurisprudence explain three kinds of expiations for those who cannot fast during the month of Ramadan due to illness, and a *mukallaf* can choose among them. But as for the acts which God per-forms, He may create for a person a son who will be *lutf* for him, or He might create another son, quite separately and distinctly from the first one, as a *lutf* for him. In such a case, it is not incumbent for God to perform either of these acts in exactly the same manner; rather, the state of His *lutf* will be appropriate to the incumbent act in which choice is incorporated.

A corollary of the fifth governing principle is that the acts on which *lutf* is bestowed, and which can substitute for each other, are required to be equally good and void of any evil aspects. On this point, according to al-Hilli, the theologians differ in opinion. A group of the Mu'tazilites *('adliyya)*, says al-Hilli, maintained the permissibility of the existence of evil in *al-maltuf*, such as the existence of oppression in an act performed by a *mukallaf* and the existence of illness in the act of God, the *Mukallif*. They contend that pain in God's act is *lutf*, which occurs in order to make a person go through the hardship and remember the penalties. A similar end is achieved by oppression in man's action, and therefore, oppression can also be *lutf*. The Imamites do not agree with the Mu'tazilites on this point. They argue that the existence of *lutf* in an action is because of its being incumbent, whereas evil cannot be incumbent. Furthermore, the *lutf* mentioned in the oppression is actually not in the oppression itself; it is in the knowledge of the one who has been oppressed, just as in the case where the knowledge about the goodness of slaughtering the animals for food is *lutf* for mankind, and not the slaughtering itself.

[*127*]

The Kinds of *lutf*

Lutf is bestowed in order to procure God's purpose, and without its occurrence the purpose in creation is invalidated. Therefore, it is incumbent on God to bestow *lutf*, so that the *mukallaf* will draw closer to obedience and refrain from disobedience. At this point al-Hilli commences to explain three kinds of *al-lutf al-muqarrib* (that which causes to draw near [to obedience]):

The first *lutf* constitutes God's action because of His liberality and generosity, which make it necessary for Him to do the most salutary thing for his servants. The bestowal of this *lutf* is incumbent upon Him. This *lutf* is more evident in the matters pertaining to *al-taklif al-sam'i*, the carrying out of which enables a person to perform *al-taklif al-'aqli*. The institution of the guidance of mankind through prophets and Imams is the manifestation of this divine grace.

The second *lutf* concerns the act of the *mukallaf*, because God knows that the obedience rendered to Him by the *mukallaf* is dependent on its occurrence. This *lutf* is also incumbent upon God to bestow so as to make the *taklif* known to the *mukallaf* and to make him aware of its imposition and incumbency on him. Without this *lutf* the procurement of God's purpose would be impossible.

The third *lutf* concerns the act of someone besides God, the *Mukallif* and the *mukallaf*. As such it is not incumbent upon God. It is a prerequisite in the implementation of *taklif* and concerns someone on whom *lutf* is bestowed by other than God, such as parents, teachers, and so on, who perform their duties in preparing a person to perform the *taklif*. This third kind of *lutf* makes the *mukallaf* aware that others besides God can bestow *lutf*, without which the purpose of imposing *taklif* would have been defeated.

The first kind of *lutf*, which was incumbent on God to bestow and which was evident in the institution of religious guidance, necessitated the conclusion that it was incumbent upon God to send a prophet or appoint an Imam at all times. The Ash'arites, who because of the latter implication did not consider *lutf* to be incumbent upon God, refuted the Imamite stand by saying that *lutf* was incumbent only when the Imam was manifest *(zahir)* and dominant *(qahir)*, while the Imamites did not consider this to be necessary. Therefore, that which the Imamites consider to be *lutf* was not *lutf*.[25] On the other hand, Mu'tazilites, such as al-Qadi 'Abd al-Jabbar, who regarded the Imam more as a temporal ruler invested with worldly power, did not consider that the principle of *lutf* proved the obligatory necessity of the Imamate on God.[26]

The Ash'arites also refuted the argument, based on *maslaha* (general good), which the Imamites brought forward in support of their statement, that since the Imam was the *lutf* of God, it was incumbent upon Him to appoint him. They argued that *lutf* could be considered incumbent when it was void of evil aspects, and that *maslaha* alone was not sufficient to render it incumbent. So long as the evil aspects were not removed, it was not permissible to maintain, as Imamites did, that the *lutf* whose evil aspects were unknown should be considered incumbent. To this the Imamites replied that the evil aspects had already been explained by the Religious Law and that we have been asked through *taklif* to refrain from performing these. Thus the problem of not having the knowledge of them did not arise. The Ash'arites then raised another objection. A non-believer is made to follow *taklif* either by the help of *lutf* or without it. The first premise was false, they said, because if it were accepted that a person endowed with *lutf* was under its effect, then how could he still remain a non-believer? The very meaning of *lutf* is that which is attained by *al-maltuf*, on whom *lutf* is bestowed, at that moment when it is bestowed. The second premise was also false, because the non-existence of *lutf* might either require the conclusion that God had no power to bring it into existence, which would render Him imperfect, or that He could but did not do so. This would mean that God had failed to do that which was incumbent.[27]

The Imamites replied that *lutf* did not mean that which is attained in *al-maltuf*, nor did it guarantee that a person favored with it would not commit sin; rather bestowal of *lutf* itself was *lutf*, which created potentialities in its recipient by drawing him closer to that of greater weight and preponderance. The non-believer who did not accept guidance even after having been blessed with *lutf* remained so because some other forces were obstructing the effectiveness of *lutf*; these obstructing forces were his evil actions and unbelief and were of his own choice. The kind of *lutf* with which he was blessed was in the form of knowledge of the *Mukallif* (i.e. God), and of the reward accruing from obedience to Him and the punishment resulting from disobedience to Him.

The Ash'arites, according to al-Hilli, then went a step further in their refutation of the doctrine that the Imam was the *lutf* of God. This time their objection concerned one of their basic tenets about *al-fiʻl*—action. They argued that informing a person that he would be among the people of Paradise or the Fire is a cause of corruption because it will instigate him to do evil. God's informing a person in this manner, they said, was not compatible with *lutf* because, if a person was already informed whether his destination was Paradise or the Fire, *lutf* became unnecessary.

The Imamites replied that informing a person that he would be among the dwellers of Paradise did not instigate him to take steps to do evil, since he was associated with other kinds of *lutf* which would prevent him from doing evil. Nor is informing a person about his going to the Fire corruption, because this informing could apply to the case of an ignorant person who did not know whether God was speaking the truth. For instance, Abu Lahab (the Prophet's uncle), as mentioned in the Qur'an, because of his ignorance about the truthfulness of God's promise, persisted in unbelief and was thus informed of his going to the Fire. Alternatively, it could apply to the case of a person who knew about the truthfulness of God's promise. For example, Iblis (Satan) persisted in nonbelief although being aware that by such persistence God's punishment would be even more severe. So, in neither case, they said, did God's informing a person became a cause of corruption, invalidating *lutf*.[28]

The *lutf* and the Imamate of the Hidden Imam

The Imamites, who established the necessity of the Imamate on rational as well as revealed grounds, made it incumbent on God to appoint an Imam, since the bestowal of *al-lutf al-muqarrib* necessitated the designation of an authority who would be responsible to draw people closer to obedience. Just as the Prophet was a *lutf* from God, sent for the purpose of elucidating *taklif*, so is the Imam another *lutf* from Him, appointed to continue the teachings of the Prophet. For the procurement of God's purpose it was incumbent upon Him to bestow the *lutf* in the Imamate. This Imamite contention was refuted by those who did not consider that the investiture of an Imam was rationally necessary. This latter group included the Ashʻarites and some of the Muʻtazilites, especially those who belonged to their Basra school. The Muʻtazilites of Baghdad agreed with the Imamites in that they maintained the establishment of an Imam on rational grounds; unlike the Imamites, they did not consider it incumbent upon God to perform this. According to al-Hilli, those who refused to accept the Imamite doctrine of the Imamate being *lutf* of God criticised the Imamites in the following manner.

First, they contended, the establihsment of the Imamate as comprising a form of the *lutf* could not be regarded as being incumbent on God to bestow. The case of the Imamate was unlike the *ma'rifa*–the knowledge (of God) which fulfilled all the requirements for its being classified as incumbent on the *mukallafun*. The purpose of creating *al-ma'rifa* was to remove any evil aspect which might arise in our supposition *(zann)*. There was no sufficient reason to consider the Imamate as incumbent on God when it was not known that all evil aspects that might cause corruption had been removed. One cannot rely on supposition in such a crucial matter. Therefore, when it was not permissible that the Imamate might comprise evil aspects unknown to us, it could not be incumbent upon God to appoint an Imam.

To this the Imamites replied that it was well known that there did not exist any known evil aspect in the Imamate, because evil aspects were confined and known to the *mukallafun*. It was not incumbent upon them to avoid all the evil aspects; rather, they had to keep away from those aspects that were known to them, because imposing *taklif* without apprisal was impossible. Since such known evil aspects were absent in the Imamate, what remained was the consideration of *lutf*, free from the cause of corruption. Thus, it is incumbent on God. Moreover, had the cause of corruption been a necessary part of the Imamate, then it would not have been separated from it. This was false, because God says in the Qur'an: "I will make you (Abraham) Imam for the people." This proved that the cause of corruption was not a necessary part of the Imamate, and in this way it was proper to declare the appointment of an Imam as incumbent on God.

Second, the establishment of the Imamate could be incumbent only when the way to the *lutf* was confined to the Imamate, whereas it was permissible that there be another *lutf* which could take place of the Imamate. Thus it was not specified that the Imamate was the only *lutf*, and hence, it was not incumbent on God to appoint the Imam.

The Imamites replied that the *lutf* which was confined to the Imamate was *al-lutf al-muqarrib* (which caused the *mukallaf* to draw closer to obedience and refrain from disobedience), known to all rational beings.

[*131*]

Through the Imamate the causes for corruption arising from disputes among the people could be removed. Therefore, the appointment of the leaders at all times and for all regions was necessary for the well being of all mankind.[29]

The Imamites, having established that the Imam was the *lutf* of God, had then to deal with the question of whether this *lutf* was in the existence of the Imam himself or in his discretionary control *(tasarruf)* over command and interdiction. The Imamites maintained that the Imam was *lutf* both in his existence and in his discretionary control. The existence of the Imam was *lutf* for several reasons, of which two were important: first, he was the protector of the Shari'a and did not allow any addition or omission in it; second, the belief of the *mukallafun* that there was an Imam who could at any time summon them to carry out his will was a cause preventing them from committing wicked deeds and drawing them to that which was salutary. This latter reason was known necessarily. But his discretionary control was dependent on three conditions, and only if these conditions were met could the Imamate work to the advantage of the community. The first condition concerned God; that is to say, He was responsible for creating an Imam and consolidating him with power, knowledge, and the means by which he could carry out that which had been entrusted to him. It was incumbent upon God to designate him by name and descent and require him to undertake the charge of the community. The second condition concerned the Imam, who should accept the *taklif*, shoulder the burden of the Imamate, and take upon himself the accomplishment of its function. The third condition concerned the *mukallafun* (i.e. the people), who should assist and support the Imam in the performance of his duties and the removal of obstacles from his way in order to facilitate the performance of the *taklif*. They should render him obedience and follow his instructions, without which he could not lead them to *al-thawab*. Obedience to the Imam had been made incumbent upon the *mukallafun* by God and has been prescribed as a duty toward the Imam.[30]

This argument makes clear that the performance of the duties of the Imamate was conditional on the existence of the Imam, since *taklif* in regard to something that does not exist is evil when judged by rational criteria. Hence, his appointment by the will of God was the main condition, while the obligation of carrying out the duties of the Imamate was dependent on it; the incumbency upon his followers to aid him was conditional on both of these, since obedience to the Imam was incumbent only when the Imam existed and performed his duties as an Imam.

This leads one to the inevitable conclusion that during the *ghayba* of the twelfth Imam the principle of *lutf* was invalidated, since there was no Imam to carry out the functions of the Imamate. This was the principal criticism made by the Mu'tazilites of the principle of *lutf* as maintained by the Imamites. Al-Qadi 'Abd al-Jabbar, commenting on this principle says, ". . . and as for those who say there is a need for the Imam because he is *lutf* in the religion . . . how do they permit the Imam to be in occultation from the *umma* for such a long time, when his existence is *lutf* in the religion and when he is needed so badly?"[31]

The objection raised by al-Qadi 'Abd al-Jabbar is found in most of the other non-Imamite sources dealing with this subject. The entire Imamite argument that the Imam was *lutf* because he could command and interdict and impose legal punishment on those who failed to carry out his guidance crumbles under the weight of the prolonged *ghayba* of the twelfth Imam. So in the case of the Imamate of the Hidden Imam, the only way to justify his *ghayba* was to offer a division of *lutf* as applied to this Imam. The *lutf* applied to this Imam in particular was of two kinds. First, the very existence of the Imam was *lutf*, and secondly, his discretionary control over absolute power became another *lutf*. The first *lutf* was effective in the belief of the *mukallafun*, who by believing in his existence are prevented from violating the Religious Law and are encouraged to perform the religious injunctions prescribed therein. They are possibly also helped by this belief to abstain from evil deeds. So this *lutf* is present even when the Imam is in occultation. The other type of *lutf*, namely his discretionary control in the affairs of the *umma*, was not possible unless he were known to exist. According to the Imamites, those who said that because of the absence of his discretionary control he did not exist were not in the right. The Imam, they said, did exist but, because the third condition required in the discretionary control, namely the need for the support and assistance to be accorded by the people, was not fulfilled, he was unable to benefit the people by his existence. Consequently, the *mukallafun* should be blamed for this situation which had compelled the Imam to remain in occultation. Thus the *lutf* of God was present to enable the people to follow *taklif*. The suggestion, says al-Hilli, that during the *ghayba*, *taklif* becomes evil is incorrect. *Taklif* would become evil if the things which were required to be performed as *taklif* were not known. However, the majority of the injunctions were known, and for those things which were not known, there could be no *taklif*—since *taklif* in regard to an unknown thing was impossible.[32]

Al-Sharif al-Murtada, in his *Treatise on the Occultation of the Twelfth Imamite Imam*, has summarized the Imamite argument about the Imam being *lutf* even during the *ghayba* as follows:

If it is said, "What is the difference between his (the Imam's) existence when he is in the *ghayba* and no one can reach him nor benefit from him, and his non-existence? [Furthermore,] would not his being rendered non-existent until the time when God knows there will be support for him from the people be as permissible as [His] allowing concealment until that time when God knows there will be support for him from the people?"

Then it should be said to those [making such objections]: "First, we consider it allowable that many of his friends and those upholding his Imamate would reach him, and thus benefit from him; and those among them, the adherents of his *shi'a*, and believers in his Imamate who neither reach nor meet him, they too benefit from him during the *ghayba* [by that] benefit which we say is required [in the state of] obligation (*al-taklif*). [This is] because with their awraeness of his existence among them and their being certain about the incumbency to obey him, they will inevitably fear him and respect him [so that they would not] commit an evil deed. They are afraid of being chastised or reprimanded by him. In this manner, the [performance of] vile deeds will decrease among them and the good deeds will increase, or, [at least] they will be closer to such a thing."

This then is the rational argument in support of the necessity of the Imam. Thus, even though the Imam does not appear to his enemies, because of fear from them and because they have blocked the way to benefit from him against themselves, we have, nonetheless, shown in this discourse the way his friends benefit from him in the two ways mentioned above.

In addition, here we say: "The difference between the existence of the Imam [who is in the *ghayba*] because of the fear from his enemies and who is waiting in this state for them (the people) to consolidate him so that he may appear and take the command of that which God has entrusted him, and his non-existence is as clear as the day-light; because, if he were non-existent then whatever good the people relinquished, or whatever guidance they abandoned and whatever benevolence they were deprived of, would be imputed to God. [In this way] there would be no argument against the people and no blame. But, if the Imam is present, although in concealment because of their alarming him, whatever benefits are removed from them will be imputed to them. They are to be blamed for that and criticized for it."[33]

The Principle of *'isma* and the Twelfth Imam

In his *Fusul al-'aqa'id*, Nasir al-Din Tusi explains two kinds of *lutf*: *al-'amm* (general) and *al-khass* (particular). The general *lutf* is the one bestowed on all *mukallafun* to enable them to perform the *taklif*. But the particular *lutf* is specially conferred on prophets and their rightful successors. By this kind of *lutf* a prophet is enabled to abstain from wicked deeds and perform those which are made obligatory on him, and to remain within the boundaries *(hudud)* set by God. This special favor to prophets is meant to attract people toward them. This *lutf* is called *'isma*.

The Imamite theologians, in proving the incumbency of *'isma* in the Prophet, begin by discussing the purpose of the prophethood *(al-nubuwwa)*. Prophets, they maintain, are sent with a mission to guide mankind towards attaining *al-thawab* by elucidating to them God's requirements of them—*taklif*. In this capacity they are the leaders of the people among whom they are appointed to carry out the duty of the prophethood. The purpose of *al-nubuwwa* could be defeated if the people to whom they are sent thought it permissible for the prophets to commit sins and tell falsehoods, because then they would also think the same about their teachings and their commands and interdictions. As a consequence, they would not follow them and would not be able to attain *al-thawab*, which is the main purpose of the *bi'tha* (sending the prophets). Furthermore, obedience to them is made incumbent by God, and if they sin, then men by following them would also necessarily be guilty of sin; this, however, is not possible, because God cannot command man to do evil, nor can He make obedience to such a person incumbent. Finally, if the prophet sins, it will be incumbent on his followers to stop him from doing so, since commanding to do good and interdicting from doing evil are incumbent on every *mukallaf*. Refraining the prophet from doing evil would cause a harmful act and the goal of prophethood would not be achieved. For these reasons, they hold, the purpose of sending a prophet is dependent on his *'isma*; unless he is infallible, the confidence which is required in the prophethood cannot be attained.[34] So al-Mufid defines *'isma* as *al-tawfiq* (divine aid), *al-lutf* (divine grace), and *al-i'tisam* (divine protection) for the *hujaj* (the proofs, i.e. the Prophet and Imams) from God against sinning and committing errors in promoting the religion of God.[35]

There is a difference of opinion among the theologians regarding the necessity of *'isma* in the prophets. A group of Mu'tazilites, according to al-Hilli, permitted the occurrence of minor sins *(al-sagha'ir)* in prophets, which were committed inadvertently, while others among them permitted minor sins, which were open to interpretation as not being sins at all; still others allowed them to occur in light of their numerous deeds of merit, which cancelled out the minor sins. The Ash'arites and the Hashwiyya (the people of *hadith*, who were contemptuously known as such because of their recognition of some anthropomorphic traditions as genuine and their literal interpretation of these without criticism), adds al-Hilli, held that the prophets could commit both minor and grave *(al-kaba'ir)* sins, with the exception of *kufr* (disbelief) and *kadhib* (falsehood). The Imamites believed that the prophets should be immune from both types of sins.[36]

The institution of guidance, according to the Imamites, includes both the Prophet and the Imams, to whom the term *hujja* is applied in their dogmatics. They are all considered to have been divinely appointed, rightly guided leaders of the community. As a result, the principle of the necessity of *'isma* in prophets is also extended to include the Imams, who, being upheld as the rightful successors of the prophetic mission, were required to be infallible from the time they matured intellectually to the end of their mission on earth. In justifying *'isma*, stress was laid on protection of the Religious Law, which could be accorded only by an infallible leader.[37]

The Imamites attached great importance to this principle and made it a condition for the procurement of God's purpose in sending or appointing His *hujja* on earth. From the early days of Islam, there was a group of Muslims sympathetic to the claims of the Banu Hashim in general and of the *ahl al-bayt* (the family of the Prophet) in particular, which propounded and looked forward to the leadership of a perfect man and was always eager to attribute such heightened characteristics to their leaders among the Banu Hasim.[38] A careful study of the evolution of this doctrine reveals that, as the Imamites moved away from the period of their Imams, the doctrine of *'isma* was redefined along even more precise lines than before. The classic example is that offered by Ibn Babuya (d. 992), who represents the view of the Imamite traditionists. On the question of *'isma*, he affirmed that the prophets and Imams, though infallible as far as both grave and minor sins were concerned, were liable to inadvertence *(sahw)*, which God might induce in them in order to remind mankind that they were merely human beings.[39] His opinion was modified by al-Mufid (d. 1022), who held that the Prophet and the Imams, being the *hujja* from God, were endowed with *'isma* from the time they matured intellectually until they died. They were not liable to inadvertence in anything concerning religion or to forgetfulness concerning any of the injunctions, because they were appointed to protect the Religious Law and take people to task if they failed to observe it.[40]

'Isma, the Imamites believe, cannot be known externally by the help of the senses *(al-hiss)* or by perceiving the outward natural disposition, since it is the psychic power *(al-malakut al-nafsaniyya)* possessed by the prophets and the Imams after they have received the revelation or have been designated as Imams respectively; according to al-Hilli, it is the *lutf* of God to the prophets and the Imams, so that they may not have the motivation to forsake obedience and to commit sin, although they have the power to do so. *'Isma* can be known only by God, who has the knowledge of hidden things, but He can guide man towards the knowledge of such a thing. This He does by the explicit designation *(nass)* of the Imam through His prophet, who is infallible. Thus only God, through the Prophet, can designate an infallible *(ma'sum)* Imam. After the Prophet it can only be another *ma'sum*, and only he knows the rightful successor.[41] Any person other than an infallible Imam claiming the prerogative of knowing and appointing his successor needs another person, who as his Imam must be infallible and who can designate the following Imam without error. This is so because, as al-Sharif al-Murtada argues, if we accept a leader who might be fallible, the needs of society are not fulfilled, and a leader is needed above that fallible leader who himself should be in infallible. If he is again fallible, another infallible person would be needed by him and so on. This would necessitate either belief in an unlimited number of Imams, which is impossible, or the existence of an Imam with whom the cause for the need of an infallible Imam has disappeared.[42] Thus *'isma* can be known only through a clear designation, and only an infallible person can take the place of the prophet or another Imam. With the establishment of the principle of *'isma*, and its relationship with *nass*, and the necessity of the Imamate in every age, there remains no alternative, says al-Sharif al-Murtada, "but to maintain that he (the twelfth Imam) is the Master of Age *(sahib al-zaman)* himself;

and in the absence of his discretionary control and his emergence *(zuhur)*, there is no way but to uphold the view about his *ghayba.* . . . Otherwise the truth will be removed from the Imamate."[43]

By this substantion of the view that only the son of al-Hasan al-'Askari was the *ma'sum*, the *ghayba* of the infallible Imam became even more difficult to justify. Al-Sharif al-Murtada undertook to vindicate the Imamate of the infallible Imam in *ghayba* by comparing the explanation of the *ghayba* with that of the ambiguous *(mutashabih)* verses of the Qur'an, for which no rationally-arrived-at reason could be offered. In such cases one had to trust the wisdom of God, who called upon the twelfth Imam to go into occultation for some reason equally unknown. Acquiring the knowledge of this reason "has not been imposed upon us as a duty." The plausible reason for the *ghayba* of the Imam, in spite of his being infallible, according to al-Sharif al-Murtada, is

> fear for him from the unjust people, and their obstructing his hand from discretionary control over that which has been meant to be his right of discretionary control. [This is] because one attains total benefit from the Imam when he is firmly established and obeyed [by the people] and when there is no obstruction between him and his goals, so as to enable him to lead troops, fight the oppressors, administer legal punishment, protect the boundaries, and see that justice is done to the oppressed. All this cannot be accomplished except when he is firmly established. So if something comes between him and his purpose, the duty of carrying out the Imamate becomes null and void on him; and when he is afraid for his life, his *ghayba* becomes incumbent. To guard oneself against harm is incumbent both by tradition and by reason.[44]

This emphasis on the infallibility of the Imam requires an explanation of the role of the infallible Imam in reaching *ijma'* (consensus) in the Imamite legal system. If *ijma'* is reached without an infallible Imam's participation *(dukhul)* as one of the members of the group who have come together to reach a consensus, the Imamites do not consider the *ijma'* valid. The validity of *ijma'* is ensured only by the participation of the infallible Imam, who is the *hujja* and the successor of the Prophet. This was the way, it seems, the Imamites sought to invalidate the principle of *ijma'* as maintained by the Sunnites, and which was the main basis for legitimizing the caliphate of Abu Bakr after the death of the Prophet.

The Concept of *ijma'* and its Relationship to the Hidden Imam:

The basic meaning of *ijma'* is "agreement." As a technical term it signifies a special kind of agreement, namely, agreement of either the Muslim jurists or the elders among the Muslim community *(ahl al-hall wa al-'aqd)* or the whole community as such on a particular legal issue. The latter meaning was never really taken literally. This defintion of *ijma'* necessarily excludes the general members of the community because it is the agreement of those individuals whose opinion is effective in the promulgation of a law and who are actually followed by the general membership. This is the way the Sunnites understand the concept of *ijma'* and they regard it as one of the four sources of Islamic law, besides the Qur'an, the Sunna, and *qiyas* (analogy). However, *ijma'*, for the Imamites, is a source of Islamic law only in form and name, as will be discussed below, since, according to them, *ijma'* is not an independent source equivalent to the Qur'an and the Sunna. In fact, *ijma'* is regarded as the process of discovering the Sunna, which is the opinion of the infallible Imam. Consequently, *ijma'* in itself is neither an authoritative nor an infallible source of the Law. In reality, the opinion of the infallible Imam is the source of the Law, provided that such an opinion can be discovered. For this reason the Imamites have employed the term *ijma'* even when the consensus comprised a small number of jurists, as against the basic requirement of the technical usage of *ijma'*, namely, agreement of the majority of the jurists. *Ijma'* in Imamite jurisprudence, then, is used to designate that opinion which has been discovered with certainty as being the Imam's opinion. Thus it is the formal use of the term *ijma'*, in a substantially different sense, which characterizes the Imamite legal system, and which is crucial in comprehending its value in the enactment of law in this school.[45]

An opinion arrived at by *ijma'*, according to the Imamites, in order to become an authoritative source of the Religious Law, must bring to light the utterance of the infallible Imam. Only when the utterance of the infallible Imam is revealed with certainty does the consensus become authoritative; that which is revealed in the form of consensus becomes authoritative, not the person who reveals the utterance. The infallibility of the *umma* as maintained by the Sunnites, the Imamites contend, cannot be substantiated. It is far-fetched to think that the *umma* would discover and agree upon an opinion of the one endowed with infallibility, such as the Imam. The reason for this contention is that the infallibility in regard to *ijma'* is to be ascertained in the opinion which has been revealed and not in the person of the one who revealed it. In this sense, then, a statement arrived at by *ijma'* is similar in status to the tradition reported in an unbroken line *(al-mutawatir)*, which was handed down by numerous chains of narrators, on the authority of the infallible Imam. The function of such a tradition is to direct a jurist to the opinion of the infallible Imam, and as such the authenticity is that of the report itself and not the narrators. Hence, a *mutawatir* tradition is not in itself directly a proof for the enactment of a religious injunction but rather an evidence of the proof for the injunction. Similarly, *ijma'* in its function is not a proof in itself but an evidence for the proof. Nevertheless, there is one basic difference between a *mutawatir* tradition and *ijma'*: the former is the verbal proof of the utterance of the infallible Imam; that is, it demonstrates the exact wording of the Imam handed down by very many distinct chains of narrators. The *tawatur* is of an utterance as such, although it is possible that it could be a *tawatur* relating to the sense of the utterance. The latter is a definite proof of an opinion of the infallible Imam itself and not a proof of the particular wording of what had been uttered by him, because it is not proved that the Imam uttered particular words in explaining a particular injunction. For this reason in Imamite jurisprudence *ijma'* is named as essential proof, similar to the rational proof. In other words, by applying either of these proofs one can obtain the sense and the purport of a legal injunction, similar to the gist as compared to the exact words of the utterance.

When *ijma'*, through the discovery of the opinion of the infallible Imam, becomes an authoritative source of the Law, it is not necessary to attain the agreement of all the jurists without exception, as maintained by the Sunnites in accordance with their concept of *ijma'*. It is sufficient that all those searching for the opinion of the Imam should concur that the opinion revealed is that of the Imam, regardless of their number. The important thing is that their cognition can be rendered reliable only through the discovery of the opinion of the Imam.

Najm al-Din al-Hilli, known as al-Muhaqqiq (d. 676/1277–78), in his work entitled *al-Mu'tabar*, after mentioning the condition for the *ijma'* regarding the inclusion of the infallible Imam's opinion in order for it to become authoritative, says: "If one hundred of our jurists reached an opinion which was far from the opinion of the infallible Imam, then such an opinion has no evidential value; on the other hand, if such an opinion were arrived at by even two jurists, then their opinion is authoritative."[46] This and other such statements in the Imamite jurisprudence explicitly mention the Imamite position regarding the validity of the *ijma'*. However, according to some procedures, to arrive at *ijma'* it is necessary to obtain the agreement of all the jurists of one single period.[47]

For this reason naming the discovery of the opinion of the infallible leader as *ijma'* is apparently unwarranted in the Imamite legal system, although such indulgence is common among some prominent Imamite jurists. Thus the term *ijma'* in Imamite law signifies any agreement, whether of all or some jurists, as long as it reveals with certainty the opinion of the Imam. The *ijma'* cannot be considered the source of law if it attains merely a strong probability *(zann)*; it must attain the highest degree of certainty to become authoritative.

How does one discover through *ijma'*, with certainty, the opinion of the Imam? This question must now be discussed. The Imamites have mentioned several ways to this end, among which the following four are the most important:

(1) *Tariqat al-hiss* (The Method of [Direct] Sensory Perception)[48]

This method was known among the ancient Imamite jurists, including al-Sharif al-Murtada and those who followed him in this. This method states that it should be known with certainty that the Imam was among *(dimn)* those who had agreed upon a consensus, without his person being revealed among them. For example, if forty opinions were found on a particular issue, it should be ascertained that one of them was the *fatwa* (legal opinion) of the infallible Imam.

This method is applicable only when a person trying to discover the *ijma'* should himself investigate and trace the opinions of the jurists and discover their agreement on a particular issue. This requires one of two procedures to be followed. According to the first, this person, who is investigating an *ijma'*, should contact all the jurists of the period and "hear" their opinion himself on the issue in question. During this process, it is possible that he might hear the Imam of the Age replying to his inquiry; thus, his ultimate discovery is authenticated by the inclusion of the Imam's opinion. Nevertheless, he has to make sure that one of those whom he heard was the Imam himself; otherwise his finding has no legal value. According to the second procedure, a person, in trying to reveal the Imam's opinion, may arrive at successively related opinions among the residents of one city or a single period. Thus he may ascertain through its being successively related that the Imam was one of those who had given this opinion, although he might not know his opinion as such. The latter is known as *al-ijma' al-manqul bi al-tawatur* (the consensus that has been related consecutively), as compared with the former, which is named *al-ijma' al-muhassal* (the consensus which is attained through investigation directly). In both cases the *ijma'* includes the Imam's opinion, and because of the "inclusion" of the Imam's opinion, it is also known as *al-ijma' al-dukhuli*.

It is clear that this method of revealing *ijma'* is almost impossible to attain except for one who is a contemporary of the Imam. During the period of occultation of the Imam, it is not possible to attain the *muhassal* type, which required it to be "heard" directly from the Imam. As for the *manqul* type, what happens if out of all the jurists one of them disagrees concerning the *ijma'*? Does the *ijma'* then retain its validity or not? If the jurist who opposed the view is a well-known person, then it can be ascertained that the twelfth Imam's opinion was among those others who had agreed. In other words, if, for instance, there were forty opinions of which one opposite view belonged to the well-known jurist, while the rest belonged to known as well as unknown persons, the opinion of the latter group would be considered to include the Imam's opinion. On the other hand, if thirty-nine opinions concurred, and one opinion belonging to an unknown person opposed the concurrence, such an *ijma'* would be regarded as invalid. The reason is that, according to this method, this unknown opinion is to be taken as the opinion of the Imam himself.

(2) *Tariqa qa'idat al-lutf* (The Method Based on the Principle of *lutf*):

This is an important method of finding out the opinion of the infallible Imam in *ijma'*. While the previous method was based on "hearing" (*al-sama'*), this one is based on "reason" (*al-'aql*) through the process of mental inference. This method mentally discovers the opinion of the Imam, through an agreement reached by a number of the jurists present during the Imam's time or in later periods (during the *ghayba*), in such a way that no impediment occurs from the direction of the Imam in any possible way, whether secretly or openly. Just as the principle of *lutf* requires the appointment of an infallible Imam, it also necessitates that the Imam reveal the truth about any problem on which a wrong agreement may have been reached; otherwise *taklif* regarding that particular injunction would be nullified. This situation would lead the Imam to give up one of the most important duties for which he was appointed, namely, the teaching of the revealed injunctions.

This method was preferred by Tusi and those who followed him. In fact, he considered this method as the only way to discover the Imam's opinion in *ijma'*. Since al-Sharif al-Murtada refuted this method (he preferred *tariqat al-hiss*), it appears that even before Tusi, the method was well known among the Imamite jurists. Shaykh al-Ansari (d. 1281/1864–65), a leading Imamite theologian of the middle Qajar period, mentions al-Sharif al-Murtada's refutation in his *Rasa'il*, where he says that towards the end of his life the latter maintained that it was not incumbent upon the Imam to reveal the truth of a matter. Since the people were the actual cause of his concealment, the blame for not knowing the truth was to be imputed to them, not to the Imam. If and whenever the cause for the *ghayba* will be removed, maintains al-Sharif al-Murtada, the Imam will appear and clarify the matter on which there happens to be a controversy or disagreement.[49] Tusi refutes this contention by saying that such belief necessitates that there be no valid *ijma'* among the Imamites, because there is no way to ascertain that the Imam was among those who have reached an *ijma'*. The only way to ascertain the inclusion of the Imam's opinion is through the principle of *lutf*.[50]

However, there are two requirements in affirming the validity of *ijma'* arrived at by the method of employing the principle of *lutf*: first, once it is ascertained that the opinion is the Imam's, and that there is no proof that could support a contrary *fatwa*, then one should not be concerned with the unsoundness of the opinion. Second, where there exists a verse of the Qur'an or an authentic tradition contrary to the view held by those who have agreed upon an issue, such an *ijma'* cannot be considered as the discoverer of the infallible Imam's opinion, even if the reason for the contrariety is not evident for the jurists. It is possible that the Imam might have based his opinion on these very sources in explaining the truth of the matter, which the jurists ought to look for in the sources.

The *ijma'* attained by the method of *lutf* is of two types. One is *al-ijma' al-dukhuli*, which states that in the absence of the Imam, as is the case with the twelfth Imam, if a group of the jurists come to an agreement on a certain solution to a problem, then it is maintained that one of those present on such an occasion was the twelfth Imam himself. In this case he was *dakhil* when the agreement was reached; hence it is called *al-ijma' al-dukhuli*. The other kind is *al-ijma' al-kashfi*, which states that when a group of the jurists agree on a point which is not right, one of them is made to disagree with them by the *lutf* of the Imam; this ensures that the group will discover *(kashf)* the right point to agree on and hence is known as *al-ijma' al-kashfi*.

(3) *Tariqat al-hads* (The Method of Intellectual Intuition)

This method states that on whatever decision the Imamite jurists may have agreed, it should be ascertained that it has reached them from their Imam, in an unbroken personal contact. Compared with *tariqat al-hiss*, this method depends on obtaining the gist of the opinion, not on its actual "hearing." In spite of the differences that might exist in the legal opinions of the Imamite jurists, their agreement reached by *ijma'* through this method is held to rely on the opinion of their Imam and not to derive from their personal opinion or independent comprehension. Their agreement is comparable to the agreement of groups who follow a certain opinion uniformly, conveying their agreement with the opinion of the leader whom they follow. The term *hads* implies this sort of "intuition" on the part of the jurists.

This is the method adopted by the majority of the *'ulama'* in the modern period. The method requires that this agreement should be arrived at in all ages, beginning from the period of the Imams to the present time, because the agreement reached in one period when taken with a disagreement in another period impairs the attainment of the required certainty. The disagreement of any jurist, even if well known, hampers this attainment.

(4) *Tariqat al-taqrir* (The Method of [Silent] Confirmation)

This is the *ijma'* that should occur in the presence of the infallible Imam, with the possibility of his preventing the jurists from agreeing either by explaining the truth of the matter or by casting a difference of opinion among them. Thus an agreement of the jurists in respect to a certain injunction is brought to light by the Imam's confirmation of their agreed opinion. This confirmation is interpreted as a proof that their decision was in accordance with the command of God.

But the *taqrir* has certain prerequisites which include the ability of the Imam to reveal the truth on certain questions without endangering his life, and his not being short of time to express his opinion. Other conditions also are treated at length in the books on Imamite jurisprudence in the section dealing with the Sunna, where *taqrir* is discussed as one form of the Sunna. The prerequisites of *taqrir* must be fulfilled in order for it to become a valid method in discovering the *ijma'*. Only after the conditions are met is the Imam's agreement attainable. In this method it is sufficient to discover an opinion of a single person who, in the presence of the Imam, might have explained an injunction with the full knowledge of the Imam and with the possibility of his rejecting his explanation or confirming it by silence. His silence in this case is interpreted as *taqrir* — confirmation, revealing his opinion. But it should be pointed out that during the *ghayba,* when the Imam has to live in *taqiyya* all the time for fear of his life, it does not seem to be possible to prove the rejection or even the casting of a dispute among the jurists on a particular issue. As a matter of fact, during the *ghayba*, as maintained by al-Sharif al-Murtada, it is not incumbent on the Imam to reveal the truth of the matter.

This is the summary of the most important methods through which one can discover the opinion of the Imam in *ijma'*. The various opinions arrived at through *ijma'* in Imamite jurisprudence were concluded by employing one of these methods. Thus it is not necessary that all the *ijma'* mentioned in the Imamite books on jurisprudence were the result of one single method, although al-Sharif al-Murtada seemed to confine *ijma'* to the *tariqat al-hiss,* whereas Tusi believed: "Had it not been for the principle of *lutf* there would have been no way of knowing the agreement of the Imam with those who had reached a consensus."[51] At any rate, according to al-Hilli, for the purpose of validating the *ijma'* reached at one time, the *ijma'* had to include the sanction of the infallible Imam in every age, who is the chief of the *umma*, and only his opinion is the authoritative source for the imposition of *taklif*.[52] Hence the important phase of any *ijma'* is the "discovery" of the Imam's opinion with certainty. For that reason any method is equally valid if it can serve the required purpose.

[145]

It is rare to obtain the infallible Imam's opinion in *ijma'* which has been reached by employing the methods stated above. The *ijma'* in most cases is through inference *(muhassal)*, because it involves searching through the opinion of all the jurists who had contact with the Imams. But as one draws closer to the period of the *ghayba*, most of the *ijma'* opinions lose their authoritativeness, because it is even more difficult to ascertain the inclusion of the Imam's opinion in a consensus when the Imam is in occultation. The situation that might occur during the *ghayba* in case of *ijma'* can be explained as follows.

Those who have reached an agreement on a particular problem have either based their opinion on textual and rational proofs or have given their opinion without recourse to these proofs. The second premise is impossible because it is customarily improper for a jurist to give a *fatwa* without using as his basis textual or rational proofs. If it were permissible for him to do so, then his opinion would not be considered authoritative. Consequently, the first premise is established. In other words, the jurists who had issued their *fatwa* had relied on certain proofs which are unknown to other jurists. The sources of the Law, according to the Imamites are four: the Qur'an, the Sunna, *ijma'*, and *al-dalil al-'aqli* (rational proof). The source for the group who claims to have discovered the *ijma'* cannot be other than the Sunna. The Qur'an could not have been their source, because it is not possible to conceive a passage which is known to them and concealed from others. If it is assumed that they comprehend some special sense conveyed in a particular verse which others do not, their comprehension cannot become authoritative for other jurists. Their *ijma'*, although documented, cannot be held as valid in order to promulgate a particular injunction. The same consideration applies to the other sources—*ijma'* and the rational proofs used in the Imamite principles of Law. It is impossible to imagine, especially regarding the rational proofs, that all the jurists would not be aware of the rational principles used in establishing an injunction. Consequently, the documentation used as basis for a particular *ijma'* is limited to the Sunna.

The Sunna in this respect can be of two kinds: first, the jurists who reach an *ijma'* must have heard the injunction directly from the Imam or have seen him performing the act or silently confirming it. This is impossible to attain during the *ghayba*, even at the level of supposition, not to speak of certainty *('ilm)*, although, according to the Imamites, direct contact of some individual jurists with the twelfth Imam cannot be ruled out. But a situation resembling the period of *ghayba*, including the present time, was current even during the times of the other Imams. Sometimes the traditions reported on the authority of the Imams were not directly heard from them. They were related by the followers of the Imams because of their trust in their being authentic; thus, their being received from the Imams was a probability and even an assumption. Besides, the *ijma'* of the jurists at the time in question is impossible to obtain, since not all of their *fatwas* were recorded. Those that were written down have been collected in the work entitled *al-Usul al-arba' mi'a*, which formed the basis for Ibn Babuya's comprehensive work, *Man la yahduruh al-faqih.*[53]

Second, the jurists who reached an agreement must have relied on a tradition from the Imam which others have not seen. It is possible that such a tradition can with certainty establish the validity of a particular injunction, either because of the rules that govern its *sanad* (chain of authorities) or the reasoning that accompanies it. As for the *sanad*, it is possible that the jurist who cites a tradition of the Imam as proof for the *ijma'* may be citing a report classified as either reliable *(muwaththaq)*, or good *(hasan)*, but not authoritative *(sahih)*, which alone can be accepted in the promulgation of an injunction. Thus it may lack the necessary validity recognized by the jurists in order for it to be cited as a proof for the *ijma'*. In the reasoning that accompanies the report, there are two kinds of traditions as far as contents are concerned: *nass* and *zahir*. A *nass* (textual proof) refers to a tradition that contents of which cannot be possibly contradicted, while a *zahir* (alleged) is a tradition the contents of which can possibly be contradicted. The content of a tradition that can be used as a proof for the *ijma'* has to be of the *nass* type. If the jurists in their *ijma'* have relied on a *zahir* tradition, then that *ijma'* is useless for the purpose of the Law.

It is evident that in Imamite jurisprudence no *ijma'* can discover the opinion of the Imam except the one based on *tariqat al-hiss*, and even that is not possible to attain at all times. The method based on the principle of *lutf*, which stated that the Imam must have given his sanction to the *ijma'* of the jurists, even if the latter adhered to a single tradition, likewise does not stand the test of the *sanad* and the reasoning are elucidated above. Shaykh al-Ansari and many other Imamite jurists maintain that the reason for which the Imam went into occultation is also the reason why the Imam cannot reveal the truth when people concur on something false. The blame in this case, as in the case of the forced *ghayba* of the Imam, should be imputed to the people and not the Imam himself. As a result, there is no way of ascertaining that the Imam must have revealed the truth during the occultation by reliance on the principle of *lutf*, in a case where the jurists might have agreed on something false.

As indicated above, one of the reasons for subjecting the validity of *ijma'* to the presence of an infallible Imam, as far as *kalam* was concerned, was to invalidate the election of Abu Bakr to the caliphate. The other reason appears to be the need to answer a question frequently put to the jurists concerning the Islamic Law, in which *ijma'* becomes a significant source for religious injunctions besides the Qur'an and the Sunna. The question was: How does the infallible Imam in the state of *ghayba* protect the Religious Law, when it is in the power of the jurists to agree on something that may prove detrimental to the Religious Law? The Imamite jurists like Tusi and those who follow him in this contend that the *lutf* of God was the Imam himself and that he was appointed to advance the *umma* towards *al-thawab*, which was obtained by following *taklif*. Therefore, the Imam was responsible for all the solutions of religious problems which arose from time to time and which could not be solved by the Qur'an and the Sunna. His infallibility alone ensured the validity of *ijma'*, which otherwise might be reached by individuals who might follow their personal will rather than the will of God.

The Implications of the Theological Vindication of the Imamate of the Hidden Imam

The Imamite theologians have discussed the *ghayba* of the twelfth Imam as part of their exposition of the doctrine of the Imamate, which inevitably raised the question of the Imamate of the Hidden Imam and the reason for believing in his Imamate. Relying on the *asalat al-'aql*, the theologians tried to discuss those arguments which supplemented arguments based on the *asalat al-sam'*, such as traditions which stated that the Imams were twelve in number, and that they were al-Qa'im, al-Mahdi, and so on; such considerations formed the main theme of the traditionists' approach. References to the twelfth Imam and his occultation, which was under attack, were incorporated in the general discussion on the doctrine of the Imamate, the necessity of the Imamate, and so on. This offers a further point, which arose because of the prolonged *ghayba* of the Imam, who was expected to reappear in the near future as the Mahdi of the people, justifying, at least, his religious role during the prolonged, enforced occultation.

The purpose of the *kalam* vindication of the Imamate of the Hidden Imam was to meet the criticisms of the non-Imamite *mutakallimun* who attacked the whole doctrine of the Imamate as propounded by the Imamites. But the ordinary Imamites, it seems, were satisfied with the traditionists' defense of the Imamate and the occultation of the twelfth Imam as the awaited Mahdi. It is plausible to suggest that it was because of this satisfaction of the ordinary believers, or, to put it differently, because of their inability to comprehend the complexities of *kalam* and their preferences for the traditional argument, that Tusi's methodology is one of compromise between the two forms of the defense of the whole problem. His *Kitab al-ghayba* contains all the main points made by *al-dalil al-sam'i* as propounded by the traditionists, with an occasional introductory clause like, "The Shi'ites say . . . instead of "We say. . . ." Tusi did not completely discard the method of the traditionists, but maintained an attitude of selectivity in accepting their traditions and supplemented the approach with the summary of the *kalam* arguments vindicating the Imamate and the *ghayba* of the twelfth Imam. The blending of the two *asalas* in his approach has rendered his work an indispensable source for an understanding of the *ghayba* of the twelfth Imam.

5. The Return of the Mahdi

The return of the Mahdi, the Islamic messiah, after a long *ghayba*, was a direct corollary of the doctrine of *ghayba*. The occultation, however prolonged, was still a temporary state for the twelfth Imam chosen by God, in order to consolidate his position before he rose as the restorer of Islamic purity. As a consequence, from the early period discussion on the return of the Mahdi was an integral part of the doctrine of the *ghayba*. The messianic role of the Imam was emphasized in his return, when the true Islamic rule would be established. But the obvious inability of the Shi'ite leaders to fix the time when the events foretold in apocalyptic traditions would be fulfilled led to much confusion over the explanation of the nature of the Mahdi's return. This inability is well reflected in a widely quoted tradition concerning the prohibition of fixing the time of the rise of the twelfth Imam.[1] The difficulties of the Imamite theologians in the matter of elucidating the final revolution to be launched by the eschatological Mahdi are evident in the use of the terms for this process of transformation. The most frequently used terms for the Mahdi's reappearance in the early works are *qiyam* (rise), *zuhur* (appearance, emergence), and *khuruj* (coming forth). Bearing in mind the chiliastic hopes of the Shi'ites, who had ceased to attempt immediate and direct political action, it was obvious that the messianic Imam al-Qa'im was expected to "rise" in order to fill the world with justice and equity. But the accentuation of the eschatological role of the Imam as al-Qa'im al-Mahdi apparently gave rise to the consideration of a much wider connotation of his function at the End of Time. How was the resurrection (*qiyama*) going to be related to the "rise" (*qiyam*) of the Mahdi? What was the relationship between his rise and the rising of the dead? Will the Mahdi rise before or after the general resurrection of the dead? All such questions had inevitably arisen during the time when the Imamites were engaged in giving final form to the doctrine of the Imamate of the Hidden Imam. The term *raj'a*, which signifies "the returning to the present state of existence after death, before the Day of Resurrection," elucidated the universal role of the Mahdi as the leader of the Final Days. Early Shi'ite factions, such as the Kaysanites, the Waqifites, and others, had maintained that their messianic Imam had not died but had departed to "return" at some future time. The Imamites explained the doctrine of *raj'a* as the return of a group of the loyal followers of the Imam to this world before the final resurrection occurs, during the days of al-Mahdi's rule, or before or after that period. The main function of the *raj'a* will be to demonstrate to the adherents of the Imamite faith the rule of their infallible Imam and to exact revenge from the enemies of the *ahl al-bayt*.

The Rise *(qiyam)* of the Mahdi

The tradition of the rise of the Mahdi grew and developed with the disintegration of the caliphate, both Umayyad and 'Abbasid, and the flowering and disappointment of successive hopes which the Shi'ites had nurtured for the establishment of the ideal rule. The oppression of the caliphs and their administrators added much to the dark events foretold in apocalyptic traditions. On the other hand, the inability of several Shi'ite leaders to fulfill their claimed role as the Mahdi afforded new details and characteristics to the promised *(al-maw'ud)* Mahdi. The Imamites had worked out their own traditions, in which many ideas and beliefs concerning other messianic figures from other religions passed through various channels into their traditions. The impatience of the Shi'ites in their expectation of the rise of the Mahdi is well attested in all the early sources. The crumbling of the 'Abbasid caliphate was taken as the sign of the reappearance of the Imam, and many other events taking place at that time were identified with the vague prophecies and traditions handed down by the Imams about the days before the Mahdi will appear. Under these circumstances most Imamite authors who wrote on the *ghayba* of the twelfth Imam also included an apocalyptic chapter or two at the end of their works. The purpose of including the apocalyptic material in works on *ghayba* was twofold: first, it consoled the followers of the Imam with hopes of a final restoration of the Islamic rule; second, it justified the delay in the appearance of the Imam because the signs foretold, of the imminent triumph of the Mahdi, had yet to be fulfilled. The method of the Imamite authors in such chapters of their writings usually follows three stages: first, some apocalyptic traditions are reported from the Sunnite collections of *hadith*, dealing with the *fitan* (plural of *fitna*, meaning "trial"), in which seditions and civil strifes of the Final Days are mentioned; second, to these are appended details of the political and social turmoil of their own time, in the form of prophecies; and finally, the prophecies are further expanded and developed to give details about the final outcome of the *fitan*, namely the establishment of justice and equity in the world. The prophecies are, in most cases, attributed either to the Prophet himself or to the fifth and sixth Imams, al-Baqir and al-Sadiq, the latter being the eminent figures of the Imamite *hadith* literature. The Imams, being heirs to the prophetic knowledge, were supposed to have been endowed with esoteric knowledge (*al-'ilm*) which enabled them to prophesy future events, especially those connected with the destiny of their followers. The notion of the divine prophetic knowledge of the Imams also represented the Mahdi, the last in the lines of these heirs, as the only leader destined to bring true Islamic justice to the oppressed. The question asked time and again concerned the "hour" when the final restoration would take place.

"The Near Future" and the Rise of the Mahdi

The rise of the Imam was described in numerous traditions from the early times in Imamite history, and the signs related there, as mentioned above, encompassed the contemporary tumultuous situation in the form of prophecy. Consequently, the adherents of the Imam interpreted the time of the rise as being in the near future. In some traditions attributed to al-Baqir the number of the years which had to elapse before the emergence of the Mahdi was specified. For instance, a close associate of al-Baqir by the name of Abu Hamza Thabit b. Dinar recalled in the presence of this Imam what 'Ali had said about the end of the period of trial for the Shi'ites after seventy years, which would be followed by a period of ease and comfort. Abu Hamza complained that the period had elapsed without the prophecy being fulfilled. Al-Baqir explained: "O Thabit, God, the Exalted, had set a time to the seventy years. But when al-Husayn was killed God's wrath on the inhabitants of the earth became more severe and that period was postponed up to a hundred and forty years. We had informed you [our close associates] about this, but you revealed the secret. Now God has delayed [the appearance of the Mahdi] for a further period for which He has neither fixed any time nor has He informed us about it, since [He says in the Qur'an]: 'God blots out and establishes whatsoever He will; and with Him is the essence of the Book.' "[2]

The alteration of an earlier prophecy of seventy years, then of one hundred and forty to an indefinite future time implied a change of the earlier divine determination. In Imamite dogmatics this divine alteration is known as *bada'*. The doctrine of *bada'* was propounded by the early Shi'ite leaders, who, in order to justify their failure to establish a rule of justice in spite of their self-declared prophecies about their victory in a particular political venture, sought to explain the change in circumstances which caused God to alter His determination in their own interest. Al-Mukhtar seems to have been the first person to have mentioned the divine intervention, when, contrary to what God had revealed to him about his victory, he was defeated in his fight against the superior forces of Mus'ab b. al-Zubayr.[3] The failure of various Shi'i revolts was conveniently explained by accepting the *bada'* — the intervention of new circumstances which had caused God to alter His early determination. *Bada'* also explained the delay in the appearance of the rightful successor of the Prophet to deliver the *umma*, which the prophecies like the one cited above had predicted and which should have taken place at a certain moment. Furthermore, it served to demonstrate the limitations of the Imam's knowledge, more particularly when the succession to the Imamate was contested by more than one person. This happened in the case of Isma'il, the son of al-Sadiq, who was previously designated as the Imam by his father and who predeceased him. The change in the decision about the Imamate of Isma'il, designated by the Imam endowed with infallible knowledge, and which was now vested in al-Sadiq's other son, was explained as *bada'*. It implied God's change of mind because of a new consideration, caused by the death of Isma'il. However, such connotations in the doctrine of *bada'* raised serious questions about the nature of God's knowledge, and indirectly, about the ability of the Imams to prophesy future occurrences. The Imam themselves appear to have denied any such knowledge, as is attested in the tradition about a man from

Fars who is reported to have asked al-Baqir if he knew *al-ghayb* (the hidden knowledge), and the Imam replied: "We apprehend the knowledge *(al-'ilm)* when it is unfolded to us and we do not apprehend when it is taken away from us," and added, "It is the secret of God, the Exalted, which He confides to Gabriel (peace be on him); and Gabriel confides it to Muhammad (peace be on him and his progeny), and Muhammad may confide it to whomever God wishes [to be informed]."[4]

The Imamite theologians, in general, had adopted an essentially Mu'tazilite theology which included their thesis on *bada'*. The Mu'tazilites related *bada'* to the principle of *aslah* (the most salutary), which states that God does the best for His creatures, and His planning is based on what is most salutary and in the best interest of His slaves. But the Ash'arites rejected the doctrine because it was interpreted as implying a change of mind on the part of God due to what He earlier did not foresee and hence a denial of divine omniscience.[5] The Imamites had to exercise much ingenuity to reconcile the theological contradictions which the doctrine implies, especially assumptions of the occurrence of new determining moments in God's knowledge. Ibn Babuya, taking *bada'* in the sense of "creation," which connoted abrogation of previous faiths and commands by the creation of the Prophet and his Shari'a, protested against those who charged the Imamites with such a doctrine, and likened them to the Jews, who apparently leveled similar charges against the Muslims. In vindicating the Imamite position Ibn Babuya cites a tradition in which the sixth Imam, al-Sadiq, says: "He who asserts that God, the Mighty and Glorious, does something new which He did not know before,—from him I dissociate myself," and he added, "He who asserts that God, after doing something, repents concerning it,—then he, in our opinion, is a denier of God, the Almighty." But the question of the change concerning the Imamate from Isma'il to Musa al-Kazim, the sons of al-Sadiq, remained unsettled. Ibn Babuya quotes the Imam al-Sadiq concerning this matter, saying: "Nothing manifested [itself] from [the will of] God, Glory be to Him, concerning any affair like which appeared regarding my son Isma'il when He cut him off by death before me, so that it may be known that he was not the Imam after me."[6]

But a more subtle argument in defense of *bada'*, as maintained by the Imamites, was given by al-Mufid, the *mutakallim*. According to him, the Muslims, in general, took the word *bada'* to mean *naskh* (abrogation), whereas the attribution of such meaning to *bada'* was unnecessary, because the Qur'an uses the term *naskh* when it intends "abrogation" and not *bada'*. The 'Adliyya (Mu'tazilites), in particular, says al-Mufid, have understood the term in the sense of "increase" *(ziyada)* and "decrease" *(nuqsan)* of the life term and subsistence as a result of a person's good or bad actions. The Imamites, contends al-Mufid, have used the term *bada'* relying on the textual source *(al-sam')*, as related by the Imams, who are the mediators between God and His slaves. This source reveals that God becomes angered or pleased; He loves or becomes astonished. These states cannot be denied in God by any rational being, and as such there is no conflict between the Imamites and other Muslims in the implication of the above revelation about God. The only difference lies in the usage of the term *bada'*. In other words, according to the commentator of al-Mufid, while *naskh* explains abrogation in the matters pertaining to the Religious Law, *bada'* signifies the "occurrence" of the events which were not anticipated beforehand in the matters pertaining to the creation *(takwin)*. Thus, al-Mufid concludes, the difference lies in the usage, but not in the meaning of the term *bada'* as implied therein.[7]

Tusi, in his vindication of the tradition in which the prophecy about the seventy and the hundred and forty years occurs, elucidates the alteration caused by the change of circumstances and the consideration of "the most salutary" for the creatures on the part of God. He takes *bada'* in the sense of "occurrence" *(zuhur)*, in addition to its generally accepted meaning of "abrogation," in the instances where such abrogation is permissible (e.g. religious injunctions), or in the sense of "the alteration of circumstances" if the report that recounts *bada'* deals with the creation. Thus, maintains Tusi, it is possible that we may find in God's actions things that we did not anticipate or were simply contrary to what we had expected without knowing the reason behind such occurrences. In a tradition which he cites to support his elucidation, the Imam al-Rida is reported to have said: "How can we inform about the future when the verse of the Qur'an says: 'God blots out and establishes whatsoever He will; and with Him is the essence of the Book.' " But as for the one, says Tusi, who maintains that God's knowledge appears on the realization of the object, he has indeed become a non-believer and is outside the belief in *tawhid* (unity of God). Thus the fulfillment of the prophecy about the Mahdi, which was announced by 'Ali in the tradition, was delayed for another seventy years because of the martyrdom of al-Husayn; further *bada'* postponing the matter for an indefinite period was caused by the revealing of the secret which was entrusted to the disciples of the Imam al-Baqir. The secrecy in the matter of the rise of al-Mahdi was a necessary condition on which depended the fulfillment of the prophecy. This leads one to doubt all the traditions which predict the appearance of the Imam. Nevertheless, Tusi distinguishes two types of reports in this connection. First are those reports in which it is impossible for alteration to occur, such as the traditions which recount the attributes of God, the past events, and the promise of God that He will reward His creatures with *al-thawab*. Second are those traditions in which it is possible that due to expediency and change of circumstances alterations may occur. These traditions recount future events. But even among the latter group there are reports that have been known to be certain, and the events mentioned in them are definitely going to be fulfilled, without alteration.[8] That the Mahdi will appear was among the definite occurrences, but fixing of the time was in the hand of God. In an account in which a disciple of al-Sadiq asked him if the Mahdi would appear in his lifetime, the Imam replied that he would have done so, but since the disciples of the Imam al-Baqir had publicized the event, God had delayed the emergence of the Qa'im until a favorable time in the future.[9]

As a result of the postponement that may occur until the conditions change to bring about the fulfilment of the victory of the twelfth Imam, fixing the time of the Mahdi's rise was prohibited and those who did (*al-waqqatun*) were declared as liars.[10] Nevertheless, among these accounts were reports that described the events that were bound to happen at the future time, and these formed the subject matter of the sections that dealt with the universal signs (*al-'alamat al-ka'ina*) of the Mahdi's rise. The vast literature on this aspect of the Mahdi doctrine shows the aspirations of the followers of the Imamite school. The associates of the Imam who wanted to know the set time of the Mahdi's rise more often than not prefaced their questions with the reason for their inquiry, namely "the knowledge [of the time] will console our grieving hearts in the separation from the Imam and will help us to await his appearance in peace." A disciple of Imam al-Baqir related an occasion when he rose to leave the presence of the Imam, and, leaning on the latter's arm, he wept. The Imam asked him the reason for his weeping. The disciple said, "I had hoped to witness the great event [of al-Qa'im's rise] while I still had strength in me." The Imam answered angrily, "Are you [*shi'a*] not satisfied that your enemies kill one another while you sit peacefully in your homes? For when that event shall come, each man among you will be given the strength of forty men. . . .

You will be the foundations of the earth and its treasures."[11] The report on the one hand discourages fixing of any particular time of the appearance of the Mahdi in the near future; on the other hand, the reference to the conflict among the enemies, which reflected the political turmoil of that period, assured the Shi'ites that the great event—the *zuhur*—would take place. Thus the knowledge of the time, even in vague terms, of the appearance was necessary to sustain the Shi'ites during the difficult days of trials and seditions of the *ghayba*. Consequently, the signs of the *zuhur* related in the form of apocalyptic vision became a source of solace for the Imamites, and every generation, having known these through the literature available to them, expected the *qiyam* to take place during their lifetime.

In spite of the prohibition regarding the fixing of al-Mahdi's emergence at a particular moment, many reports related the day on which the Mahdi would appear. Apparently fixing the day was theologically less problematic than appointing the year, when the Imamites had to resort to the doctrine of *bada'*. As a consequence, many traditions report various days of the year, according to their significance in the Shi'i piety, when the *zuhur* will take place. The most often cited day in all our sources is the tenth of Muharram, the day of 'Ashura, which would fall on a Saturday, in one of the odd numbered years of the *hijra* calendar. The 'Ashura' occupies a significant position in Shi'i history as well as in its piety. The martyrdom of al-Husayn on this day, in the year A.D. 680, stands as a climax of Shi'i suffering and passion. As a result, the day generates more than anything else the belief in the redemption of the *umma* through the sufferings of the son of 'Ali and Fatima. It is the promise of God, says a tradition on the authority of al-Sadiq, that He will raise the cry of al-Qa'im for those who killed al-Husayn, and He will take vengeance against those who wronged him.[12] The year by year commemoration of the 'Ashura' by the Shi'i community indicates not only their sorrow for the afflictions suffered by the family of the Prophet, but also their yearning for the descendant of this Imam to rise against unbearable social circumstances and establish the rule of justice and equity.[13] This is clearly evident in the condolences that the Shi'ites offer each other on the occasion of 'Ashura', saying: "May God grant us great rewards for our bereavement caused by the martyrdom of al-Husayn (peace be on him), and make us among those who will exact vengeance for his blood with His friend *(wali)* the Imam al-Mahdi, from among the descendants of Muhammad (peace be on him)."[14] The martyrdom of al-Husayn, thus, embodies for the Shi'ites not only their vision of suffering and revenge, but also their final hope for justice, through the rise of his descendant.

Before the Mahdi rises on the day of 'Ashura', his name will be called out on the twenty-third night of the month of Ramadan.[15] This night, in the Shi'i liturgy, is considered to be the *laylat al-qadr* (The Night of Power in which the Qur'an was revealed), in which the angels descend with the decrees from God about the events that will take place during that year from God to al-Qa'im, His *hujja*.[16] Following this call in Ramadan, the Mahdi will rise in the month of Muharram, on the day of 'Ashura'.[17]

The Problem of "Where?" in regard to the Rise of the Mahdi

The question of "near future" in the emergence of the Qa'im was in some ways resolved by the emphasis laid on the events that had to occur preceding the *qiyam*. These formed the apocalyptic signs of the appearance of the messianic Imam, such as the rise of the sun from the west, and the occurrence of the solar and lunar eclipses in the middle and the end of the month of Ramadan, respectively, against the natural order of such phenomena. Accompanying these traditions were reports relating the merits of waiting for the appearance of the Imam in patience. Al-Sadiq is reported to have described the merits of the latter in these terms:

> That which causes the servants of God to get closer to Him at the time when people will search for the *hujja* of God, who will not appear for them nor will they know of his whereabouts, will be their faith [in the fact that] neither His *hujja* nor His promise [about the *faraj* (freedom from grief)] have been annulled. At that time they should expect *faraj* day and night, because the most severe thing to cause the wrath of God on His enemies [is the loss of their faith] when they will be looking for him and he will not appear for them. [God] knows that His friends will not doubt, [and] if He knew that they would, He would not have concealed His *hujja* from them even for a moment. This is so only for those who are the most wicked among mankind.[18]

In another tradition the Prophet is reported to have addressed his companions and informed them about the future generations of believers, of whom each individual will be entitled to the reward equal to that of fifty among them. The reason for such *thawab* will be their ability to bear patiently the difficult circumstances caused by the disappearance of their Imam.[19] Thus endurance was far more rewarding than being impatient about the rise of al-Qa'im. In the course of a tradition al-Sadiq asked his disciples:

> "Why have you fixed your eyes [on the rise of the Qa'im] and why do you wish to expedite [his appearance]? Do you not feel secure now? Is it not so that a man among you leaves his home and having finished his tasks returns without being forcibly arrested? I wish those who were before you had had [the same security] as you, because [in those days] a person was seized by force and his hands and legs were cut off and he himself was crucified between the palm trees, and cut into two pieces with a saw. [After all this] he used to consider [this torture] as expiation of his sins." [Then he read this passage from the Qur'an:] "Or do you think you would enter the garden while yet the state of those who have passed away before you has not come upon you; distress and affliction befell them and they were shaken violently so that the Apostle and those who believe with him said, 'When will the help of God come?' Now surely the help of God is nigh." (2:214).[20]

These traditions indicate the frustration of the Shi'ites at the delay in the appearance of the Mahdi. But the consequences of the *qiyam* were obvious to them, since they were repeatedly reminded that the rise of the Mahdi would be no less than the sword and death under the shadow of the sword of al-Qa'im, the Master of the Sword *(sahib al-sayf)*. Hence, Abu Basir and other close associates of the Imams al-Baqir and al-Sadiq were often asked by the latter: "Why are you in haste about the rise of al-Qa'im?"[21]

Another remarkable theme in these apocalyptic traditions is consideration about the place where the Imam will rise, whenever he does. Most of the traditions that report the rise on the day of 'Ashura' also mention the place of *zuhur*. Since the significance of the 'Ashura' is tremendous in the pious literature of the Imamites, one would have expected Karabala', the battlefield of al-Husayn's martyrdom, to have been designated as the most likely place for the messianic Imam to rise and commence his mission of conquering the evil forces obstructing his ultimate establishment of the kingdom of God. There are traditions which describe the Mahdi's triumphant entry into Kufa, from where he will dispatch troops to the other parts of the world; even though there is no reference in the early sources about the Imam's residence after his rise, according to a tradition cited by Majlisi, Kufa will be his place of residence, the mosque of

[*159*]

Kufa his seat of government, and the mosque of Sahla, in the vicinity of Kufa, his treasury. Furthermore, since most of the traditions are concerned with the details of al-Qa'im's revolution in Kufa, it is assumed to be his capital. Historically, this was also 'Ali's seat of government, whose rule is idealized in the Shi'ite writings.[22] The importance of Kufa is reflected in the tradition which says: "The Hour will not commence until all the believers have assembled in Kufa."[23] Karbala' will be joined with Kufa by digging a canal from behind the shrine of al-Husayn which will provide water for the people in Kufa.[24] But the *zuhur* proper will take place in Mecca, the birthplace of Islam. Al-Mahdi, like the Prophet, will come with a new order and will call the people to follow that order, as did the Prophet in the beginning of Islam.[25] That new order will restore the purity of Islam as taught by the Prophet and the Imams. The order will carry within itself the religio-socio-political aspects of the pristine Islam. Thus the commencement of the appearance of the Mahdi in Mecca, more specifically in the Ka'ba, between the Rukn and Maqam, the two holy spots in the precinct, not only increases the significance of the twelfth Imam's mission, but also preserves the symbolic unity of the *umma* by launching it in Mecca. This is the import of the phrase *mahdi al-anam* — the Mahdi of the People — the title on which the Imamite scholars placed great emphasis during the early years of the Complete Occultation.

Both Kufa and Karbala' hold an extremely elevated position in Imamite history, because of their being the places where 'Ali and al-Husayn, the two symbols of opposition to the unjust acts committed by the Umayyads, died as martyrs. Numerous traditions describe the rise of the Qa'im in the same manner: When al-Qa'im rises he will proceed toward Kufa. The absence of any mention of the rise commencing in Mecca, which seems to have been inserted in some traditions, corroborates the argument that those traditions which emphasize Kufa are the early versions of those reports which accentuate Mecca as the starting point of al-Qa'im's rise, especially following the prolonged occultation of the twelfth Imam, which also necessitated the accentuation of his eschatological role as the *mahdi al-maw'ud*. While it was impossible to find a more emotionally inspiring and significant day than 'Ashura' in the whole history of Islamic religion which would minimize the highly Shi'i connotation in the rise of the Mahdi, Mecca held symbolic precedence over Kufa and even Karbala', as the place from which the Mahdi would emerge as the messianic leader of the Islamic peoples. Significantly, the people of Mecca (i.e. non-Imamites) are asserted to be the first group on earth who would be called upon by the Mahdi to pay allegiance to him. The ninth Imam, Muhammad al-Jawad, informed his associates of this by saying: "I see [in future] that al-Qa'im is standing between Rukn and Maqam, on a Saturday, the day of 'Ashura', and Gabriel is standing in front of him calling out, "Alegiance belongs to God. Indeed, he (al-Qa'im) will fill the earth with justice as it is filled with tyranny and wickedness.' "[26]

In a long tradition reported on the authority of al-Mufaddal b. 'Umar,[27] one of the most eminent and close associates of the Imams al-Sadiq and al-Kazim, it is related that al-Mufaddal had once asked al-Sadiq to inform him about the *qiyam* of al-Qa'im al-Mahdi. The sixth Imam said: "I see him that he has entered the city of Mecca wearing the apparel of the Prophet and a yellow turban on his head. He has put on the patched sandals of the Prophet and the latter's stick is in his hands, with which he is directing some goats before him. In this manner he will enter the Ka'ba, without anyone recognizing him. He will appear as a youth."[28] The Imam then proceeds to give details about the Mahdi's appearance. He will, relates the Imam, emerge alone, and having proceeded toward the Ka'ba, he will remain there until it is dark at night. When the people fall asleep, Gabriel and Michael will descend on earth in the company of groups of angels. At that time Gabriel will speak to the Mahdi: "O my Master, whatever you say is acceptable and your commands will be carried out." The Imam will stroke Gabriel's face and say: "Praise be to God whose promise concerning us is fulfilled, and who appointed us as heirs to the earth and we will settle in the Paradise wherever we wish to do so. Verily, what a recompense for those who act according to His injunctions!" Then he will stand between the Rukn and Maqam and in a loud, clear voice he will announce: "Oh the chiefs and the people who are close to me! O you who were preserved on earth by God in order to help me when I emerge! Come toward me to obey me!" His voice will reach these people, who at that time will assemble close to him between the Rukn and Maqam, having arrived from the east and the west, from their places of worship and sleep, after hearing the call from the Mahdi. After that God will command the light to raise itself in the form of pillars, rising from earth upward to the heavens, so that the inhabitants of the earth will see it. The light will enrapture the believers, who will not know that the Qa'im has appeared. But when the morning sets in all these believers, who will reach three hundred and thirteen in number (of which fifty, according to one tradition, will be women)—the number of those who had fought on the Prophet's side in the Battle of Badr—will be assembled in the presence of the Qa'im.

At this point al-Mufaddal asks the Imam al-Sadiq if those seventy-two persons who were killed with al-Husayn in Karbala' will rise with those three hundred and thirteen believers. Al-Sadiq says that only al-Husayn among the martyrs of Karbala' will rise, wearing a black turban on his head, with twelve thousand *shi'a* of 'Ali. Then al-Mufaddal asks if people will pay allegiance to al-Husayn before the appearance and the rise of al-Qa'im with the latter. The Imam says: "Any allegiance before the rise of al-Qa'im is disbelief, hypocrisy and fraud. May God curse anyone who receives or pays allegiance [before the rise of al-Qa'im]." Al-Sadiq then proceeds to describe the manner in which the twelfth Imam will receive allegiance. He will lean his back on the wall of Ka'ba and stretch out his arm. There will be light emanating from his hand, and he will say: "This is the hand of God; it is from His direction and through His command," and will read this verse of the Qur'an: "Surely those who swear allegiance to you do but swear allegiance to God; the hand of God is above their hands. Therefore whoever breaks [his faith], he breaks it only to the injury of his own soul" (48:10).

The first being to kiss his hand as a sign of paying allegiance will be Gabriel, who will be followed by all other angels and the noble ones among the *jinns*, who will, in turn, be followed by the other beings of high rank. The inhabitants of Mecca will exclaim and ask about this person and those who are with him and will inquire about the sign they will have seen in the previous night, the like of which they will not have witnessed before. Some among them will tell each other that he is the man with the goats. Some others will say: "Look, do you recognize any of these persons accompanying him?" The people will say that besides the four persons from Mecca and the other four from Medina, who are so and so, they do not recognize any others.

All this will take place at the beginning of sunrise on that day. When the sun is up, a caller from the direction of the sunrays (i.e. east) will call out in eloquent Arabic, which will be heard by all the inhabitants of the heavens and earth. The announcement will be: "O inhabitants of the Universe! This is the Mahdi from among the descendants of Muham-

[*162*]

mad," and the voice will address him by the name and patronym of his forefather, the Prophet, and will relate him through his father al-Hasan al-'Askari to al-Husayn. After this introduction the voice will ask the people to pay allegiance to him in order to be saved and will warn them against opposing him, since their opposition will lead them astray. At that all the angels, the *jinns*, and the chiefs of the people, in that order, will kiss his hand, saying: "We heard the call and we are obeying." There will be no soul on earth on that day who will not hear this announcement. Those who are far in distant lands will cross the lands and seas, will arrive in Mecca, and will relate to each other the call they all had heard.

At sunset on that day someone will call out from the west side, saying: "O inhabitants of the world, your lord by the name of 'Uthman b. al-'Anbatha, the Umayyad, among the descendants of Yazid, the son of Mu'awiya, has appeared in the dry desert of Palestine. Go and pay allegiance to him so that you might be saved." At that all those who will have paid allegiance to the Mahdi will refute his call, declaring it to be false, and will reply to the announcer by saying: "We heard the call and we are disobeying." Those who will have some doubts in their minds about the appearance of the Mahdi, including those who disbelieved him and the hypocrites, will be led astray with this second call. At that time the Qa'im, leaning on the wall of the Ka'ba will say:

Truly, anyone who wishes to see Adam and Seth, should know that I am that Adam and Seth. Anyone who wishes to see Noah and his son Shem, should know that I am that Noah and Shem. Anyone who wishes to see Abraham and Ishmael, should know that I am that Abraham and Ishmael. Anyone who wishes to see Moses and Joshua should know that I am that Moses and Joshua. Anyone who wishes to see Jesus and Simon, should know that I am that Jesus and Simon. Anyone wishing to see Muhammad and 'Ali, the Amir of the Believers, should know that I am that Muhammad and 'Ali. Anyone who wishes to see al-Hasan and al-Husayn, should know that I am that al-Hasan and al-Husayn. Anyone who wishes to see the Imams from the descendants of al-Husayn, should know that I am those pure Imams. Accept my call and assemble near me so that I will inform you whatever you wish to know. Anyone who has read the heavenly scriptures and divine scrolls, will now hear them from me.

Thus he will begin to read that which God had revealed to Adam and Seth. The followers of Adam and Seth will acknowledge the authenticity

[*163*]

of the Mahdi's recitation and will confirm that he read and taught even those sections which were omitted or distorted. Then the Mahdi will read the books revealed to Noah and Abraham, and will also read the Torah, the Gospel, and the Psalms; the followers of all these scriptures will acknowledge the truthfulness of the Mahdi and will attest that the Mahdi knew the original scriptures before they were distorted or altered. Then the Mahdi will read the Qur'an, and the followers of the Qur'an will say: "By God, this is the true Qur'an that was revealed unto the Apostle of God and nothing has been omitted from it and no changes or distortion have taken place."[29]

Al-Mufaddal goes on to ask about al-Qa'im's program in Mecca. Al-Sadiq replies that the twelfth Imam, having invited the Meccans to respond to his call and they having accepted it, will appoint a person from his family as his deputy in Mecca, and he himself will move towards Medina. Al-Mufaddal then asks what the Imam will do to the Ka'ba. Al-Sadiq answers that the Mahdi will demolish the Ka'ba and will rebuild it as it was originally done during the time of Adam, will raise it as Abraham and Ishmael had done, in accordance with the will of God. He will destroy anything built by the oppressive caliphs and their representatives, in Mecca, Medina, Iraq, and other places, so that no sign of their wicked rule will remain on earth. He will destroy the mosque of Kufa also and will rebuild it on its original foundation. Al-Mufaddal asks if al-Qa'im will reside in Mecca. The Qa'im, says the Imam, will not remain in Mecca as he will have appointed his deputy for that city. However, when the Meccans see that the Mahdi has left, they will attack his deputy and will kill him. The Mahdi will return and the people of Mecca will plead guilty and repent for their act of transgression. The Qa'im will exhort them with sermons and the fear of God. Subsequently, he will appoint a Meccan to represent him and will leave the city once again. The Meccans will treat this person the same way as they had done before and will kill this person. On learning this the Mahdi will send a group of his helpers among the *jinns* to Mecca with instructions to kill everyone except those who are steadfast in their belief. The Mahdi will declare to his followers that had it not been for the consideration about the mercy of God, which encompasses everything and of which he is the manifestation on earth, he too would have returned to Mecca, whose residents have cut themselves off from the mercy of God by committing evil deeds. The troops of the Imam will return to Mecca; and then, al-Sadiq declares solemnly, not a single person among every hundred or even a thousand will escape this punishment.

The Mahdi will then enter Medina, where he will have such status that the believers will be pleased to witness it. On the other hand, the adversaries of the Imam will resent it. At this point al-Sadiq informs al-Mufaddal about a strange occurrence connected with the first two caliphs, Abu Bakr and 'Umar, who are buried beside the Prophet. The whole episode, as reported by al-Mufaddal, reveals the Shi'i polemics against the Sunnis and the ultimate fate of the two caliphs who usurped the right of the *ahl al-bayt*. The Mahdi will then proceed to Kufa, which will be his capital. On that day, all the believers will be assembled in that city and the surrounding areas, which will expand immeasurably to the neighborhood of Karbala', to accommodate all the Shi'ites. Karbala' that day will be the frequenting place of the angels and the believers.[30]

The *hadith* of al-Mufaddal continues to describe the condition of Baghdad at the time and relates the rise of a *sayyid* among the descendants of al-Hasan in the land of the Daylamites. The *sayyid* will announce in a loud, audible voice the appearance of the one whose prolonged occultation had disappointed the Shi'ites: "O people, respond to his call which is coming from the direction of the Prophet's grave." The brave and faithful people of Taliqan (in Khurasan) will respond to this call by riding their swift horses and carrying weapons. On their journey toward Kufa, they will fight the enemies of God and wipe them out, until they enter the city and settle there. When the actual news about the appearance of the Mahdi reaches the *sayyid* and his disciples, the latter will ask about the identity of the person who is said to have alighted in Kufa. The *sayyid* will ask them to follow him, and together they will go and meet with the Mahdi. He will ask the Mahdi to show them the symbols of the Prophet in his possession, such as the Prophet's ring, his coat of mail, sword, and so on, including the Qur'an, which was compiled by 'Ali. The Mahdi will show them three things, and they will all pay allegiance to him, except for the forty thousand Zaydites, who will have their own Qur'an and who will refuse to acknowledge the Mahdi. The latter will try to persuade them for three consecutive days, but they will persist in their rejection of him, so he will order them to be killed.

Following this the troops will be sent to Damascus to arrest al-Sufyani, the Umayyad messiah. The soldiers of the Mahdi will seize him and behead him on a stone. This will be the time for al-Husayn to "return" with his twelve thousand *shi'a*, in addition to the seventy two persons who were killed with him in Karbala'. This will be the illuminated *raj'a*, to be distinguished from the *raj'a* to be discussed below. Following al-Husayn, 'Ali will return and take his place in a huge tent, which will stand on four pillars, of which one will be in Najaf, one in the precinct of the *Ka'ba*, one on the hill of Safa near the Ka'ba, and the other in Medina. The earth and the heavens will be illuminated. The secrets of each person will be revealed. The mothers who will be nursing their infants will abandon them in fear. At that time the Prophet, with his companions, both the Ansar and the Muhajirun, and those who believed in him and acknowledged his prophecy and sacrificed their lives for him, will return. With the believers, those who falsified his mission and doubted it will also return so that proper vengeance for their disbelief can be exacted from them.[31]

This is perhaps the longest tradition ever recorded in the Imamite *hadith* literature. But before we continue to describe the rule of the Mahdi following his *zuhur*, as related in al-Mufaddal's account, we should turn to the consideration of the doctrine of *raj'a* (return) of the Imams, to which al-Sadiq alludes in al-Mufaddal's *hadith*.

The Doctrine of *raj'a* and the Return of the Mahdi

One of the salient features of Shi'ite doctrine is the belief in *raj'a*, meaning "the return to the present state of existence after death, before the Day of Resurrection."[32] Nearly every sect of the Shi'ites maintained the belief that the Imams had not died but would appear on earth to establish the rule of justice and equity.

The belief in *raj'a* seems to have gained wide currency in Shi'ite circles at a quite early period. In the early sources some persons are specifically mentioned as having maintained belief in this doctrine. Ibn Tahir al-Baghdadi, for instance, mentions Jabir b. Yazid al-Ju'fi (d. 128/745−46) as the one who believed in the *raj'a* of the dead before the Day of Judgment.[33] He also mentions Bashshar b. Burd (d. 167/783−84), the poet, who maintained the belief in *raj'a*.[34] From the sources on Islamic sects it can be discerned that as a rule the belief in *raj'a* was held in connection with the Shi'i Imams beginning from 'Ali. It is sometimes found in connection with the Prophet himself, more particularly in the incident when 'Umar rebuked those who believed that the Prophet was dead, and he emphatically expressed his belief that the Prophet would return after forty days "just as Moses had done."[35] Next to 'Ali the belief was held in connection with his son Muhammad b. al-Hanafiyya, whose followers, the Kaysanites, believed that Muhammad b. al-Hanafiyya had not died but would reappear on earth. In the later development of the Shi'ite sects the belief is found in respect to nearly every Shi'ite Imam. The Imams were sometimes asserted to be in concealment and not dead, as in the case of the Waqifiyya, in distinction from the Qat'iyya, who believed the Imam was dead and had a successor to continue the Imamate.

Although all the Shi'ite sects held a belief in *raj'a*, they differed in their exposition of the doctrine. Al-Mufid, commenting on the belief, says: "The Imamites agree on the necessity of the *raj'a* on earth of a great number of the dead before the day of resurrection. But there is a difference of opinion among them concerning the meaning of *raj'a*."[36] Al-Ash'ari touches on one of the basic differences among the Shi'ites concerning the doctrine of *raj'a*. He says that the Shi'ites are divided into two groups in their opinion about the *raj'a* of the dead on earth before the Day of Judgment. The first group asserts that the dead will return to earth before the Day of Judgment, and this is maintained by the majority of the Shi'ites. In support of this belief, says al-Ash'ari, this group holds that there will occur among the Muslims the like of what has occurred among the children of Israel. Just as God brought to life a group of the children of Israel, so will He bring to life the dead among Muslims and return them to the world before the day of resurrection. The second group among the Shi'ites, whom al-Ash'ari mentions as *ahl al-ghuluww* (the extremists), rejects the doctrine both of resurrection and the hereafter. They maintain belief in the transmigration of the soul in different forms. Their belief takes the following form: those who were righteous will be rewarded after death in such a way that their souls will be transferred to bodies not afflicted by harm or pain; those who were sinful will be punished after death in such a way that their soul will be transferred to bodies which will be afflicted by harm and pain. This is the way, they assert, things will be, and the world will continue in this manner forever.[37]

The Imamites belong to the first group mentioned by al-Ash'ari. *Raj'a* in the Imamite creed means the return of a group of believers to this world before the final resurrection occurs, during the days of al-Qa'im's rule, or before or after that period. The *raj'a* will take place in order to show the believers the rule of the righteous Imam and to exact revenge from the enemies of the *ahl al-bayt*.[38] The purpose of *raj'a* would also require that a given number of non-believers and enemies of the *ahl al-bayt* also be returned to earth so that revenge may be exacted from them.

In regard to the *raj'a* of the Imams themselves, there is a difference of opinion between the Imamites and other Shi'i groups: the latter hold the belief that those of their Imams who disappeared will return eventually to establish their rule; the former hold the belief that *raj'a* actually means the return of the dead Imams, as in the case of 'Ali and al-Husayn. In respect to the twelfth Imam, who is the Hidden Imam of the Imamites, it is his appearance or emergence *(zuhur)* which is awaited rather than his "return" *(raj'a)*, as in the case of the other Imams or even the Prophet. The concept of *raj'a* when applied to the twelfth Imam refers to his function as the eschatological Imam. This can be clearly construed from the *hadith* of al-Mufaddal. As stated above, the delay in the appearance of the Imam, as al-Qa'im, the redresser of wrongs committed against the family of the Prophet, resulted in the accentuation of his function as al-Qa'im al-Mahdi of the Last Days.

The difference of opinion among the Imamite writers on the meaning of *raj'a* to which al-Mufid alludes is centered on two points: first, whether *raj'a* will take place simultaneously with the *zuhur* of al-Qa'im, or before or after it; second, the duration of the period of the rule of al-Qa'im and the question of the *raj'a* of other Imams.

It is reported on the authority of the sixth Imam, al-Sadiq, that the first person for whom the earth will open up and who will return will be al-Husayn. This is not to be a general return of the dead, which will take place on the Day of Judgment; rather, this will be a partial return of only the genuine believers and the total non-believers.[39] Another report quotes the fifth Imam, al-Baqir, who told a group of Kufans that al-Husayn will be the first person to return, and he will rule until such a time that his eyebrows will fall on his eyes (i.e. until the skin of his forehead becomes so slack as a result of old age that his eyebrows will begin to slide down over his eyes). Furthermore, a report from al-Sadiq adds that al-Husayn will be responsible for judging the people's deeds before and after the final resurrection, when people will enter heaven or hell according to the judgment passed by al-Husayn.[40]

Al-Sadiq, in explaining the passage of the Qur'an which says "Then,

[*168*]

returned We unto you the turn [to prevail] against them and aided you . . . ," (17:6) says that by "returned" is meant the return of al-Husayn, who will be accompanied by his seventy-two companions who were killed with him on the battlefield of Karbala'. The companions will announce the return of al-Husayn to the people. At the same time, the Imam says, the believers should not doubt him, since he is neither Antichrist (al-Dajjal) nor the Devil. The Qa'im will be among the people. When the people have gained certainty about his being al-Husayn, the Qa'im will die, and al-Husayn will perform his funeral rites and bury him.[41]

Al-Mufid in one place explains his own position regarding the meaning of *raj'a*. In this exposition he does not include the traditions concerning the return of the rule of the other Imams, but affirms the rule of al-Qa'im, upon whose emergence the *raj'a* will take place. This *raj'a*, al-Mufid says, will be of only a given number of the dead, who will return to life in the forms which they possessed before their death. Among those whose *raj'a* will have occurred will be some whom God will raise in esteem and others whom He will lower. Those who were in the right will be given ascendancy over those who were unfaithful; those who were oppressed will be given the upper hand over the oppressors. This will occur upon the rising (*qiyam*) of al-Mahdi from among the progeny of Muhammad. Al-Mufid then goes on to divide those who will have returned into two groups on the basis of their faith and actions. There is that group who will have returned to earth because of their high status in the faith and the numerous good deeds performed in their first lives, and who died after lives spent in trying to avoid the commission of grave sins. God will show this group the rule of truth and will honor its members by granting them all they wished to possess. The other group will be those persons who were thoroughly corrupted and who had gone to the extreme in opposing those in the right, even killing the friends (*awliya'*) of God. Thus God will aid those who were transgressed against by this group before death and will assist them to vent their anger and take revenge on them. Then both these groups will die and be brought to life again at the final Day of Judgment, when they will be entitled to the continuance of their reward or punishment. Al-Mufid concludes with the remark that the Imamites with few exceptions were unanimous on this exposition of *raj'a*.[42]

The above Imamite view of *raj'a* came under severe attack by the Mu'tazilites, as is evident in al-Mufid's description of an encounter with them and his vindication of the Imamite stance on the particular question of the return of the dead to enable the believers to exact their vengeance from the non-believers. The Muʻtazilites, in a meeting with the Imamites, raised the following question: How can the Shiʻites be certain that Yazid (the Umayyad caliph), al-Shimr (or, al-Shamir, the one who killed al-Husayn) and ʻAbd al-Rahman b. Muljam (ʻAli's assassin), when returned, would not repent, and thereby begin to obey the Imam—which would require the Shiʻites to befriend them and would assure them of reward? Such a possibility, said the Muʻtazilites, renders the Imamite belief unsound. Before al-Mufid undertook to vindicate the Imamite position, another prominent Imamite scholar, whose name is not given in the source, answered the Muʻtazilite criticism by saying that since belief in *rajʻa* was derived through the *samʻ* (sources based on the revelation), there was no place for *al-nazar* (discursive knowledge) to attempt to reply to this question. In the absence of the proper *nass* (textual proof) in support of the particular issue, it was improper for him to take upon himself to answer the question. The Muʻtazilites, on hearing this, began to belittle the Imamites and denounce them for maintaining such a belief. At that point al-Mufid offered a twofold reply to their question.

First, he said, the intellect *(al-ʻaql)* does not consider it impossible for faith *(iman)* to occur in Yazid, al-Shimr, and the likes of them. But *al-samʻ* (the traditional sources), especially *hadith* from the Imams, affirm their permanent abode in the Fire and have ordered the followers of the latter to curse and disavow them up to the Last Days, without having any doubt about their ultimate fate. It is undisputed that they will not believe as a result of their own choice, just as had happened in the case of Pharaoh, Korah, and Haman, about whom God has made declarations in the Qur'an (29:39). That which definitely corroborates this point is the verse: "And even if We had sent down to them angels and the dead had spoken to them and We had brought together all things before them, they would not believe unless God willed; but most of them are ignorant" (6:11)—which implies that they will not believe unless God compels them to do so. Furthermore, God says to Satan: "I shall assuredly fill hell with you and with those among them who follow you, all together," (38:85) and, "Surely My curse is on you to the Day of Judgment" (38:78). These and other verses invalidate the Muʻtazilite objection.

Second, when God returns the non-believers during the *rajʻa*, in order to permit the believers to exact their revenge from the non-believers, He will no longer accept their repentance, as happened, according to the testimony of the Qur'an, in the case of Pharaoh: "When the drowning overtook him, he said, 'I believe that there is no god but He in whom the Children of Israel believe, I am of those who surrender.' What! Now? And indeed before you rebelled, being of those that did corruption" (10:90). Thus God rejected his repentance and his remorse, just as He will do with these people on the Day of Judgment, since repentance on that day will be of no avail. God has set a particular time in man's life when his repentance will be accepted. However, it is well established in His wisdom that repentance after death will be of no benefit. "On that day when one of your Lord's signs comes, it shall not profit a soul to believe which did not believe before, or earn good through its belief. Say, 'Watch and wait, we too are waiting'" (6:159). The "sign" in this verse, according to the Imamite exegetes, is al-Qa'im; when he emerges, the repentance of the adversary will not be accepted.[43]

The *raj'a*, then, can be interpreted as a prelude to the final resurrection. While the function of al-Mahdi is to commence the *zuhur* and launch the revolution in the final days, it is 'Ali and, more particularly, al-Husayn who will establish the Islamic rule after returning to life, following the *zuhur*. The traditions of this aspect of *raj'a* are unanimous in according al-Husayn, the martyr *par excellence* of Shi'ism, the honor of initiating the rule of justice and equity, in collaboration with 'Ali and al-Qa'im.

The Imamite doctrine of the Mahdi at one point merges with the return of Jesus, another prominent figure of Islamic eschatology. The doctrine of the return of Jesus, as described in the Sunnite sources and cited by the Shi'ite traditionists is explained in a more or less uniform manner. ner.

He will descend in the Holy Land at a place called Afiq with a spear in his hand; he will kill with it al-Dajjal (the Antichrist of Islamic eschatology) and go to Jerusalem at the time of the morning prayer. The Imam will seek to yield his place to him, but Jesus will refuse and will worship behind him according to the Shari'a of Muhammad. Thereafter he will kill the swine, break the cross, and kill all the Christians who do not believe in him. Once al-Dajjal is killed, all the Peoples of the Book (i.e. Jews and Christians) will believe in him and will form one single *umma* of those who submit to the will of God. Jesus will establish the rule of justice and will remain for forty years, after which he will die. His funeral will take place in Medina, where he will be buried beside Muhammad, in a place between Abu Bakr and 'Umar.[44]

The Muslim eschatological tradition is unanimous in assigning to both Jesus and the Mahdi a significant role in the doctrine of the *qiyama* (resurrection). As a matter of fact, many exegetes of the Qur'an in explaining the verse, "He (Jesus) is surely a knowledge of the Hour" (43:61), state that the descent of Jesus during the rulership of the Mahdi will make the approach of the Hour known.[45] In the development of the eschatological role of the Mahdi in Shi'ite traditions, much emphasis was laid on the function of the Mahdi as the descendant of Muhammad and the Imam, who will be followed in the prayer by Jesus. The latter point is repeatedly emphasized in the Shi'ite eschatological tradition. This distinguished the roles of the Mahdi and Jesus, which at times became confusingly alike. On the other hand, some Sunnites, in their polemics against the Shi'ites, related a tradition attributed to the Prophet: "There is no Mahdi save Jesus, son of Mary." This tradition was evidently used to undermine the chiliastic hopes of the Shi'ites and to minimize the eschatological importance of the Mahdi, which was emphatically maintained by the Shi'ites. The group who used the above tradition in their polemics argued that while there was no mention of Mahdi in the Qur'an, the return of Jesus was well established in the signs of the Hour,[46] and he, not the Mahdi, would kill the Dajjal.

In the Shi'i traditions the function of killing the Dajjal is reserved for al-Mahdi. In a long tradition 'Ali is reported to have answered a question regarding al-Dajjal, whose features are vividly described thus: He is one-eyed, his eye being in his forehead and shining like the morning star. On his forehead is written: "This is the *kafir* (non-believer)," which will be legible to both literate and illiterate persons. His emergence will be preceded by a time of great hardship. Then 'Ali describes the manner in which he will appear on a donkey, and his call will be heard from one end of the earth to the other. He will tell the people that he is their creator and their lord. Those who follow him on that day will be the enemies of God, who will be wearing something green on their heads. God will cause them to be killed in Syria at a spot named Afiq, on Friday, three hours after the sunrise, at the hands of "the one behind whom Jesus will worship. Beware that his death will be followed by a great event." This great event is the revolution of the twelfth Imam, commencing from the direction of Safa in the precinct of the Ka'ba. Thereafter no rependance will be accepted.[47] Al-Dajjal's role at the End of Time is almost identical with that of Satan, as explained in traditional sources, because he will tempt people by bringing food and water, which will be scarce at that time. The Prophet is reported to have said that since the time of Noah there has been no *umma* on earth who did not fear al-Dajjal and his temptations; every prophet has warned his community against this tempter.[48] The episode of al-Dajjal's emergence, at the time of the *zuhur*, has been interpreted as a test for sifting the true believers of God from the false ones.[49]

The Rule of al-Qa'im al-Mahdi:

"Hasten up, hasten up O son of the Virgin (*al-batul*, the title of Fatima; i.e. the Mahdi from among her descendants through al-Husayn),
Thy Shi'a are ever in mourning garb,
At the lateness of the coming of thy rule."

These are the lines from the famous *ghadiriyya* epic, in which the twelfth Imam is called upon to bring an end to the mourning of al-Husayn by establishing his rule.[50] These lines, which also form an integral part of the most repeated Shi'i prayer, "May God hasten release from suffering through his (Mahdi's) rise," reflect the aspiration of the Shi'ites for the rule of "justice and equity," embodied in the promise of the appearance of the Mahdi. Under such a rule the loyal shi'a of the twelve Imams will find their exalted position, and under the just government of al-Qa'im they will be able to share the blessings of a world free from "oppression and tyranny." The main purpose of the *zuhur* is to humble or destroy the evil forces of this world and establish the fully just Islamic rule. Indeed, the establishment of the rule of the twelfth successor of the Prophet is reckoned as the climax of Imamite history—a history full of struggle and radical social protest; a history of sufferings, afflictions, and the martyrdom of its leaders and loyal adherents, who, in the course of centuries and under unbearable social and political circumstances, persisted in their faith in the *faraj* (freedom from grief) through the emergence of the messianic leader. The *faraj* depicts the function of the Mahdi, namely to establish justice and redeem the whole world from oppression, suffering, and war and to introduce a period of spiritual and physical bliss. Hence al-Mahdi's rule personifies the chiliastic vision of

[*173*]

the Shi'ites, who believe that all their dreams will come true "when God will lay his (al-Mahdi's) [blessed] hand on the heads of the people, through which He will bring their intellects together."[51] The Shi'ites will, as a result of this blessing, be able to use the accumulated experience of mankind to remove imperfections in their society. As a successor of the Prophet, who held both spiritual and temporal power in the early Islam, al-Mahdi was the only leader who could accomplish the creation of an ideal Islamic society. Thus the foundation of the Shi'i piety is the acknowledgement of the Imam who can ensure the *faraj* through his rise, and in whom culminates the peculiarly Shi'i vision of Islamic history.

We have seen in al-Mufaddal's tradition the overall significance of Kufa as al-Qa'im's seat of government and the subjugation of the east and west by the troops of the Imam, in order to establish the kingdom of God. The Mahdi will rule from Kufa assisted by three hundred and thirteen of his close associates. The first thing that will occur under the rule of the Mahdi will be the Islamicizing of the whole world. The followers of all other religions will embrace Islam and profess faith in one God, just as He has said in the Qur'an: ". . . to Him submits *(aslama)* whoever is in the heavens and the earth, willingly and unwillingly, and to Him shall they be returned" (3:82).[52] Consequently, there will be no place on earth where testimony, "I bear witness that there is no god but God" and "I bear witness that Muhammad is the Apostle of God," will not be heard.[53] The faith that will be presented by the Qa'im will be the pure religion of Muhammad, Islam without any omission or innovation. Al-Baqir is reported to have said, "I can see your religion mixed with blood [in the future]. No one will be able to return it to its pristine purity except a man among the *ahl al-bayt* who will distribute gifts twice a year. . . . In his time the knowledge of religion will be spread to such an extent that a woman, sitting in her home, will be able to give rulings according to the Book and the teachings of the Prophet."[54] In another tradition, 'Abd Allah b. 'Ata', an associate of the fifth and sixth Imams, asked al-Baqir regarding the manner in which al-Qa'im will proceed among the people. He said: "He will raze that which existed before him just as the Prophet did (before him) [when he began his mission], and will revive Islam once again."[55] However, al-Qa'im will not follow the Prophet's example of gentleness and flexibility and winning over the people by uniting them; rather, the Qa'im will kill, in accordance with the text of the testament *(wasiyya)*, which each Imam, beginning with 'Ali to the Mahdi, was required to follow.[56] He will also not follow the example of 'Ali, who adopted the path of forgiveness and benevolence in his dealings with the people, because he knew that there would follow after his death the rule of tyrants who would oppress his *shi'a*. The Qa'im, on the other hand, is assured that his *shi'a* will not ever be dominated by wicked rulers, and consequently he will fight with his enemies and put them into prison.[57] Al-Qa'im will rise with a new authority, a new Book, and a new order, which will be severe on the Arabs (his main supporters, according to some traditions, will be the non-Arabs). His state of affairs will be the sword (he is known as the *sahib al-sayf*, Master of the Sword), and he will not accept repentance from anyone, nor will the rebuke of his adversaries deter him from carrying out the command of God.[58] The Islamicizing and restoring of the purity of the faith will be visible throughout the dominion of al-Qa'im. In the mosque of Kufa there will be tents pitched, and the followers of the Mahdi will learn to recite the Qur'an the way it was revealed unto the Prophet. The *qibla* (direction of the prayer) of the mosque will also be restored—an indication that the previous rulers had distorted even the direction of the prayer, in addition to all other atrocities committed against the *umma*.[59] The banner of the Prophet, which was spread for the last time in the Battle of the Camel (36/656–57) by 'Ali, will once again be spread by al-Qa'im, as a symbol of the 'Alid victory and hegemony.[60]

The above description gives immeasurable importance to the Mahdi's role as the restorer of faith which was sometimes attacked by the Sunnites, as appears in the attempt to reply to such criticisms in the Shi'ite sources. Al-Tabarsi (d. 549/1154–55) has mentioned one of these objections in his biography of the twelve Imams. The objection reads: All the Muslims are of the belief that there will be no prophet after Muhammad, the seal of the prophets. But the Shi'ites believe that when the Qa'im rises, he will not accept the *jizya* (poll tax) from the Peoples of the Book; anyone over twenty years of age who does not know his religious obligations will be put to death. The mosque and other religious edifices will be demolished, and the Mahdi will judge according to the method of David, who did not require witnesses. All such traditions, assert the critics, are recounted in the Shi'i books, which are tantamount to the abrogation of the Islamic religion and invalidation of the religious injunctions. In fact, they say, such beliefs require maintaining the continuation of prophethood after Muhammad, although the term "prophet" is not used for the Mahdi.

Al-Tabarasi denies having seen any reports about the non-acceptance of the *jizya* from the Peoples of the Book, or of the killing of the youths who did not know their religious obligations. As for the demolishing of the mosques and other religious buildings, argues al-Tabarsi, it may be that these buildings will have been constructed against the requirements of piety; the precedent of such an act is provided by the Prophet, who ordered the mosque of al-Dirar in Medina to be demolished because it was constructed by the hypocrites to disunite the community. The administration of justice according to David's method, says al-Tabarsi, is not substantiated in the Shi'ite writings. If one accepts such traditions, they can be interpreted thus: In those cases when the Imam has the required information personally, he can judge relying on it, because Islamic Law stipulates that whenever the Imam or the ruler ascertains the truth of the matter, it is necessary to give the ruling according to his own information without requiring witnesses. This provision does not abrogate religion. Moreover, the traditions about not accepting the *jizya* or not requiring witnesses, provided they are proved to be authentic, cannot render religion abrogated, because abrogation can take place only when the reason for abrogation follows the ruling about abrogation, and not simultaneously with it. If both reason and ruling for an abrogation occur simultaneously, then the former cannot be considered as abrogating the latter, however contradictory they might appear in meaning. It must be remembered, says al-Tabarsi, that the information about al-Qa'im was given by the Prophet himself, who exhorted the Muslims to follow his commands. As a result, it is incumbent upon the *umma* to obey him and carry out his orders. When the *umma* does so, even if al-Qa'im's orders might appear to contradict the earlier injunctions, they do not abrogate Islam, as argued above. On the contrary, they are the original, unadulterated rulings of Islam.[61]

There is no consensus in the Imamite sources on the duration of the Mahdi's rule. According to one report, al-Baqir is said to have related that the Mahdi will rule for three hundred and nine years. This is the number of years the Companions of the Cave *(al-kahf)*, as mentioned in the *sura* eighteen of the Qur'an, slept in the cave. During these years, adds the Imam, the rule of justice and equity will spread in the world.[62] Another tradition mentions al-Sadiq saying that the Mahdi will rule for seven years, "each year of his rule being equivalent to your seventy years."⁶³ In al-Mufaddal's tradition the sixth Imam was asked about the length of the period of the Mahdi's rule. The Imam cited the following passage of the Qur'an: "The day [when] it (the appointed term) arrives, no soul shall speak but by His leave; then [some] of them shall be wretched and [some] blessed. Then as for those who shall be wretched, they shall be in the (Hell) fire, for them therein shall be sighing and groaning. They shall abide therein so long as the heavens and earth endure, except [as] what wills your Lord; verily your Lord is the [Mighty] Doer of whatsoever He wills. And as for those who will be blessed, they shall be in the garden (of Paradise) abiding therein so long as the heavens and earth endure, except [as] what your Lord will; [it will be] a gift incessant" (11:105–08). The Imam added, "After that there will be the day of resurrection,"⁶⁴ meaning there was no time limit to the rule of justice as established by al-Mahdi. According to a tradition reported by Ibn Babuya, Abu Basir, a close associate and a narrator of numerous Imamite traditions, once asked al-Sadiq: "O son of the Prophet, I have heard from your father that there will be twelve Mahdis after al-Qa'im." The Imam said, "However, my father said 'twelve Mahdis' and not 'twelve Imams.' But they will be a group among our Shi'a, who will call people to friendship with us and inform them about our rights."⁶⁵ Tusi reports a variant of this tradition on the authority of the Prophet, who informed 'Ali on the night before his death about the twelve Imams who will follow him and the twelve Mahdis who will follow the twelfth Imam.⁶⁶

Al-Mufid affirms that there will be no government subsequent to that of al-Qa'im, except that reported in some traditions in which there is an allusion to the government of the descendants of al-Qa'im, if God wills so. But even these traditions, cautions al-Mufid, are not established as authentic. Most of the reports, clarifies al-Mufid, confirm that the Mahdi of the *umma* will die forty days prior to the day of resurrection. In those forty days chaos and general confusion will prevail, which will be followed by the signs of the resurrection of the dead and the Day of Judgment. "And of course, God knows best what is going to happen."⁶⁷

In another account al-Baqir told one of his disciples, Jabir b. Yazid al-Ju'fi, that a man from the *ahl al-bayt* would rule for three hundred and nine years after his death. Jabir asked, "When will this happen?" Al-Baqir said, "After the death of al-Qa'im." Jabir went on to ask, "How long will al-Qa'im remain in the world?" The Imam replied, "Nineteen years from the time of his rise until his death." Jabir asked if his death would be followed by chaos. The Imam said, "Yes, for fifty years. At that time the Imam al-Muntasir (al-Husayn, as mentioned at the end of the tradition) will return and exact revenge for himself and his follow-ers. . . ."[68]

The above reports indicate the difficulty of determining the length of time for which al-Mahdi will rule. The confusion also appears to have been intensified because of the tradition about the *raj'a,* which was the rule of the Imams before the day of resurrection, and because of the eschatological role of the Mahdi before the Day of Judgment. Some later Imamite scholars have attempted to interpret these traditions in two ways.

First, the rule of the twelve Mahdis means the rule of the Prophet and the rest of the Imams, with the exception of al-Qa'im, when they "return" to the world and rule in succession. The term Mahdi, according to these scholars, has been used for all the Imams; al-Qa'im, according to some reports, will also return to the world after his death. All these variant traditions together afford explanation for different versions of the time period of al-Mahdi's rule.

Second, these Mahdis might well be the successors of al-Qa'im, who, during the period of *raj'a* when other Imams will be ruling, would call the people to the path of God, so that the world might not remain void of the *hujja* of God. The successors of the Prophet and the Imams are also considered *hujja.*[69]

There is no doubt that the doctrine of *raj'a* was a subsequent development in the Mahdi doctrine, as indicated in the difficulty of disentangling confusing reports on the two aspects of the doctrine: the *raj'a* and the *zuhur,* especially the former. The function of the twelfth Imam as the Mahdi during the *zuhur* was sufficient to save the whole of humanity and the entire creation from degeneration. The rule of the Mahdi alone will establish the era of absolute prosperity which will obtain until the final resurrection takes place and the cycle of creation is completed. Al-Mahdi will thus accomplish the return of creation to its original purity. The Imamite aspirations are best voiced in the following lines composed by the Shi'ite poet Di'bil b. 'Ali al-Khuza'i (b. 148/765–66):

Were it not for him, who I hope will come today or tomorrow, my sighing for them could cut my heart.

No doubt an Imam will rise—an Imam who will govern according to the name of God and the Blessings.

He will distinguish the false and the truthful among us; he will requite with favors and punishments.[70]

Conclusion

The most important point about the Islamic messiah, al-Mahdi, is that he will come forth from his occultation and appear for the sight of all mankind. The appearance *(zuhur)* of the twelfth Imam absorbs the interest of the Imamites in general and their traditionists in particular, and as seen in the previous chapter, they behold this appearance in numerous apocalyptic visions. They long and pray for the fulfillment of these visions. The message conveyed in the numerous traditions about the appearance is that the *zuhur* of the Mahdi is at hand, and that the righteous and elect adherents of the Imam who long for it should not despair at the seemingly prolonged *ghayba* of the messianic Imam. When the time is at hand, the Promised Mahdi will appear in "a twinkling of the eye, or nearer" (16:77). The faithful must wait until all that is promised, preceding the appearance of al-Mahdi, is accomplished and the signs of the *zuhur*, of which they have been informed in the tradition, have come. The conception of *zuhur* in Shi'i piety conveys an important aspect of the faith *(iman)* concerning the Awaited Imam. The twelfth Imam, according to this faith, will not merely come forth from the earthly obscurity of the *ghayba* and reveal himself to launch his program of messianic works; rather, he, as the Imam of the believers, who will emerge from the pre-existent state of occultation to the longing Shi'ites, has remained in their vision as long as their earthly lives. The *zuhur* of the Mahdi is undoubtedly the great change of the ages, which will inaugurate the final judgment and the new eon. As such, it is also a cosmic event involving the whole creation. The signs and wonders which precede the appearance of the Mahdi form the omens of the universalistic Islamic eschatology to which explicit reference is made in Islamic tradi-

[*180*]

tions. However, the eschatological Mahdi, in the Shi'ite faith, is primarily the twelfth Imam from among the descendants of the Prophet, in whom the primordial light of the prophethood has continued to shine through the ages. He is the light of God in the darkness of the world. This latter belief has not allowed maintaining any idea regarding the inaccessibility of the Hidden Imam in the state of occultation. The Imamite works on the twelfth Imam have, as a rule, included a chapter or two on "those who have seen or met with the Sahib al-zaman (Master of the Age)." Consequently, however significant the eschatological role of the Mahdi might have been defined in the Shi'ite exposition of this doctrine, his function as the Imam of his Shi'a is of paramount importance in the pious lives of his followers. Salvation is guaranteed to the one who acknowledges the true Imam of his time, to whom devotion *(walaya)* and obedience *(ita'a)* are incumbent, since he alone can bring a true Islamic rule of justice and equity on earth.

The endeavors of the Imamite scholars, especially the early *wukala'* (deputies) of the Imam, at different times, in regard to the elaboration, systematization, and crystallization of the Imamite doctrine of the Mahdi Imam, succeeded in establishing a sort of spiritual link in the lives of the Imamites who looked forward to the appearance of their Imam. The belief in the appearance of the Hidden Imam as the Mahdi helped the Shi'ites to endure under unbearable situations and to hope for a just future pending the return of the Mahdi. It would not be an exaggeration to suggest that without such a belief in the role of the twelfth Imam, the Imamite religion might not have been able to survive persecutions under different dynasties in the course of Islamic history, before it became established as the official creed of the Safavid empire at the beginning of the sixteenth century. The spiritual aspect of the Mahdi doctrine was destined to gain importance in the face of the failure to establish temporal rule by the Imam. Already the often quoted Shi'i tradition describing the temporal function of al-Qa'im al-Mahdi of "filling the earth with justice and equity as it is filled with tyranny and wickedness" sometimes assumed an esoteric interpretation. Sayyid Haydar al-Amuli (d. 1385), in explaing this tradition says: "By 'filling the earth with justice' is meant that al-Qa'im al-Muntazar (the Awaited Qa'im) will fill the hearts with knowledge [and affirmation] of the Unity of God *(tawhid)*, after they had been filled with polytheism and ignorance."[1] This aspect of the Mahdi doctrine has become nothing less than the cornerstone of the Imamite spiritual edifice. It reflects the hopes and visions of its believers for a better existence. The phenomenon of salvation through the rise of the divinely guided savior Imam, who is believed to have been endowed with the divine prophetic knowledge, has thus dominated the Imamite outlook throughout the period of the Complete Occultation. Moreover, the persistent faith in the *faraj* (freedom from grief) through the *zuhur* required the Shi'ites to be on alert at all times and also to pave the way for the Imam's reappearance by constantly re-evaluating contemporary historical life. Hence the prolongation of the *ghayba*, in Shi'i piety, is interpreted as a time of travail, a period of testing and sifting of the believers, a period of disintergration which must precede the final restoration when the Savior of Islam appears. The Mahdi thus embodies all that for which the religious experience of the Muslims stand. The basic emphasis of this experience is the establishment of the ideal religio-political community, the *umma*, under the guidance of the Islamic revelation.

The idea of al-Mahdi has, as a result, enabled the Imamites to give full rein to their hagiographical imagination. In many cases, some of the traditions concerning the birth of the Imamite Mahdi and his reappearance reflect Shi'i piety, its hopes, disappointments, and aspirations for a prosperous future. For the believers in the Imamate of the twelfth Imam, neither his *ghayba* nor the delay in his reappearance as the only true Mahdi seemed unusual. Even the limitation of the number of the Imams to twelve is taken to be normative as the number of the legatees *(awsiya')* of all the major prophets, who also had a period of occultation, and their followers a period of trial culminating in the final triumph and establishment of justice.[2] In Shi'i piety, the role assigned to al-Mahdi, descended from al-Husayn, the martyr, at the end of human history, is the fulfillment of the mission of all these great prophets.[3] He is the victorious Imam who will restore the purity of the Faith, which will bring true and uncorrupted guidance to all mankind, creating an adequately just social order and a world free from tyranny and wickedness. The chiliastic vision of history in Shi'ism continues to be expressed, even today, in terms of radical social protest in the face of political oppression. Had it not been this deep sense of paving the way for the reappearance of the Imam, the Shi'ites would not have felt the need to re-evaluate their social circumstances and the shortcomings of their present lives. Thus, the *ghayba* of the Imam has acted as a creative force in the lives of the Imamites in order not only to help them bear with patience the difficult times, but also to prepare them to fulfill their historical responsibility of establishing a true Islamic rule, even before the Imam assumes the leadership of the Imamiyya. The realization of this responsibility from the time of the Short Occultation (873–74) has provided the Imamites with a religious as well as a social structure, and the *wikala* (deputyship) of the Imam, direct or indirect, provided the crucial guardianship of that community.

Appendix: Index of the Imam and the Imamate in al-Kulayni's Kitab al-hujja in al-Kafi

(The sub-headings of *kitab al-hujja* are not numbered in any edition of *al-Kafi*. But for the sake of convenience they are numbered in this index, and the sub-titles will appear at the end of the index. The first number indicates the *bab* and the second number the *hadith*, which is properly marked in the book.)

The Creation of the Imams

    created in the best shape and form, 11/6;
    like the prophets created from special matter, 94/2;
    birth described, 93/1;
    conception described, 93/1;
    after the fortieth day of conception listen to what is said, 93/2;
    before conception the preceding Imam is sent through an angel heavenly syrup which he drinks, 93/3;
    born pure and circumcised, 93/5;
    the mother of the Imam-to-be-born experiences light and noises before the birth of the Imam, 93/5;
    ten signs of the Imam when he is born and after he is in the world, 93/8;
    created from *'illiyin* (sublime matter) and their spirits created from a matter above that, 94/1;
    created from the light *(al-nur)* which shows the greatness of God, 94/1;
    lived under the green shadow before anything else was created, glorifying God, 111/7;
    do not become *muhtalim* (one who experiences an emission of the seminal fluid in sleep) in their sleep, 124/12.

[*184*]

The Acknowledgement of the Imams

no one will enter Paradise without acknowledging the Imam—and no one will be put into the Fire except those who have refused to recognize them, 7/9;

those who do not acknowledge them are in darkness, 7/13;

should be acknowledged, whether he appears now or later, 84/1;

the one who dies without acknowledging his Imam dies a death of ignorance (*jahiliyya*), 84/5;

all the twelve must be acknowledged, and not the last or the first one only, 85/7;

the one who has not acknowledged the living Imam has not acknowledged the past ones either 85/8;

acknowledgement of the righteous Imam is like possessing the light of Islam, 86/3;

acknowledgement of the Imam is crucial, 87/1;

Imams from the descendants of 'Ali and Fatima should be acknowledged, 88/1;

those who do not acknowledge the one from among the descendants of Fatima will be punished twice as much (for their sins) as those who do, 88/2.

The Imam and His Successor

The Imam:

hands over the Books, knowledge, and weapons to his successor, 59/1;

does not die without seeing his successor, to whom he entrusts the tokens of the Imamate, 59/5;

does not become an Imam without having a son to succeed him, 73/4;

in case of his death, the people are obliged to look for his successor, 89/1;

in case of his death, those in distant lands should make every effort to travel to the place of the last Imam's residence and find out his successor, 89/2;

his successor may be known in the same manner as 'Ali, al-Hasan, and al-Husayn were known, 89/2;

his successor can be known by three signs, 89/2;

his successor can be recognized by his outstanding personality, 89/3;

knows about his Imamate when the preceding Imam is dying; if he is away, he knows about his succession by inspiration from God, 90/4;

his dead body is washed by his successor, a tradition established by Moses, 92/2;

does not die before appointing a successor to the Imamate, 99/1.

The Imams and Their Followers

The Imams:

know their helpers by looking at their countenances since they are *al-a'raf* (the elevated places) mentioned in the Qur'an, 7/9;

their opponents will not receive the intercession of the Prophet, 19/3;

know their followers and whether they are true believers or hypocrites, 33/1;

there exists a *mithaq* (covenant) made by God between them and their followers, 33/1;

knew all that was going to befall their followers, but since they would not control their tongues, the Imams refrained from revealing it, 51/1;

like their followers to speak when they speak and to keep quiet when they keep quiet, 52/1;

make it lawful for their followers to benefit from that which belongs to them, 105/3;

whatever belongs to them belongs to their followers, 105/5;

will make *shafa'a* (intercession) for their followers on the Day of Judgment, 108/91;

know when their Shi'a will die, 120/7;

accept *dirhams* in order to purify the wealth of their followers, 129/7.

The Imam and the Prophets

The Imams:

compared with the Prophet, 3/1;

in them is the tradition of past prophets and the Prophet, 11/4;

are the signs [celestial] *('alamat)* and the Prophet is the star, 17/1;

in their bodies runs the Prophet's spirit; their blood and flesh is the Prophet's blood and flesh, 19/4;

the names and the names of their fathers and the names of their devotees revealed to the Prophet through Gabriel, 19/4;

the Prophet will complain against those who refused to recognize their excellence and severed relations with them, 19/5;

are the *rasikhun fi al-'ilm* (firmly founded in knowledge), but the Prophet is superior to them in this respect, 22/2;

'Ali, among the Imams, was taught by the Prophet in accordance with the command of God, 49/1;

used to stop people who thought they were prophets, 53/2;

are not prophets but resemble the close associates of the Prophet, 53/1, 4;

are the learned but not prophets, 53/5;

have the status of the Prophet but are not the prophets, and the number of wives lawful to the Prophet was not lawful to them, 53/7;

endowed with five souls like prophets, 55/2;

'Ali and the Prophet hold a special excellence over the rest of the Imams in comprehending the Law, 58/3;

their *walaya* (devotion, love) elucidated by the Prophet, 64/4;

entrusted with the knowledge, the faith, the *ism al-akbar* (the greatest name), and the knowledge of the prophets by the Prophet, 65/2;

their rights acknowledged by all the prophets, 109/4;

and the Prophet created from the light, that is, spirit without body before anything was created, 111/3;

and the Prophet created first in order to bear witness over the entire creation, 111/5;

and the Prophet supported by the angel Gabriel when in the light form, 111/10;

will be from 'Ali's descendants, according to the tidings given to the Prophet, 111/4.

The Knowledge of the Imam

The Imam:

the *'alim* (learned authority), on whom depends the knowledge of truth and falsehood, 5/5;

the treasurer of God's knowledge in the heavens and on earth, 11/2;

knows the inner meanings *(ta'wil)* of the Qur'an, 22/1;

endowed with the knowledge, which is firmly established in his breast, 23/1;

possesses such knowledge that it increases from day to day and from hour to hour, 33/3, 4;

possesses the knowledge of the Torah, the Gospels, the Psalms, and the exegesis of that which was revealed on the Tablets, 33/3, 4;

inherited the knowledge of the Prophet and the Qur'an, 33/7;

inherited all the revealed books in their original languages and knows how to read them as they were [originally] read and how to interpret them, 34/1;

speaks other languages besides Arabic, 34/2;

collected the whole Qur'an as it was revealed, in chronological order, 35/1;

only can claim to possess the knowledge of all that is manifest and hidden in the Qur'an, 35/2, 45/3;

possesses the knowledge of the Book, 35/5;

is endowed with the knowledge of the exegesis and the injunctions of the Qur'an and the changes that will take place and the events that will occur, 35/3, 41/1;

possesses *al-Jami'a*, *al-Jafr*, and *Mushaf Fatima*,[1] 40/1;

being the *hujja*, possesses the esoteric meanings of the Qur'an, 41/1;

his knowledge increases every Thursday night, 42/1, 2, 3;

before being endowed with any new knowledge, that knowledge is first given to the Prophet, who then passes it on to him, 43/3;

equal in knowledge, and no Imam is more learned than the other, 43/4;

receives all the knowledge of God which He bestows on the angels, prophets, and apostles, and the knowledge of *bada'* (a change in the divine ruling caused by the emergence of new circumstances)[2], 44/1;

denied possession of the knowledge of hidden things, 45/1;

denied the knowledge of hidden things but was informed about anything he wished to know, 45/4;

[*187*]

The Characteristics of the Imam

after the Prophet, 7/5;

necessary for the acceptance of prayers, 7/8;

without him a person is like a sheep without a shepherd, 7/8;

the *bab* ("gate"), *sirat* (way), *sabil* (path), and *wajh* (countenance, meaning favor)[3] of God to lead the people towards Him, 7/9;

the *a'raf* through whom God can be known, 7/9;

resembles the clear spring which flows at the command of God, 7/9;

the guide *(dalil)* to give directions, 7/10;

the light towards which people walk, 7/13;

to him belongs *anfal* (the booty, etc.) and *safw al-mal* (the best portion of the booty which goes to the chief), 8/6;

the firmly rooted in knowledge, 8/6;

the learned authority *('alim)* of the *umma*, 8/14;

the witness of God to His creatures, 9/1;

the witness to the people, and the Prophet witness to him to what he has delivered to him from God, 9/2;

the witness of God, indirectly, 9/2;

the chosen one, 9/4;

with the Qur'an and the Qur'an with him, 9/5;

pure and immune to sin before being made the witness and the *hujja*, 9/5;

the *hadi* (guide) for the *umma*, 10/1;

the *hadi* for the century in which he lives, 10/1;

wali al-amr (responsible for the command), the keeper of His knowledge, 11/1;

the interpreter of the revelation of God, 11/3;

the *hujjat al-baligha* (i.e. the Proof which has reached the people)[4] for all under the sky and on earth, 11/3;

his name and his father's name given to the Prophet by Gabriel, 11/4;

the *Qa'im bi al-amr* (one who upholds the Command), 11/5;

had he not been created, God would not have been worshipped, 11/6;

God makes the tree to speak for him, 11/6;

from the household of the Prophet is the light of God, 13/1;

the revealed light of God, 13/1;

his love and the effects it can produce on the lovers of him, 13/1;

the pillars of earth, 14/1;

not recognizing his right results in being drifted away from the right path, 14/3;

all equal in status, 14/3;

the support of Islam and the link to the path of guidance, 14/3;

can be found only among *ahl al-bayt*, 15/1;

resembles raincloud in blessings and kindness, 15/1;

through him the religious endeavors are accomplished, 15/1;

the pure one endowed with knowledge and faith, 15/1;

from the progeny of *al-Batul* (the Virgin, i.e. Fatima), 15/1;

the infallible, confirmed, divinely aided and guided, 15/1;

protected by the Angel *(al-ruh)*, 56/4;

acted according to the instructions laid down in the *wasiyya* (testament)[6], 61/1;

revolted or chose political quietism in accordance with the *wasiyya*, 61/3;

informed of the time he would die by the Prophet who appears in his dream, 61/5;

possesses a note-book *(sahifa)* which outlines the course of events connected with him during his term as an Imam, 61/5;

three proofs for his claim to the imamate, 62/2;

cannot be defamed with wicked deeds, 62/3;

his signs, 62/4;

al-Qa'im in relation to each other, 70/7;

does not indulge in amusement and pleasure-seeking, 71/15;

sees with the light of God and listens with the understanding endowed by God, 72/14;

he alone washes the dead body of the preceding Imam, 72/14;

respected even when he dies by the reading of the *takbir* (i.e. the saying of *allah akbar* [God is the great]) nine times instead of five in the funeral prayers, 62/14;

inherits the Imamate even if very young, 73/2;

there cannot be two (Imams) at one time, 73/7;

removed when God is enraged with the people, 80/31;

should be able to make impression on stone, 81/3;

the hidden meaning of that which is lawful in the Qur'an, 85/10;

for him God erects a minaret in every city from where he watches the deeds of the slaves of God to present them to God, 93/3, 4;

should be contacted after the *hajj* and referred to in regard to the religious difficulties, 96/1;

frequented by the angels, who are kinder [than people in general] to the children of the Imam, 97/1;

also Imam to the *jinn*, who come and ask him about their religious difficulties, 98/1;

jinn work for him when there is urgency about a matter, 98/4;

will rule according to the command of God and the method set down by David, 99/3;

encourages unity among the Muslims, 103/4;

his right, which is incumbent on the people, is that he be listened to and obeyed, 104/1;

the father of the orphans, 104/5;

responsible for the repayment of any debts left by a believer, provided his debt was not for any corrupt reason, 104/7;

to him belongs all the land because he has inherited it according to the covenant of God, 105/1;

must receive the *kharaj* (land tax) on all land cultivated by the Muslims, 105/1;

does he pay *zakat*? 105/4;

to him belongs all the fresh waters on earth, 105/5;

extremely simple in his food and clothes so that the poor thereby get a consolation [from seeing him like themselves], 106/1;

his simplicity is because of his position as a righteous man, 106/3;

when he sneezes, those who are present must say, "May God bless you," 107/1;

warns with the help of the verses of the Qur'an, as did the Prophet, 108/61;

gives the tidings of al-Qa'im's appearance, 108/83;

knows by looking at a person whether he has true faith or is a hypocrite, 110/2;

replies to each person according to his comprehending capacity, 110/3;

to him belongs the treasures on earth, 119/4;

twelve in number, in accordance with the tradition of Jesus, who had twelve
apostles, 126/10;

all are *al-Qa'im, al-Mahdi, Sahib al-sayf*,[7] *Warith al-sayf*, 128/1;

does not need what the people possess; rather the people need what he possesses, 129/1;

the fifth *(khums)* payable to him on all that is in earth and under the sea, if used
with the permission of the Imam, 130/1.

The Imamate:

more important than prophethood, 2/2, 4;

is the light, 13/6;

the part of the completion of Religion as revealed to the Prophet at the end of
his mission, 15/1;

part of the Prophet's mission on earth without which religion would not have
been perfected, 15/1;

cannot be based on the principle of *ikhtiyar* (choice by election), since the *umma*
is not aware of the importance of it, 15/1;

a position which Abraham attained after his prophethood, 15/1;

the highest status attained by Abraham after prophethood and the friendship
(khulla) of God, 15/1;

cannot be vested in the oppressor, until the Day of Judgment, 15/1;

the status of the prophets and the inheritance of the legatees *(awsiya')*, the
khilafat allah (vicegerency of God) and the *khilafat al-rasul* (vicegerency of the
Prophet), 15/1;

fully described, 15/1;

being coveted by others, 16/1;

should be sought in the house where the weapons of the Prophet are found,
38/1, 62/1;

like prophethood must be announced at the set time by the will of God, 41/6;

of every Imam announced by God alone, 60/1;

the covenant of God and His Prophet for a person, until it reaches its right
owner, 60/2;

the covenant of God for specified persons, and the Imam has no right to con-
ceal that, 60/3;

The *babs* of *Kitab al-hujja* in *al-Kafi*:

1. *al-idtirar ila al-hujja*
2. *tabaqat al-anbiya'* . . .
3. *al-farq bayn al-rasul wa al-nabi* . . .
5. *anna al-ard la takhlu min hujja*
7. *ma'rifat al-a'imma* . . .
8. *fard ta'at al-a'imma*
9. *fi anna al-a'imma shuhada' allah* . . .
10. *anna al-a'imma hum al-hudat*
11. *anna al-a'imma wulat amr allah*
13. *anna al-a'imma nur allah*
15. *nadir jami' fadl al-imam* . . .
16. *anna al-a'imma wulat al-amr wa hum* . . .
17. *anna al-a'imma hum 'alamat* . . .
19. *ma farada allah wa rasuluh min al-kawn* . . .
20. *anna ahl al-dhikr alladhina amara allah* . . .
21. *anna man wasafah allah fi kitabih* . . .
22. *anna rasikhin fi al-'ilm* . . .
23. *anna al-a'imma qad 'utu al-'ilm* . . .
24. *fi anna man astafah allah* . . .
25. *anna al-a'imma fi kitab allah imaman*
27. *anna al-ni'ma allati adhkaraha allah* . . .
28. *anna al-mutawassimin* . . .
29. *ard al-a'mal 'ala al-nabi* . . .
30. *anna al-tariqa allati huththa* . . .

31. *anna al-a'imma ma'din al-'ilm* . . .
33. *anna al-a'imma warithu 'ilm al-nabi* . . .
34. *anna al-a'imma 'indahum jami' al-kutub* . . .
35. *annahu lam yajma' al-qur'an kulluh illa* . . .
36. *ma 'u'tiya al-a'imma ism allah* . . .
37. *ma 'inda al-a'imma min ayat al-anbiya'*
38. *ma 'inda al-a'imma min silah* . . .
40. *fihi dhikr al-sahifa* . . .
41. *fi sha'n inna inzalnah fi* . . .
42. *fi anna al-a'imma yazdadun fi* . . .
43. *law la anna al-a'imma yazdadun* . . .
44. *anna al-a'imma ya'lamun jami' al-'ulum* . . .
45. *nadir fih dhikr al-ghayb*
46. *anna al-a'imma idha sha'u an ya'lamu* . . .
47. *anna al-a'imma ya'lamun mata yamutun* . . .
48. *anna al-a'imma ya'lamun 'ilm ma kan* . . .
49. *anna allah lam yu'allim nabiyyah 'ilm* . . .
50. *jihat 'ulum al-a'imma*
51. *anna al-a'imma law sutira 'alayhim* . . .
52. *al-tafwid ila rasul allah wa ila al-a'imma* . . .
53. *fi anna al-a'imma biman yushbihun* . . .
54. *anna al-a'imma muhaddathun mufahhamun*
55. *fih dhikr al-arwah* . . .
56. *al-ruh allati yusaddid allah* . . .
57. *waqt ma ya'lam al-imam jami' 'ilm* . . .
58. *fi anna al-a'imma fi al-'ilm wa al-shuja'a* . . .
59. *anna al-imam ya' rifu al-imam* . . .
60. *anna al-imama 'ahd min allah* . . .
61. *anna al-a'imma lam yaf'alu shay'* . . .
62. *al-umur allati tujibu hujjat al-imam*
63. *thabat al-imama fi al-a'qab* . . .
64. *ma nass allah 'ala al-a'imma* . . .
65. *al-ishara wa al-nass 'ala amir al-mu'minin*
66. *al-ishara wa al-nass 'ala al-Hasan b. 'Ali*
70. *al-ishara wa al-nass 'ala abi 'abd allah* . . . *al-Sadiq*
71. *al-ishara wa al-nass 'ala abi al-Hasan Musa*
72. *al-ishara wa al-nass 'ala abi al-Hasan al-Rida*
73. *al-ishara wa al-nass 'ala abi Ja'far al-thani*

The Imamite Imams

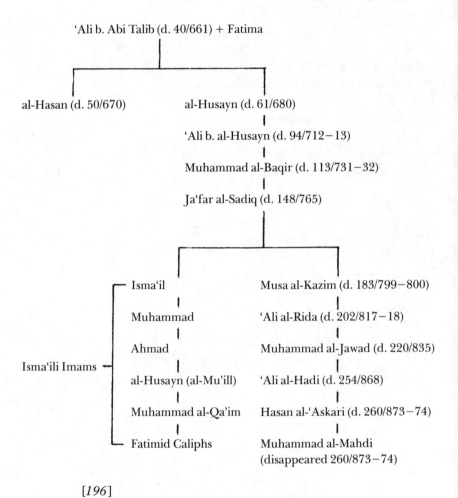

'Ali b. Abi Talib (d. 40/661) + Fatima

al-Hasan (d. 50/670)   al-Husayn (d. 61/680)

'Ali b. al-Husayn (d. 94/712−13)

Muhammad al-Baqir (d. 113/731−32)

Ja'far al-Sadiq (d. 148/765)

Isma'ili Imams

Isma'il   Musa al-Kazim (d. 183/799−800)

Muhammad   'Ali al-Rida (d. 202/817−18)

Ahmad   Muhammad al-Jawad (d. 220/835)

al-Husayn (al-Mu'ill)   'Ali al-Hadi (d. 254/868)

Muhammad al-Qa'im   Hasan al-'Askari (d. 260/873−74)

Fatimid Caliphs   Muhammad al-Mahdi
                                   (disappeared 260/873−74)

Glossary

The following is a glossary of the technical terms which occur most frequently in the book. The meanings of the terms are confined to the context in which they appear in the book.

al-'abath: "futile." In theological works it occurs in the discussion on the purpose of creation. God is wise and just, and therefore no futile action can be attributed to Him. Also in *kalam* theories of moral acts where *al-'abath* is an act that neither produces a position beneficial nor prevents harm was considered by some as bad.

abwab: pl. of *bab* (q.v.) "gate," mediator between the Imam and his followers. Al-Kulayni also uses the plural form for all the Imams, meaning the "gates" of God through which He is approached.

ahl al-bayt: "the People of the House." In the Shi'i writings (and in some Sunni references) it includes the Prophet, 'Ali, Fatima, al-Hasan and al-Husayn, and the other Imams from among the descendants of al-Husayn (see articles *ahl al-bayt* and *ahl al-kisa'* in *EI2*, 1:258, 264).

ahl al-ghuluww: the extremist among the Shi'ites who believed in the divinity of 'Ali and the other Imams (see article *ghulat* in *EI2*, 2:1093ff.).

amir al-mu'minin: "the Commander of the Faithful." In the Shi'ite writings the title is reserved for 'Ali exclusively.

amwal: pl. of *mal*, goods taken as the one fifth *(al-khums)* (q.v.).

asala: abstract noun derived from the form *ASL* meaning "firmness or soundness of judgment" *(Lisan al-'arab*, 9:16). But in this work the meaning is something between authenticity and fundamentality, for which it is hard to find a single equivalent in English.

aslah: "more" or "most salutary." Al-aslah forms a theological discussion in *kalam* and is associated with Mu'tazilism. The doctrine states that God is just and therefore does the best for His creatures. His planning is guided by that which is most salutary and to the best interest of His servants. Both the Basra and Baghdad schools agreed that God preferred the *aslah* for man's religious

[197]

welfare, but disagreed on whether He does that for their worldly benefit, i.e. whether He simply does *salah* (salutary) (q.v.), but not the *aslah*. See also *bada'*.

al-'aql: "reason, intellect, intelligence." In *kalam* it is discussed as a source of knowledge through which man learns of the first principles and ethical axioms, independently of the authority of *al-sam'* (q.v.) (Hilli, *Bab*, p. 40; see also the discussion on *taklif* in Chapter IV).

bab: pl. *abwab*, "gate," is used in a technical sense in the early Imamite writings. It signifies the means of communcation with the Hidden Imam. The deputies of the twelfth Imam were thus termed *abwab* between the Shi'ites and their Imam, being the authorized disciples of the Imam (see article *bab* in *EI2*, 1:832).

bada':   "occurrence"; "to become apparent." In Shi'ite theology it signifies the intervention of new circumstances which bring about a change in an early divine ruling (Mufid, *Awa'il*, p. 53). In the Imamite writings *bada'* serves to explain, on grounds of expedience which God exercises in His planning, the Imamate of Musa al-Kazim (d. 183/799). It also explains the delay in the appearance of the Mahdi (see Chapter V). The doctrine of *bada'* is based on the discussion of *al-aslah* (the most salutary), which states that God does the best for His creatures and that His planning is based on what is most salutary and in the best interest of His slaves (see article *bada'* in *EI2*, 1:850ff.; Kulayni, *Kafi*, 1:262–66). But it was rejected by Ash'arism because it was interpreted as implying a change of mind on the part of God due to what He earlier did not foresee and hence a denial of divine omniscience.

baqiyyat allah: the title of the twelfth Imam derived from the verse in the Qur'an (11:86): "That which is left by God."

al-dalil al-'aqli: argument based on reason independent of revelation. Usually inference from effect to cause; however, when the philosophers use the term *dalil*, they mean by it inference from cause to effect, See *al-'aql*.

al-dalil al-sam'i: argument based on traditional sources such as the Qur'an, Sunna, *qiyas*, and *ijma'*. See *al-sam'*.

faqih: pl. *fuqaha'*, "jurist" or, in the original sense of the term, "theologian," and sometimes both. See *fiqh*. The lowest degree of *faqih*, according to al-Ghazali, is one who possesses only the knowledge that hereafter is better than this world (Jabr, *Essai*, p. 224).

fiqh: originally meant "comprehension" or "intuitive intelligence" (*Lexicon*, 1/6, 2429; Jabr, *Essai*, p. 224). In the technical sense of the term it is knowledge of the religious law in Islam. In the earlier period the term *fiqh* also included the speculative side of the religion in addition to jurisprudence, and was used in the sense of comprehending religious sciences through independent exercise of one's well-informed judgment. (This was never open to just anybody.) This process became necessary in the absence of a ruling based on the Qur'an, or in cases which the existence of such a ruling was not known, or in cases involving the interpretation of the Qur'anic texts in the light of the traditions (see article *fikh* in *EI2*, 2:886).

ghayba: "disappearance, occultation" of the twelfth Imam, with the under-standing that there would be no Imam after him and that he would appear as the Qa'im al-Mahdi.

ghaybat al-qasira: The Short Occultation, also known, in the later period, as *ghaybat al-sughra* (the Lesser), which lasted for some sixty-eight years (874–941).

ghaybat al-tamma: The Complete Occultation, also known as *ghaybat al-kubra* (the Greater) in the later period. This occultation began from 941 and will continue until the reappearance of the twelfth Imam.

hadd: pl. *hudud*, "legal punishment" of certain acts which have been forbidden or for which punishments have been prescribed in the Qur'an (*Lexicon*, 1/2, 525; article *hadd* in *EI2*, 3:20ff.).

al-haqq: "suitable to the reality" or "reality" (*Lexicon*, 1/2, 607). In the context of this book its secondary meaning, "the truth," which has *al-batil* as its oppo-site, is more appropriate (Jabr, *Essai*, p. 69; article *hakk* in *EI2*, 3:82).

al-hiss: The term basically means "the sense," i.e. the five senses taken collec-tively. As a theological and philosophical term, it means "the principle of intel-lectual knowledge," that is, that knowledge attained by intellectual process. For its use in the context of *ijma'* in the Imamite *fiqh*, see Chapter IV.

hujja: The "Competent Authority" in the matters pertaining to religion. Also "Proof" in the sense that the Imam who is the Proof of God stands as a proof of His existence and the existence of His revelation on earth (Kulayni, *Kafi*, 1:361).

husn: "goodness" used as the antithesis of "evil" (*qubh* or *qabh*) in *kalam*; ac-cording to the Shi'ites and Mu'tazilites, *husn* was objective in nature, more spec-ifically an objective attribute or state of the moral act; that is, it belongs to the theory of moral acts. In other words, our reason unaided by revelation is capa-ble of knowing it (see Chapter IV and also Hourani, *Islamic Rationalism*, p. 103).

ijtihad: "A lawyer's exerting the faculties [of the mind] to the utmost for the purpose of forming an opinion in a case of law [respecting a doubtful and different point]" (*Lexicon*, 1/2, 475). *Ijtihad* is an independent estimation of the *faqih* in a legal or theological question, based on the interpretation and applica-tion of the four sources of the Islamic Law: the Qur'an, Sunna, *ijma'*, and *qiyas* (Jabr, *Essai*, pp. 62ff.).

ikhtiyar: "choice by election" concerning the question of the Imamate. This is in opposition to *nass* (clear designation) of the Imam by the Prophet as main-tained by the Shi'ites (Baghdadi, *Usul*, p. 279; see article *ikhtiyar* in *EI2*, 3:1062).

al-'ilm al-daruri: "necessary" or "immediate knowledge" (see Chapter IV, fn. 7).

al-'ilm al-nazari: knowledge which results from an inquiry; also known as *al-muktasab* (acquired) (see Chapter IV, fn. 7).

imam al-gha'ib: "The Hidden Imam": one of the earliest titles of the twelfth Imam.

imam al-natiq: "The 'speaking' [the truth] Imam": this title is used for the Imams who form the source of demonstrative knowledge as compared with the Qur'an, which is *al-samit* (the silent).

imam al-samit: "The Silent Imam." This is the title used for the Imam when there are two of them at one time, one being the *natiq* and the other *samit* as was the case with al-Hasan and al-Husayn.

imam al-zaman: "The Imam of the Age." This is one of the important titles of the twelfth Imam, with the implication that he is the only living Imam of the Age.

imamiyya: Those Shi'ites who recognized the line of the Husaynid Imams up to the Imamate of al-'Askari, through 'Ali al-Rida, and later on acknowledged the Imamate of the twelfth Imam, forming the group of the *Ithna 'Ashariyya* — the Twelvers. Among the early theologians al-Mufid uses the appelation for those Shi'ites who had maintained the necessity of the Imamate among the descendants of al-Husayn, through a clear designation *(nass)* of an infallible individual (see Chapter II, fn. 1).

irada: "will" (of God) which He makes known to the *mukallafun* (q.v.) in the form of necessary knowledge and rational and traditional guidance.

ism al-a'zam: The most esteemed name of God, which, in the Imamite tradition, was supposed to have been given to the Prophet and then was passed on to the Imams. The one possessed of this name was endowed with supernatural powers and knowledge of the hidden things.

'isma: "infallibility." It is "a faculty of avoiding or shunning acts of disobedience [or of self-preservation therefrom,] with [i.e. despite] possession of power to commit them" *(Lexicon,* 1/5, 2067). It also means infallibility in the "total knowledge of the meaning of the revelation and its prescription" *(EI2,* 4:184).

i'tisam: "protection from disobedience" by the grace of God *(Lexicon,* 1/5, 2066).

kaba'ir: pl. of *kabira,* "grave sins," which the Imam could not commit at all. For example, *shirk* (polytheism) was a grave sin, and the Imam at no time in his life could commit *shirk.*

kaffara: "expiation" or "atonement" for neglected duties or sins of omission and commission.

khums: "one fifth." A form of taxation made incumbent upon all the Imamites besides the alms-giving *(al-zakat).*

lutf: "grace." In the context of this study when God imposes obligations on men, He makes the fulfillment of these obligations possible by giving them a "grace." Madelung in his article on *imama* in *EI2,* 3:1167, translates *lutf* as "benevolence." But in the context in which the term is used in *kalam* it is more appropriate to render it "grace." Moreover, "benevolence" or "acts of benevolence" is the translation of *ni'ma* (See Hourani, *Islamic Rationalism,* p. 106).

al-mahdi: "The one guided by God to the truth" *(al-haqq).* This is the proper name of the twelfth Shi'i Imam, who will come at the end of time.

mandub: "recommended act," the doing of which is more excellent than the leaving it undone, in the eye of the prescriber of the law, but which it is permissible to leave undone (*Lexicon*, 1/8, 2750).

marja' (or marji') al-taqlid: a competent authority to which a *muqallid* refers in matters of religion. (See also *mujtahid*.)

ma'sum: "infallible" in the sense that despite possessing power to commit acts of disobedience, a person is endowed with the grace of God, which makes him avoid such acts (see *'isma*).

mubah: indifferent actions for which neither reward nor punishment is to be expected, but which are permissible (*Lexicon*, 1/1, 274).

muhaddath: a person who is inspired; as though he is told a thing and says it. This is what the Shi'i Imam is held to be, namely, he hears the voice of an angel but does not see him (*Lexicon,* 1/2, 529; Kulayni, *Kafi,* 2:37ff.).

muhtadi: "guided," in the sense of being the recipient of divine guidance in the matters of religion.

mujtahid: the one who practises *ijtihad* (q.v.), that is, one who by his own exertions forms his own opinion in matters pertaining the law. In Imam ite *fiqh* a *mujtahid* is also a *mufti,* giver of *fatwas,* whose legal opinions were followed by the *muqallidun* (imitators). The *muqallidun* followed the rulings of a *mujtahid* without any necessary knowledge of its basis. Thus a learned *mujtahid* also becomes *marja' al-taqlid*, a competent authority to whom a person refers in matters of religion "firmly believing him to be right therein, without regard or consideration of the proof of evidence" (*Lexicon*, 1/7, 2557).

mukallaf: "the one on whom the task is imposed" in the form of *taklif* (q.v.) by the *mukallif* (God).

mukallif: "the one who imposes a task." In *kalam* it is God who imposes religious duties on the *mukallaf* (q.v.) in the form of *taklif*, so as to expose the latter to the great reward *(al-thawab)*.

nass: "clear designation" of a successor to the Prophet, as opposed to the principle of *ikhtiyar* (q.v.).

al-qa'im: "Redresser of wrongs"; "the one who will rise"; "the Upholder"; one of the important titles of the twelfth Imam (see Chapter II).

al-qa'im bi amr allah: "the Upholder of the Command of God"; one of the titles of the twelfth Imam, showing his function at the time of his reappearance.

al-qa'im bi'l-jihad: "the Upholder of the Holy War" (against the enemies of *ahl al-bayt* [q.v.]). The title of the twelfth Imam showing his function as the Qa'im of the Family of the Prophet.

al-qa'im bi'l-sayf: "the one who will rise with the sword" (to exact revenge from the enemies of *ahl al-bayt*). The title of the twelfth Imam used interchangeably with *al-qa'im bi'l-jihad*. The Imam also becomes *warith al-sayf* (the one who inherits the sword, for the said purpose).

qubh (or qabh):   "evil." An evil act is that which deserves blame (Hourani, *Islamic Rationalism*, p. 49). See also *husn*.

raj'a: "the returning to the present state of existence" after death, before the day of resurrection. In the early Shi'i belief it meant the "return" of the Imam who had disappeared, to establish the rule of justice and equity. But in the Imamite creed it means the "return" of a given number of believers to this world before the final resurrection occurs, during the days of al-Mahdi's rule, or before or after that period (see Chapter V).

rawi: pl. *ruwat*, "transmitters" of *hadith*. In the Imamite writings it refers to the *mujtahid*, who is considered to be the sole custodian of the teachings of the Imams.

riyasa: used as the synonym of *"Imama"* (leadership).

ruju':   = *raj'a* (q.v.).

sagha'ir: pl. of *saghira*, "minor sins" as opposed to *kaba'ir* (q.v.), that is, grave sins.

sahib al-amr: "the Master of the Command." One of the titles of the twelfth Imam.

sahib al-zaman: "the Master of the Age." One of the titles of the twelfth Imam.

salah: "benefit, propriety." Also a synonym of *maslaha* (q.v.) (*Lexicon*, 1/4, 1715). Also see *al-aslah*.

al-sam':   lit. "the hearing." It is that knowledge which becomes accessible through the traditional sources, such as the Book and the Sunna, *ijma'* (consensus) and *qiyas* (analogy), in contrast with what is known by *al-'aql* (q.v.). The Book, the Sunna, *ijma'* and *qiyas* constitute *al-sam'*, or revelations (Jabr, *Essai*, p. 127; Hourani, *Islamic Rationalism*, pp. 129ff.).

shahid: "witness," in the sense that he shall be called upon to bear witness on the Day of Judgment to what was revealed to the Prophet and those who acknowledged him and those who charged him with falsehood (see Chapter I).

taklif: "imposition of a task, obligation," the fulfillment of which carries great reward in the future life (see Chapter IV).

taklif al-'aqli: *taklif* which is based on *al-'aql*, that is, the unaided reason is capable of knowing it, independently of revelation.

taklif al-sam'i: that *taklif* which is based on *al-sam'*, that is, revelation.

taqiyya: technically "dispensation from the requirements of religion under compulsion or threat of injury"(article *takiya* in *EI1*, 4:628).E.G. Brown renders it "prudential concealment" (*Literary History of Persia*, 4:17). In the Imamite sense it means "protection of the true religion from enemies by hiding it, in circumstances where there is fear of being killed or captured or insulted" (Ibn Babuya, *Creed*, p. 110, fn. 2). This dispensation is not accepted by the Sunnites.

wahid: "rare" or "unique," a technical term used in the classification of *hadith*. It is a tradition which has not been reported with frequency, regardless of the number of transmitters who have reported it. The books on the principles of *fiqh* discuss various kinds of *wahid* traditions. Thus, for instance, one kind is known as *mashhur*, meaning that rare tradition which has attained fame because of its substance, although it is likely that the *sanad* may be completely dropped in reporting it. On the other hand, *gharib* is that *wahid* tradition for which only one narrator has been recorded.

[*202*]

wahy: "revelation." It is that knowledge transmitted through the archangel Gabriel and reserved for the prophets only. It differs from *ilham*, which is inspiration. In revelation a prophet hears the voice and sees the angel. See *muhaddath* (Kulayni, *Kafi*, 2:37ff.).

wajib: "obligatory" or "binding" in the moral sense of the term; "incumbent" or "necessary" in the sense that certain acts become logically necessary (*Lexicon*, 1/8, 2923; Hourani, *Islamic Rationalism*, p. 115).

wajibat: those acts which are made obligatory, and for neglecting which one will be punished (*Lexicon*, 1/8 2923).

walaya: "love and devotion" (Jabr, *Essai*, p. 278) towards the *ahl al-bayt* (q.v.).

wali al-amr: "the ruler, the legal guardian" (Dozy, *Supp.*, 2:843), is a title of the twelfth Imam which means that he will exact revenge from the enemies of *ahl al-bayt* (q.v.).

wasi: "legatee"; in the context of the Shi'ite writings, an Imam commissioned to execute the will of the Prophet (see *Lexicon*, 1/8 3055 for its basic meaning).

wasiyya: "testament" or "the command" (*Lexicon*, 1/8, 3055) from God, in the written form for the Imams, who were required to follow the instruction therein.

wikala: used as the synonym of *sifara* and *niyaba* in the Imamite writings, meaning "deputyship."

ziyara: pl. *ziyarat*, literally "visit"; technically, "salutations" offered at the shrines of the Imams.

Notes

Notes to Chapter 1

1. For this and other traditions on *Mahdi* see A. J. Wensinck, *A Handbook of Early Muhammadan Tradition* (Leiden, 1927), under MAHDI, p. 139.

2. M. A. Shaban, *The 'Abbasid Revolution* (Cambridge, 1970), pp. 147ff.

3. Marshall G. S. Hodgson, "How did the early Shi'a become sectarian?" in *JAOS*, 75 (1955), 9.

4. Snouck Hurgronje, *Der Mahdi, Versprede Geschriften* (Bonn, 1923), I:150 suggests that the epithet Mahdi may have been used in a purely honorific and political sense to describe 'Ali and his sons al-Hasan and al-Husayn. According to Tabari, *Ta'rikh*, 5:589, Sulayman b. Surad, the leader of the Penitents, called al-Husayn, after his death, the Mahdi son of the Mahdi. Earlier than this Hassan b. Thabit, the poet, is described to have addressed the Prophet as *mahdi* in one of his compositions (*Diwan*, ed. Walid 'Arafat, 1 [London, 1971], p. 269), but doubtless in the non-eschatalogical sense.

5. Naw., *Firaq*, p. 204; *Heterodoxies*, Vol. 28/1:44.

6. Shaban, *Islamic History: A New Interpretation 2* (Cambridge, 1976), p. 9.

7. Isfahani, *Maqatil*, p. 157.

8. Naw., *Firaq*, p. 57; *Heterodoxies*, p. 44; *Milal*, 1:273 is in doubt as to whether this name is derived from a man named Nawus or a place Nawusa.

9. W. Ivanow, *Studies in Early Persian Ismailism*, The Ismaili Society, Series A, No. 3 (Leiden, 1948), p. 2.

10. Hodgson, *The Venture of Islam* (Chicago, 1974), 2:185.

11. Ibn Khaldun, *The Muqaddima*, trans. Franz Rosenthal, 2nd ed. (Princeton, 1967), 2:156.

12. Ibn Sa'd, *Tabaqat*, 1:156−64.

13. Ibn Nadim, *Fihrist*, p. 33 mentions a *tafsir* (exegesis) of the Qur'an transmitted by Abu al-Jarud Ziyad b. al-Mudir on the authority of al-Baqir. Abu al-Jarud had seceded to Zayd b. 'Ali after the latter's death and did not acknowledge the leadership of al-Sadiq. In fact, he became the founder of the Jarudiyya faction of the Zaydites, who maintained the Mahdiism of al-Nafs al-Zakiyya (Baghdadi, *Farq*, p. 31).

14. Shaban, *Revolution*, p. 167.

15. Kulayni, *Kafi*, 2:114; Ibn Babuya, *Kamal*, 2:48.

16. Naw., *Firaq*, p. 38.

17. Kashshi, *Rijal*, p. 290.

18. Hodgson, "Early Shi'a . . .," p. 11.

19. W. M. Watt, *Formative Period of Islamic Thought* (Edinburgh, 1973), p. 54ff. discusses the line of the Husaynid Imams of whom some were not even recognized as the head of the

'Alid family. But he does not satisfactorily explain how then the line of the Twelver Imams came to be acknowledged even at the later dates. The explanation offered by Marshall Hodgson in this connection in his article "Early Shi'a . . ." is not only substantial but also convincing.

20. Ibn Babuya, *Creed*, p. 70; Hilli *Bab*, pp. 40ff.

21. *Mawaqif*, 3:261ff.

22. Kulayni, *Kafi*, 2:54ff.

23. See, for example, Kulayni, *Kafi*, 1:456. In the case of Muhammad b. al-Hanafiyya, the Kaysanites regarded him as 'Ali's successor and heir of his esoteric knowledge, which is a point of an anecdote told by Ibn Sa'd, wherein Ibn al-Hanafiyya comes to know that the people believe the family of the Prophet have some (esoteric) knowledge *(shay'an min al-'ilm)* and he says, "I solemnly swear that we have not inherited anything from the Prophet of God, save the Qur'an *(bayn hadhahyni'l lawhayn)"* (*Tabaqat*, 7:77; *Milal*, 1:236).

24. Kulayni, *Kafi*, 1:360; for a lexical explanation see E. W. Lane, *An Arabic-English Lexicon* (Beirut, 1968), 1/4, 1610.

25. Kulayni, *Kafi*, 1:361. See also R. Dozy, *Supplément aux Dictionnaires Arabes* (Beirut, 1968), p. 249. His explanation of the term is very close to the context here.

26. Ibid., 1:387.

27. Ibid., 1:448ff.

28. Ibid., 1:337.

29. Ibid., 1:333.

30. Shaban, *History 2*, p. 47.

31. Mas'udi, *Ithbat al-wasiyya* (Tehran, 1343 Sh.), p. 507.

32. Shaban, (2History 2, p. 54; H. A. R. Gibb, "Government and Islam under the early 'Abbasids: The political collapse of Islam," in *L'elaboration de l'Islam, Colloque de Strasbourg*, 12–13–14 juin 1959 (Paris, 1961), pp. 120ff.

33. Gibb, "Government and Islam," p. 126.

34. Ibn Khallikan, Ahmad b. Muhammad, *Wafayat al-a'yan* (Beirut, 1961), 3:424–25; Mufid, *Irshad*, p. 641.

35. Isfahani, *Maqatil*, pp. 395–96.

36. Tusi, *Ghayba*, p. 214.

37. Tusi, *Fihrist*, p. 204. See also a recent article by Wilferd Madelung, "A Treatise of the Sharif al-Murtada on the Legality of Working for the Government," in *BSOAS*, 43 (1980), Part I, 18–31, which discusses the Imamite position on the question of the lawfulness of holding office under the illegitimate caliphate. Such a discussion was prompted because of the fact that many Imamites were known to have held office in the imperial 'Abbasid court throughout formative period of Imamite history, the second/eighth and third/ninth centuries.

38. Kashshi, *Rijal*, index pp. 4ff.

39. Hilli, *Khulasat al-aqwal*, p. 101.

40. *Kamil*, 9:350.

41. Ibid., 8:619, 628, 9:94.

42. Ibid., 8:134 where it is related that when the great scholar Tabari died in 310/923, the Baghdadians demonstrated against him and he was denied a decent burial because he had refused to recognize Ahamd b. Hanbal as a jurist.

43. Tusi, *Fihrist*, p. 186.

44. *Ta'rikh*, 3:23.

45. Tusi, *Rijal*, p. 485.

46. Tusi, *Fihrist*, p. 162.

47. *Kamil*, 9:637.

48. Ibn Hajar al-'Asqalani, Ahamd b. 'Ali, *Lisan al-mizan*, 2nd ed. (Beirut, 1971), 5:135.

49. Tusi, *Ghayba*, p. 2.

1. I have used the term *imamiyya* here and at other places for those Shi'ites who had recognized the line of the Husaynid Imams up to the Imamate of al-'Askari, through 'Ali al-Rida, and later on acknowledged the Imamate of the twelfth Imam, forming the group of the Ithna 'Ashariyya—the Twelvers. Among the early theologians al-Mufid had used the appelation of the *imamiyya* for those Shi'ites who had maintained the necessity of the Imamate among the descendants of al-Husayn, through a clear designation *(nass)* of an infallible individual *(Fusul M*, pp. 239–40). Lahiji, a later theologian, defines *imamiyya* as every Shi'ite sect which believes in the necessity of infallibility in the Imam and considers the existence of such an Imam indispensable in all ages. Thus, adds Lahiji, Kaysaniyya and Zaydiyya are not Imamites *(Gawhar*, Tenth Chapter, third section, third discourse). The term *qat'iyya*, which is used synonymously with *imamiyya*, is older and broader than the latter term, whereas *ithna 'ashariyya* was used much later. See below.

2. Mufid, *Irshad*, p. 670.

3. Isfahani, *Maqatil*, pp. 140, 157. In his account of al-Nafs al-Zakiyya, the author clearly mentions that after the latter had been recognized as the Mahdi who would establish 'Alid rule by the majority of the Shi'ites, with the exception of Ja'far al-Sadiq, who had predicted the victory of the 'Abbasids in this venture, al-Saffah and following him al-Mansur persisted in their aim of getting their hands on him and his brother Ibrahim. This they did because they both had paid allegiance to him in the beginning and were now afraid of his rivalry in the matter of the caliphate.

4. Naw., *Firaq*, p. 94; Tusi, *Ghayba*, pp. 62, 145.

5. Kulayni, *Kafi*, 2:154; Tusi, *Ghayba*, p. 134; Ibn Babuya, *Kamal*, 1:339; *Milal*, 1:170.

6. Naw., *Firaq*, p. 79.

7. *Milal*, 1:170.

8. Mas'udi, *Muruj*, 8:40.

9. Ibn Babuya, *Kamal*, 1:124.

10. The name of the mother of the twelfth Imam has been variously recorded in the sources as Sayqal, Rayhana, Sawsan, and Narjis.

11. Ibn Babuya, *Kamal*, 2:152.

12. Ibid.

13. *Khwandan*, p. 108; Naw., *Firaq*, p. 79; Tusi, *Ghayba*, pp. 141ff.

14. For the detailed account of his life and works see *Khwandan*, pp. 125ff. See also the introduction to *Firaq* by Helmut Ritter and his sources on the life of al-Nawbakhti.

15. The word is usually translated as "the Proof." In the Shi'i terminology the Imam is the *hujja*, i.e. the Proof of God on earth, with the implication that he is "the Competent Authority" representing God on earth and standing as a proof of His existence and the existence of His revelation on earth. See Chapter I, fn. 24, and also below.

16. This title is difficult to render in English. Fyzee in his translation of Ibn Babuya's *Creed* translates it as the one "who upholds" and as the full title goes—*al-qa'im bi amrillah-*—"who upholds the command of God." But as discussed below, I would be inclined to agree with Majlisi's explanation of this title as it appears in one of the early traditions of *Kafi*. The tradition is reported on the authority of the fifth Imam al-Baqir, who was asked about al-Qa'im. So he struck his son al-Sadiq with his hand and said, "This is, by God, al-Qa'im." The reporter adds that when al-Baqir died he told the tradition to the sixth Imam al-Sadiq, who said, "This is true. Perhaps you believe that not every Imam is al-Qa'im following the preceding Imam" (Kulayni, *Kafi*, 2:114). Majlisi explains that *qa'im* as used in such reports means *al qa'im bi'l-jihad*, the one who will arise with the sword, and this applies to all the Imams. Majlisi adds that this was the way Imams had chosen not to disappoint those Shi'ites who were expecting their Imams to arise against the tyrannical caliphate. See additional comments on the same page of *Kafi*.

17. Naw., *Firaq*, pp. 79–80; *Milal*, 1:170; Tusi, *Ghayba*, p. 141; Ibn Babuya, *Kamal*, 1:24; Mufid, *Fusul M*, p. 259.

18. Naw., *Firaq*, pp. 80−81; *Milal*, 1:170; Tusi, *Ghayba*, p. 62, 142; Mufid, *Fusul M*, p. 259.

19. Naw., *Firaq*, p. 82; *Milal*, 1:170; Tusi, *Ghayba*, p. 143; Mufid, *Fusul M*, p. 259.

20. Kashshi, *Rijal*, p. 520; Najashi, *Rijal*, p. 219.

21. Louis Massignon, *La Passion de Husayn Ibn Mansur Hallaj* (Paris, 1975), 1:355; Tusi, *Fihrist*, pp. 72ff.; Qummi, *Kuna*, 2:96.

22. Naw., *Firaq*, p. 82; *Milal*, 1:171; Tusi, *Ghayba*, p. 143; Mufid, *Fusul M*, p. 259. For relevant traditions on this subject see Kulayni, *Kafi*, 2:68.

23. *Passion*, 1:346ff., where Massignon discusses the importance of the ordeal of Mubahala which took palce on 21 Dhu al-Hijja, 10/22 March 632, in which the Prophet, 'Ali, Fatima, al-Hasan, and al-Husayn took part. Thus as the participants on this occasion, which has been given great importance in Shi'i piety, both sons of 'Ali, al-Hasan and al-Husayn, were considered to have been vested with the Imamate following each other, a privilege confined to these two brothers only.

24. Naw., *Firaq*, pp. 83−84; Mufid, *Fusul M*, p. 259; *Milal*, 1:171 adds that people believed that even al-'Askari was of wicked character but in secret, while Ja'far was openly known as vicious.

25. Naw., *Firaq*, pp. 84−85; *Milal*, 1:171.

26. Mufid, *Fusul M*, pp. 259−60.

27. *Passion*, 1:355.

28. Naw., *Firaq*, p. 85; *Milal*, 1:181; Mufid, *Fusul M*, p. 261.

29. Naw., *Firaq*, p. 87; Mufid, *Fusul M*, p. 261. *Milal* does not recount this sect, but in his exposition of the tenets of the next sect he alludes to this faction.

30. *Fatra* is designated as a period between the end of one prophet and the emergence of another; more precisely, it is the period between Jesus and Muhammad. See Ibn Babuya, *Kamal*, 2:371ff., where he discusses the concept of *fatra* and argues that there have always been the *hujaj* from God to guide people, whether the prophets or their legatees. See also *EI²*, 2:97.

31. Naw., *Firaq*, p. 87; Mufid, *Fusul M*, p. 260; Tusi, *Ghayba*, pp. 51, 63, 145; *Milal*, 1:171 adds that the group confirmed al-'Askari's being childless, thus falsifying the claim of those who believed in the pregnancy of his slave girl and established the Imam after him.

32. Naw., *Firaq*, pp. 88−89; Mufid, *Fusul M*, p. 260. *Milal* and Tusi do not mention this faction.

33. Naw., *Firaq*, p. 90; *Milal*, 1:172; Tusi, *Ghayba*, p. 163; Mufid, *Fusul M*, p. 260.

34. Kulayni, *Kafi*, 2:157, 161, and Ibn Babuya, *Kamal*, 2:361, mention several traditions regarding this prohibition. See below for a discussion relating to this subject.

35. He was one of the 'Abbasid generals, who died in 260/873−74.

36. Naw., *Firaq*, pp. 91−93; Mufid, *Fusul M*, p. 259; Ibn Hazm mentions this sect as Qitti'iyya, who, according to him, belong to the Imamiyya Rawafid. See *Heterodoxies*, p. 47. *Milal* does not mention this sect.

37. For the Imamate of the eldest son see the tradition mentioned by Kashshi, *Rijal*, p. 282.

38. Compare the Isma'ili doctrine of the Imamate of two brothers and their interpretation of this. According to them al-Hasan was *imam-i mustawda'*, i.e. temporarily entrusted with the Imamate, and al-Husayn was *imam-i mustaqarr* or "regular Imam," which means that the Imamate was permanently with him. For this reason the Imamate was inherited by his descendants. The same is the case with this group with a different interpretation. See *Haft bab-i bu Ishaq*, ed. and trans. W. Ivanow (Bombay, 1959), p. 22.

39. Naw., *Firaq*, p. 93.

40. Mufid, *Fusul M*, p. 260.

41. *Khwandan*, p. 154.

42. See the "Reconstruction of Lost Works" of al-Mas'udi in Tarif Khalidi, *Islamic Historiography: The Histories of Mas'udi* (Albany: SUNY, 1975), especially pp. 157−58.

43. The framework within which the Muslim heresiographers composed their works on

milal is summarized in Watt's Introduction to *Formative Period*, pp. 3ff.

44. *Passion*, 1:369. Earlier than this Abu Muslim, the commander of Khurasan during the 'Abbasid propaganda and revolution, had used this phrase for similar reasons. See Ghulam Husayn Yusufi, *Abu Muslim, sardar-i khurasan* (Mashhad, 1344 Sh.), p. 50.

45. *Milal*, 1:172.

46. *Heterodoxies*, p. 47.

47. For the Waqifite position see *Maqalat*, 1:100; Tusi, *Ghayba*, pp. 99, 142; Naw., *Firaq*, p. 67; for the Qat'ite position see Mas'udi, *Muruj*, 8:40; Baghdadi, *Farq*, p. 23; Isfarayini, *Tabsir*, p. 42. This last author calls the Qat'iyya *ithna 'ashariyya*, i.e. the Twelvers.

48. *Milal*, 1:127.

49. Ibn Hazm does not use this term to designate the Qat'iyya, but Mas'udi in *Muruj*, 7:40; Baghdadi, *Farq*, p. 63; and Isfarayini, *Tabsir*, p. 42 use this word. Strangely enough, and proving the origin of this word as later, even al-Nawbakhti does not use this word for the Imamiyya. For the transition from Imamiyya to Ithna 'Ashariyya, see E. Kohlberg, "From Imamiyya to Ithna-'Ashariyya," in *BSOAS*, 39, (1976), pt. 3, 521–34.

50. Mas'udi, *Tanbih*, pp. 198–99.

51. Ibn Nadim, *Fihrist*, p. 219; Qummi, *Kuna*, p. 293; Tusi, *Fihrist*, 107 does not mention this.

52. Ibid.

53. Najashi, *Rijal*, p. 304.

⁵⁴Ibn Nadim, *Fihrist*, pp. 176–77. See also *Khwandan*, p. 111, where he thinks that the attribution of this belief to Abu Sahl is questionable, since no Imamite sources mention it, and that in all probability this must have been his early view which he must have modified later on. But the contentions on which the argument is built are weak. It is assumed that later Imamite authorities like Ibn Babuya would concede such a belief in their prominent theologian. Al-Nawbakhti, understandably, did not mention this view in his exposition of the fourteen sub-divisions, and Ibn Babuya might very well have purged Abu Sahl's opinion before quoting it in his *Kamal*. I would tend to support his conclusion that Abu Sahl might have held such a view which he later on modified to conform with the official Imamite view.

55. Tusi, *Ghayba*, p. 147.

56. *Passion*, 1:371.

57. Mufid, *Fusul M*, pp. 258–59.

58. Tusi, *Ghayba*, p. 282.

59. Ibid., p. 132.

60. *Bihar 2*, pp. 310ff.

61. Tusi, *Ghayba*, p. 282.

62. *Ghayba N*, p. 124. See also *Bihar 2*, p. 229, where the significance of various titles used for the twelfth Imam is discussed.

63. Kulayni, *Kafi*, 2:114.

64. *Ghayba N*, p. 164. The Battle of Camel (35/655–56) is·a symbol of 'Alid political victory.

65. Kulayni, *Kafi*, 2:114, footnote under *hadith*, no. 7. See also fn. 15 above.

66. Tusi, *Amali*, 2:33. See also Ibn Babuya, *'Ilal*, 1:218ff.

⁶⁷*Kifayat*, fl. 26–27–28.

68. *Ghayba N*, p. 98.

69. Kulayni, *Kafi*, 2:180; Ibn Babuya, *Kamal*, 2:48.

70. Ibn Babuya, *Kamal*, 1:128.

71. Ibid., 2:268; Mufid, *Irshad*, p. 700. I had an opportunity to examine a microfilm copy of a manuscript from Mecca Library of the Haram (No. 34) at Amir al-Mu'minin Library in Najaf, Iraq, which mentions even the time of appearance of al-Qa'im on the day of 'Ashura'. The tradition runs: "He will come out from Mecca in the month of Muharram, on the day of 'Ashura', after evening prayers in the year two hundred after one thousand" (al-Mutaqqi al-Hindi, *Talkhis*, fl. 4).

72. Kulayni, *Kafi*, 2:180.

73. Ahmad Zumurrudiyan, *Bayan-i haqiqat* (Shiraz, 1350 Sh.), p. 22.

74. Kulayni, *Kafi*, 2:176; see also *Ghayba N*, p. 7, where 'Ali is reported to have told one of his most renowned associates, Kumayl b. Ziyad, about the necessity of the presence of the *hujja* of God on earth whether *zahir al-ma'lum* (manifest, recognized) or *kha'if al-maghmur* (hidden, unknown).

75. *Ghayba N*, p. 68.

76. Ibid., p. 7; Ibn Babuya, *Kamal*, 2:361–62; Tusi, *Ghayba*, p. 122.

77. Kulayni, *Kafi*, 2:213; Kashshi, *Rijal*, pp. 320–21.

78. Ibn Babuya, *Kamal*, 1:217–18, 318.

79. Ibid., 1:73.

80. *Ghayba N*, p. 179.

81. Akhbat al-Muwaffaq al- Khwarazmi, *Maqtal al-Husayn* (Najaf, 1367), 1:67. The author was the chief pupil of the great commentator of al-Zamakhshari. Among the Sunnite traditionists, al-Khwarazmi accepts and cites many of the unusual Shi'ite traditions. This fact has led some of the Imamite scholars to consider him as one of their important authorities.

82. Tusi, *Amali*, 2:26, fourth part.

83. Hilli, *Nafi'*, Chapter 211, p. 78.

84. Ibn Babuya, *Kamal*, 2:9.

85. Ibid., 2:96–98.

86. Tusi, *Ghayba*, pp. 124–28.

87. *'Uyun*, p. 127. In the introduction to this edition Muhammad 'Ali Awradabadi says that the Shaykh was being consulted by the two Sharifs, al-Murtada and al-Radi, both al-Mufid's disciples.

88. *Bihar*, 102:79.

89. For the importance of this night in Imamite devotions and recommended prayers and fasting, see Qummi, *Mafatih*, pp. 165ff.

90. Sura 32 and 36. Both of these are recommended to be read at childbirth.

91. These are the seven in the *fiqh*: the forehead, the palms of both hands, both knees, and two toes.

92. Here the expression means that he was already circumcised, and that the umbilical cord had been cut and his navel was clean.

93. Ibn Babuya, *Kamal*, 2:96–98.

94. Ibid., 2:56.

95. *'Uyun*, p. 134.

96. Ibn Babuya, *Kamal*, 1:317; *Bihar 2*, p. 596.

97. Tusi, *Ghayba*, p. 152.

98. Ibid., p. 115.

99. Ibid., p. 183.

Notes to Chapter 3

1. Kulayni, *Kafi*, 1:315–18.

2. See the article "Hisham b. al-Hakam" in *EI²*.

3. Ibn Babuya, *Kamal*, 1:317.

4. Bahr al-'Ulum, Muhammad al-Mahdi, *Kitab al-rijal al-sayyid,* known as *al-Fawa'id al-rijaliyya* (Najaf, 1965–67), 3:316ff.

5. Najashi, *Rijal*, pp. 311–16; Tusi, *Fihrist*, pp. 186ff.; Ibn Nadim, *Fihrist* (ed. Bayard Dodge), 1:491.

6. *Mughni*, Vol. 20, pts. 1 and 2.

7. *Kamil*, 9:336, 341, 392, 417. On certain occasions even the caliphs sought to please the powerful *naqib* of the Talibiyyin, al-Sharif al-Murtada.

8. Ibn Babuya, *Kamal*, 2:157. See also the article "Buwayhids" in *EI2*, 2:1350–52, for the discussion of this aspect of the doctrine of *ghayba*.

9. Tusi, *Ghayba*, p. 1.

10. Kulayni, *Kafi*, 2:179.

11. Tusi, *Ghayba*, p. 142.

12. Mufid, *Irshad*, p. 673.

13. Tusi, *Ghayba*, p. 142.

14. Ibn Babuya, *Kamal*, 1:149. Majlisi in his commentary of *Kafi* explains the meaning of the *imam al-zahir* and *imam al-maghmur*, quoting Shaykh al-Baha'i: "*imam al-zahir* is like our master, Amir al-mu'minin ['Ali] during his caliphate; and *imam al-maghmur* is the one who does not call upon people to pay allegiance except the special ones, just as Amir al-mu'minin was during the caliphate of his predecessors, and the other Imams during different epochs and the Master of the Age *(sahib al-zaman)*, our master Mahdi in our times" (*Kafi*, 2:167 fn.).

15. Kulayni, *Kafi*, 2:175.

16. Ibid., 2:178; *Ghayba N*, p. 89 adds at the end "only his special slaves (friends) in his religion."

17. Ibn Babuya, *Kamal*, 1:93.

18. *Ghayba N*, p. 91.

19. See, for instance, Mufid, *Irshad*, p. 692, where signs of the reappearance of the Mahdi are recounted which include the prophecy regarding the decay of the 'Abbasid caliphate, which is found as early as Ibn Babuya (the last sections of his *Kamal* discuss the signs of the reappearance of the Mahdi). This indicates how early the *ghayba* was expected to end.

20. *Ghayba N*, p. 91.

21. The vocalization is not 'Umari. I feel confident it is 'Amri. See Tusi, *Ghayba*, p. 214.

22. Tusi, *Rijal*, p. 436.

23. Ibn Babuya, *Kamal*, 2:116.

24. Ibid., 2:151.

25. Ibid., 2:106ff.

26. *Al-khums*—the fifth—in the Imamite legal system is a form of taxation besides *al-zakat* (the alms) made obligatory on the followers of the Imam. *Al-khums* is calculated on several items after deducting one year's provision; these items are explained in the *(fiqh* works. The amount thus calculated is payable to the Imam when he is present, and during the occultation to the righteous *mujtahid*, who is considered to be indirectly the representative of the Hidden Imam. See "*Al-khums* in the Imamite Legal System" by the author in *JNES*.

27. Ibn Babuya, *Kamal*, 2:179.

28. Mufid, *Irshad*, pp. 689–90.

29. Ibid., p. 686.

30. Ibid., p. 685; also Najashi, *Rijal*, p. 299.

31. Tusi, *Rijal*, pp. 420 and 434.

32. Ibid., p. 420.

33. Tusi, *Ghyaba*, p. 215.

34. Ibid., p. 214.

35. Ibid., p. 216.

36. Ibid. See also Ibn Babuya, *Kamal*, 2:251. According to the Sunnite sources (Ahmad b. 'Ali al-Khatib al- Baghdadi, *Ta'rikh Baghdadi* [Beirut, 1966], 7:366) these rites were performed by the caliph's brother Abu 'Isa b. al-Mutawakkil. The modern Imamite interpretation of this practice of washing the dead body of the Imam and the performance of other funeral rites, which, according to them, must be carried out by the succeeding Imam, is that the twelfth Imam himself must have done everything from behind the scenes; it was only to show the people that Abu 'Amr performed the rites. See Muhammad al-Sadr, *Ta'rikh al-ghaybat al-sughra* (Beirut, 1972), pp. 399ff. In all probability, this is the reason why

Majlisi, who quotes Tusi in detail, does not include this part in his account of the First Agent (*Bihar 2*, pp. 665–66).

37. Tusi, *Ghayba*, p. 216.

38. See above, Chapter II.

39. Ibn Babuya, *Kamal*, 2:116ff.

40. Tusi, *Ghayba*, p. 218.

41. Ibid., p. 222; Ibn Babuya, *Kamal*, 2:114.

42. Ibn Babuya, *Kamal*, 2:114.

43. Tusi, *Ghayba*, p. 221.

44. Ibid., p. 222.

45. Ibid.

46. Ibid., p. 221; *Khwandan*, p. 214 treats the subject of his relationship to the Naw-bakhtis in detail.

47. Tusi, *Ghayba*, p. 227.

48. Al-Iskafi's recent ancestors were Zoroastrians. He had written a work entitled *al-Anwar*, which dealt with the biography of the Imams. He died around 332/943–44 or 336/947–48. See Najashi, *Rijal*, p. 269; Baghdadi, *Ta'rikh*, 3:365.

49. Tusi, *Ghayba*, p. 224.

50. Ibid., p. 240.

51. Ibid., p. 227.

52. Ibid., p. 236.

53. Ibn Babuya, *Creed*, p. 110.

54. Tusi, *Ghayba*, p. 236.

55. Ibid., pp. 228–29.

56. Ibid., p. 237.

57. Shams al-Din Muhammad b. Ahmad Dhahabi, *Ta'rikh al-islam*, pp. 139ff.

58. Najashi, *Rijal*, p. 293.

59. Tusi, *Ghayba*, pp. 183, 186ff.

60. *Kamil*, 8:290.

61. Tusi, *Ghayba*, p. 241.

62. Yaqut b. 'Abd Allah al-Hamawi, *Irshad al-arib ila ma'rifat al-adib*, known as Mu'jam al-udaba', ed. D. S. Margoliouth, 2nd ed. (Cairo, 1923), 1:296. Ibn Miskawayh, Ahmad b. Muhammad, *Tajarib al-umam* (Cairo, 1914), 5:123, tells us about the good relationship between the son of the vizier 'Ali b. Muhammad al-Furat, who followed the deposed Hamid b. 'Abbas, and al-Shalmaghani. Unfortunately for al-Shalmaghani and the vizier, the Qarmatians had during this period plundered the caravan of the pilgrims, and al-Furat and his son were suspected of being behind this because of their Shi'ism. For this and other reasons the vizier and his son had to pay with their lives; al-Shalmaghani went into hiding and escaped to Mawsil. See also *Kamil*, 8:292–94.

63. Tusi, *Ghayba*, p. 187.

64. Ibid., p. 252.

65. Ibid., p. 242.

66. Ibid., pp. 242ff.; Ibn Babuya, *Kamal*, 2:193. Al-Sufyani is mentioned in traditions attributed to the Prophet about a dissension which would arise between the East and the West. At that time al-Sufyani would emerge from the Wadi of Yabis. Then he will send out armies and there will be widespread destruction until Gabriel will be sent against him and will destroy him. For variant reports on al-Sufyani see Ibn Babuya, *Kamal*, 2:364ff.; also the article "al-Mahdi" in *EI1*, 3:114.

67. Ibid., p. 245.

68. Ibid., pp. 239–40. For more information on Banu Fadal see Qummi, *Kuna*, 2:96; Tusi, *Fihrist*, pp. 72ff.

69. *Ghayba N*, p. 91.

70. Tusi, *Ghayba*, p. 231; *Bihar 2*, p. 1251.

71. *Bihar 2*, p. 1251 fn. 2.

72. The modern interpretation of the tradition on the *bay'a* of the twelfth Imam appears in Safi Gulpaygani, *Navid amn va aman* (Qumm, 1349), pp. 174–75.

73. A. K. S. Lambton in her article, "A reconsideration of the position of the *marja' al-taqlid* and the religious institutions," in *Studia Islamica*, Vol. 20, p. 115 says, "In the absence of the Imam, all government, even if the holders of actual power were Shi'i, was regarded as unrighteous by the Shi'i divines." This is a much later interpretation which dates back to the Qajar period, since those Imamite jurists who wrote during or immediately after the Short Occultation do not mention anything about the unrighteousness of the government during the occultation. In fact, the illegitimacy of any form of government was maintained by all the Imams before the twelfth Imam went into occultation. The Shi'is believed that the Imam was the leader of the community and as such the government rests in his hands. As a matter of fact, government belongs to him alone (Shaykh Muhammad Hasan al-Najafi, *Jawahir al-kalam* [Tehran, 1392 A.H.], 11:157). Thus both the Umayyads and the 'Abbasids were known as *ghasibin* (usurpers) of the rights of the *ahl al-bayt*, very much earlier than this period of the *ghayba*. In his invocation the fourth Imam, 'Ali b. al-Husayn, says on the occasion of the Friday service, the convening of which is considered to be the constitutional right of the Imam as the temporal ruler: "O my God, this position (of convening and leading the Friday service) belongs to your vicegerents and your chosen ones . . . which they (the Umayyads) have taken away [from us]" (*Sahifa al-kamila* [Tehran, 1375 A.H.], p. 364). The reference made by Lambton in her article or by N. Keddie in her article entitled "The roots of the 'Ulama's power in Iran" about the illegitimacy of any state (*Studia Islamica*, Vol. 29, p. 32) should be taken as the inevitable consequence of the evolution of the doctrine of al-Mahdi as *al-qa'im bi'l-jihad*, discussed above in Chapter II.

In a recent article by Said Amir Arjomand entitled "Religion, Political Action and Legitimate Domination in Shi'ite Iran: fourteenth to eighteenth centuries A.D." (*Archives Europeenes de Sociologie*, 20 [1979]), the author speaks about the depoliticization of the Imamate and its transformation into a strictly theological doctrine, devoid of any political implication. In such an assertion it is assumed that a theological doctrine necessarily deals with soteriology and eschatology and thus becomes an abstract principle which has nothing to do with the question of legitimacy of any form of government. On the contrary, as will be seen in Chapter IV, the Imamite doctors were faced with a dilemma of not only establishing the so-called "abstract" Imamate of the twelfth Hidden Imam, but also with justifying his prolonged occultation in spite of his being the only rightful Imam who could set the affairs of the community aright. There was no need for the jurists of this school to dispute the legitimacy of the caliphs in the name of the Hidden Imam, since the occurrence of the Complete Occultation had postponed the whole question of the *bay'a* (acclamation) of the twelfth Imam as the ruler of the Muslim community, pending his return. The blame for the situation thus created through the concealment of the Imam was imputed on those who had put obstacles in the path of the Imam, who could not assume full responsibilities as the rightful successor of the Prophet. The article, on the whole, suffers from preconceived notions about Imamite doctrines; the employment of Weberian categories for the Islamic situation has caused the terminology to become dubious and misleading.

74. *Lexicon*, 1/1, 344.

75. This is the famous tradition known as *hadith al-hawd*. *Hawd* is the pool or basin at which the Prophet will meet his *umma* on the day of judgment. For details on this subject see the article in *EI2*.

76. Ibn Babuya, *Kamal*, 1:151–53.

77. His full name was 'Abd Rabbih Zurara b. A'yan (d. 150/767). Zurara was his title. A'yan, his father was a slave from Byzantium and belonged to a person from the Banu Shayban. His master taught him the Qur'an and then freed him and offered to accept him as one of his family. But A'yan preferred to remain his friend. A'yan's father was a monk in Byzantium. Zurara himself had many sons and brothers, who formed the large and well-known family of the Banu Zurara. They were all reporters of several traditions and the authors of various works and compilations. Zurara reported from the fourth, fifth, and

sixth Imams. Tusi mentions a book written by him under the title of *al-Istita'a wa al-jabr* (*Fihrist,* p. 100). Najashi says: ". . . he was a reciter (of al-Qur'an), a jurisprudent, a theologian, a poet and a man of letters. In him were combined excellence of character, piety and truthfulness in which he reported" (*Rijal,* pp. 132ff.). Kashshi mentions a tradition which is reported on the authority of the sixth Imam: "Had it not been for Zurara, I think, the traditions of my father would have disappeared" (*Rijal,* p. 133). With all these good reports about him, there are accounts which show that Zurara had on some important issues contradicted the sixth Imam, having reported something different on the authority of the fifth Imam (Kashshi, *Rijal,* p. 136).

78. Ibn Babuya, *Kamal,* 2:157.
79. Tusi, *Ghayba,* p. 63.
80. *Ghayba N,* pp. 110–11; Ibn Babuya, *'Ilal,* 1:232.
81. Ibn Babuya, *Kamal,* 2:158.
82. Ibid., 1:127; Tusi, *Ghayba,* p. 66.
83. Ibid., 1:182–83. The reference is to the boycott of the Quraysh before the Hijra.
84. Ibid., 1:365.
85. Ibid., 1:176.
86. *Ghayba N,* p. 118.
87. *Jawahir al-kalam,* 11:178.

Notes to Chapter 4

1. See the last part of his *Kamal,* entitled *Bab al-nawadir al-kitab,* which includes some *kalam* topics in crude form, 2:370ff. See above, Chapter III.
2. *Fihrist,* p. 187.
3. *Ghayba,* p. 65.
4. Mufid, *Fusul 'A,* pp. 34–35; also W. Madelung, "Imama," in *EI2,* for the views of different schools on this question.
5. *Ghayba,* p. 65.
6. Sharif, *Treatise,* p. 118.
7. The *mutakallimun,* both the Mu'tazilites and the Ash'arites, divide knowledge into *al-daruri* (necessary or immediate), *al-nazari* (that resulting from an inquiry), and *al-muktasab* (acquired) (Baghdadi, *Usul,* p. 8; for the Imamite position, Hilli, *Kashf,* p. 139). The *daruri* knowledge did not depend on revelation; rather, it presented itself to the mind in an immediate form prior to revelation. This knowledge presents itself in such a way that the person attaining it had no choice but to accept it (Baqillani, *Tamhid,* pp. 7ff.; Baghdadi, *Usul,* p. 8; Hilli, *Kashf,* p. 136). The *nazari* or *muktasab* knowledge results from a process of discursive proofs. All the knowledge in the acquired sciences, including knowledge of the Islamic Law, depends on rational proofs. The Mu'tazilites maintained that general ethical axioms were known by intuitive reason. Every rational person was capable of attaining them by the intellect and did not need revelation to explain to him what was immediately known. Thus they contended that good and evil were objective concepts and rational categories which could be known through the *daruri* knowledge. The function of revelation was to supplement the difficulties experienced by human reason in the acknowledgement of good and evil. On the other hand, the Ash'arites held that good and evil were subjective concepts whose validity depended on the revelation or something dependent on it in one way or another, such as the Sunna, *ijma',* or *qiyas* (analogy) (Baghdadi, *Usul,* pp. 24ff.; *Milal,* 1:59ff.; Hilli, *Kashf,* p. 185; also G. F. Hourani, *Islamic Rationalism: The Ethics of 'Abd al-Jabbar* [Oxford, 1971], pp. 20ff.)
8. Muhammad al-Mahdi al-Husayni al-Shirazi, *Qawl al-sadid fi sharh al-tajrid* (Najaf, 1961), p. 306 (hereafter referred to as *Qawl*). In writing this section I have mainly used Hilli's commentary on Nasir al-Din Tusi's *Tajrid* entitled *Kashf*; but in some places I have supplemented *Kashf* with *Qawl.*
9. *Qawl,* p. 307.

10. Ibid.
11. *Gawhar*, p. 250; Hourani, pp. 135ff.
12. Hilli, *Kashf*, p. 217.
13. Ibid., p. 226; see above p. 111ff.
14. Ibn Babuya, *Kamal*, 2:375.
15. Tusi, *Talkhis*, 1:90; *Ghayba*, p. 65.
16. Mufid, *Awa'il*, p. 26; Asadabadi, *Mughni*, 13:17. Among the Mu'tazilites Bishr b. al-Mu'tamir and those who followed him among the Baghdadian Mu'tazilites did not maintain *lutf* to be incumbent on God. See Asadabadi, *Sharh*, p. 520; Muhammad b. 'Ali al-Karajaki, *Kanz al-fawa'id* (Tehran, 1307), p. 52.
17. Kulayni, *Kafi*, 1:121.
18. *Maqalat*, 1:288.
19. *Farq*, p. 156.
20. *Maqalat*, pp. 287–88; Asadabadi, *Mughni*, 13:4–8.
21. J. Windrow Sweetman, *Islam and Christian Theology* (London, 1947), Pt. 1, 2:65.
22. Asadabadi, *Sharh*, p. 519. For details see his *Mughni*, 13:9–11.
23. Asadabadi, *Mughni*, pp. 15–17.
24. Hilli, *Kashf*, pp. 203–04.
25. *Mawaqif*, 2:264.
26. Asadabadi, *Sharh*, p. 750.
27. Ghazali, *Iqtisad*, p. 184 contends that it was not obligatory on God to bear in mind the most salutary for His creatures; rather, God can act in any way He pleases.
28. Hilli, *Kashf*, pp. 202–03; *Mawaqif*, 4:196.
29. Ibid., p. 226.
30. Ibid.; Tusi, *Talkhis*, pp. 106–07.
31. Asadabadi, *Sharh*, p. 751.
32. Hilli, *Kashf*, p. 226.
33. Sharif, *Treatise*, pp. 122–23.
34. Hilli, *Kashf*, p. 217.
35. Mufid, *Tashih*, pp. 60ff.
36. Hilli, *Kashf*, p. 217.
37. Mufid, *Tashih*, p. 62; Hilli, *Bab*, p. 59.
38. See Chapter I for various members of the Banu Hashim who were proclaimed as Mahdi and the sources cited therein.
39. Ibn Babuya, *Man*, pp. 74–75.
40. Mufid, *Tashih*, p. 62; *Awa'il*, p. 35.
41. Hilli, *Bab*, p. 59; *Kashf*, p. 229; Ibn Babuya, *Kamal*, 1:176; Tusi, *Talkhis*, 1:61, fn. 2.
42. *Treatise*, p. 119.
43. Ibid., pp. 119ff.
44. Ibid., pp. 120–21.
45. Mufid, *Awa'il*, p. 99; Muzaffar, *Usul*, 2:104–05. I have greatly relied on the latter work to write this section on *ijma'*, especially pp. 97–116.
46. As cited by Muzaffar, *Usul*, p. 106.
47. *Rasa'il*, p. 40.
48. Al-hiss: The term basically means "the sense," i.e. the five senses taken collectively, or "the faculty of sensory perception." But as a term in theological and philosophical writings, it is the source by which knowledge is produced in us. Our soul begins to know by way of the senses. When the sensible faculty perceives the sensible object, the figure and the apparent form of the latter are actualized in that faculty (A. M. Goichon, *Lexique de la langue philosophique d'Ibn Sina (Avicenna)* [Paris, 1938], pp. 68ff.). The knowledge attained by the sensible faculty is different from that attained by experience. Al-Ghazali gives an example to demonstrate this difference thus: "When the sun rises the stars disappear. This is known by experience *(tajriba)*. Then you say: 'It is evident that the sun has arisen.' This is apprehended by the sense" (F. Jabr, *Essai sur le lexique de Ghazali* [Beyrouth, 1940], p. 64).

The term also indicates the principle of intellectual knowledge, since the perceptual activity is not perceived by the perception but by an intellectual process (*Avicenna's De Anima*, ed. F. Rahman [London, 1959], p. 67). In this context a judgment arrived at by *ijma'* by this method implies that the jurist investigates the situation as it presents itself to his sensible faculty, especially the audible sense *(al-sama')* and then arrives at a conclusion about its being authentic or not.

49. *Rasa'il,* p. 42.
50. Ibid., p. 51.
51. Ibid., p. 42.
52. Hilli, *Mabadi,* p. 190.
53. Muzaffar, *Usul,* p. 112.

Notes to Chapter 5

1. Tusi, *Ghayba,* pp. 262ff.
2. Ibid., p. 263.
3. According to Tabari, *Ta'rikh,* 6:104, it was 'Abd Allah b. Nawf who propounded this doctrine in opposition to al-Mukhtar.
4. Kulayni, *Kafi,* 1:494.
5. *Mawaqif,* p. 348.
6. Ibn Babuya, *Creed,* p. 42.
7. Mufid, *Awa'il,* p. 53; fn. 2 on the same page by Charandani.
8. Tusi, *Ghayba,* pp. 264ff.
9. Ibid., p. 265.
10. Ibid., p. 261.
11. Kulayni, *Rawda,* p. 294.
12. Tusi, *Amali,* 2:33.
13. Mahmoud Ayoub, *Redemptive Suffering in Islam: A Study of Devotional Aspects of 'Ashura'* *in Twelver Shi'ism* (The Hague, 1978), pp. 216ff.
14. Qummi, *Mafatih,* p. 288; Ibn Qawlawayh, *Kamil,* p. 179.
15. Ibn Babuya, *Kamal,* 2:366.
16. Kulayni, *Kafi,* 1:463.
17. Mufid, *Irshad,* p. 692.
18. Tusi, *Ghayba,* p. 276.
19. Ibid., p. 275; Tabarsi, *Ihtijaj,* 2:50.
20. Ibid., p. 276.
21. Ibid., p. 277.
22. Bihar 2, p. 979.
23. Tusi, *Ghayba,* p. 273.
24. Mufid, *Irshad,* pp. 701ff.
25. Ibid., p. 705.
26. Tusi, *Ghayba,* p. 274.
27. Al-Mufaddal was among the former followers of Abu al-Khattab, the founder of the extremist Shi'i sect of the Khattabiyya, who had repented and reverted to the moderate view of the Imamate. His early views are discussed in Kashshi, *Rijal,* pp. 321–29.
28. *Bihar 2,* p. 972.
29. Ibid., pp. 973–76.
30. Ibid., p. 979.
31. Ibid., p. 986.
32. Lane, *Lexicon,* 1/3:1040. He adds, "This was a tenet of some Arabs in the Time of Ignorance, and a sect of Muslim innovators, and a sect of *rafidah* who say that 'Ali. . . .
33. Baghdadi, *Farq,* pp. 58ff.
34. Ibid., p. 54.
35. Ibn Hisham, *Sira,* 2:155.

36. Mufid, *Awa'il*, p. 13.
37. *Maqalat*, 1:114.
38. *Bihar 2*, p. 1232. Majlisi quotes al-Mufid, who cites the answer given by al-Sharif al-Murtada on the *raj'a* of the Imams.
39. Ibid., pp. 1186ff.
40. Ibid., p. 1189.
41. Ibid., p. 1220.
42. Mufid, *Awa'il*, p. 50.
43. Mufid, *'Uyun*, pp. 115–17.
44. Wensinck, *Handbook*, 'Isa, pp. 112–13 for numerous traditions in the *Sihah* and their variants. For *hadith* on Jesus in Shi'ite sources see Gulpaygani, *Muntakhab*, pp. 316–18.
45. All major *tafsir* works cite this opinion on the authority of Ibn 'Abbas and others. Tusi, among the Shi'i exegetes, quotes this opinion but favors the one which says that the pronoun *hu* in the verse refers to the Qur'an itself (*Tibyan*, 9:211).
46. *Passion*, 2:105.
47. *Bihar 2*, pp. 785–86. For various traditions on the subject of al-Dajjal, see *Handbook*, pp. 50–51; *Muntakhab*, pp. 460–62.
48. *Handbook*, p. 50; *Muntakhab*, p. 460.
49. *Bihar 2*, p. 791.
50. G. S. Godeon, *The Ashura Ceremonies in Lebanon,* unpublished doctoral thesis submitted to the School of Oriental and African Studies, University of London, 1963, 1:4.
51. *Muntakhab*, pp. 482–83.
52. Mufid, *Irshad*, pp. 705ff.
53. *Bihar 2*, p. 942.
54. *Ghayba N*, pp. 125ff.
55. Ibid., pp. 121–22.
56. Ibid., p. 121; also Kulayni, *Kafi*, 2:54ff. for the detailed description of the *wasiyya*.
57. *Bihar 2*, p. 944.
58. *Ghayba N*, pp. 122, 170.
59. *Bihar 2*, pp. 948–49.
60. Ibid., p. 953.
61. Tabarsi, *I'lam*, pp. 477ff.
62. Ibid., p. 961.
63. Tusi, *Ghayba*, p. 283.
64. *Bihar 2*, pp. 1001–02.
65. Ibn Babuya, *Kamal*, 2:27.
66. Tusi, *Ghayba*, p. 96.
67. Mufid, *Irshad*, p. 708.
68. *Bihar 2*, p. 1059 cites the *tafsir* of al-'Ayyashi.
69. Ibid., pp. 1060–62.
70. *Di'bil*, pp. 25, 99. I have made some amendments to L. Zolondek's translation.

Notes to Chapter 6.

1. Haydar ibn 'Ali al-Amuli, *Jami' al-asrar wa manba' al-anwar*, ed. H. Corbin and 'Uthman Isma'il Yahya (Tehran, 1969), p. 102.
2. Ibn Babuya, *Kamal*, 2:226ff. has a whole section devoted to the *ghayba* of the prophets and their *awsiya'*.
3. See above, Chapter V.

1. For the explanation of all these material manifestations of the Imam's knowledge, see Chapter I.

2. See also the Glossary.

3. Lane, *Lexicon,* 1/8, 3050.

4. See Chapters I and II for the full explanation of the term *hujja*.

5. *Lexicon,* 1/3, 969.

6. It is the command and injunction (*Lexicon,* 1/8, 3055) in the written form, from God for the Imam, who was required to follow the instruction therein.

7. See the Glossary for the explanation of all these terms and phrases.

Selected Bibliography and Abbreviations

Items are arranged alphabetically. Under each author, his works are arranged alphabetically according to the abbreviated forms used in the notes. Bibliographical data on secondary sources which are partially abbreviated may be found in the places where they are first cited in the footnotes.

Ansari, Murtada Muhammad Amin al-:
    Rasa'il   *al-Rasa'il al-arba'a*, also known as *Fara'id al-usul*. Qumm: Mustafavi, 1374/1954
Asadabadi, al-Qadi 'Abd al-Jabbar b. Ahmad al-:
    Mughni   *al-Mughni fi abwab al-tawhid wa al-'adl*. 20 vols. Cairo: Dar al-Misriyya, n.d.
    Muhit   *al-Muhit bi al-taklif*, compiled by al-Hasan b. Ahmad b. Matwiyya in 683/1284–85. 2 vols. Cairo: Dar al-Misriyya, 1965.
    Sharh   *Sharh al-usul al-khamsa*. Ed. 'Abd al-Karim 'Uthman. Cairo: Maktabat Wahba, 1965.
Ash'ari, 'Ali b. Isma'il al-:
    Maqalat   *Maqalat al-islamiyyin wa ikhtilaf al-musallin*. 2 vols. Cairo: Nahdat al-Misriyya, 1950.
Baghdadi, 'Abd al-Qahir b. Tahir b. Muhammad al-:
    Farq   *Kitab al-farq bayn al-firaq*. Cairo: Maktabat Muhammad 'Ali Sabih wa Awladuh, 1965.
    Usul   *Kitab usul al-din*. Istanbul: Matba'at al-Dawla, 1346/1928.
Baqillani, Muhammad b. al-Tayyib al-:
    Tamhid   *Kitab al-tamhid*. Ed. R. J. McCarthy. Al-Hikma Univ. of

Baghdad Publication, Kalam Series No. 1. Beirut: Maktabat al-Sharqiyya, 1957.

Di'bil b. 'Ali al-Khuza'i:
Di'bil   *Di'bil b. 'Ali: The life and writings of an early 'Abbasid Poet.* Ed. and tr. Leon Zolondek. Kentucky: Univ. of Kentucky Press, 1961.

Ghazali, Muhammad b. Muhammad al-:
Iqtisad   *al-Iqtisad fi al-i'tiqad.* Ankara, 1962.

Gulpaygani, Lutf Allah al-Safi al-:
Muntakhab   *Muntakhab al-athar fi imam al-thani 'ashar.* Tehran: Maktabat al-Sadr, n.d.

Hilli, al-Hasan b. 'Ali b. Dawud al-:
Kitab al-rijāl. Tehran Univ. Publication No. 857. Tehran: Univ. of Tehran Press, 1342 Sh.

Hilli, Ibn al-Mutahhar Hasan b. Yusuf al-:
Anwar   *Anwar al-malakut fi sharh al-yaqut.* Ed. Muhammad Najmi Zanjani. Tehran Univ. Publication No. 543. Tehran: Univ. of Tehran Press, 1338 Sh.

Bab   *al-Babu 'l-Hadi 'Ashar: A Treatise on the Principles of Shi'ite Theology,* with commentary by Miqdad Fadil al-Hilli. Tr. William McElwee Miller. London: Royal Asiatic Society, 1928.

Kashf   *Kashf al-murad fi sharh tajrid al-i'tiqad* of Nasir al-Din Tusi. Mashhad: Kitabfurushi Ja'fari, n.d.

Mabadi'   *Mabadi' al-usul ila 'ilm al-usul.* Najaf, 1970.

Nafi'   *al-Nafi' yawm al-hashar fi sharh bab al-hadi 'ashar,* with several other treatises by other Imamite theologians. Tehran: Markaz-i Nashr-i Kitab, 1370/1950.

Hurr al-'Amili, Muhammad b. al-Hasan al-:
Fusul   *al-Fusul al-muhimma fi usul al-a'imma.* 2nd ed. Najaf: al-Matba'at al-Haydariyya, 1378/1958.

Ibn 'Abd al-Wahhab, al-Shaykh Husayn:
'Uyun   *'Uyun al-mu'jizat.* Najaf: al-Matba'at al-Haydariyya, 1950.

Ibn Abi Zaynab, Muhammad b. Ibrahim b. Ja'far al-Nu'mani:
(see Nu'mani).

Ibn al-Athir, 'Izz al-Din:
Kamil   *al-Kamil fi al-ta'rikh.* 12 vols. Beirut: Dar Sadir, 1965.

Ibn Babuya (Ibn Babawayhi), Muhammad b. 'Ali:

Creed   *A Shi'ite Creed: A translation of Risalatu'l-I'tiqadat* of Muhammad b. 'Ali Ibn Babawayhi al-Qummi known as Shaykh Saduq. Tr. Asaf A. A. Fyzee. Islamic Research Association Series No. 9. London: Oxford Univ. Press, 1942.

'Ilal   *'Ilal al-sharayi'*. Najaf: al-Matba'at al-Haydariyya, 1963.

Kamal   *Kamal al-din wa tamam al-ni'ma*. Ed. Ayatullah Kamrahyi. 2 vols. Tehran: Islamiyya, 1378/1959.

Man   *Man la yahduruh al-faqih*. Najaf: al-Islamiyya, 1378/1958.

Ibn Hazm, 'Ali b. Ahmad:

Fasl   *al-Fasl fi al-milal wa al-ahwa' wa al-nihal*. In the margin: al-Shahrastani, *al-Milal wa al-nihal*. 5 vols. in 2; reprint of the 1317–21 ed. Baghdad: al-Muthanna, 1963.

Heterodoxies   "The Heterodoxies of the Shi'ites in the presentation of Ibn Hazm," tr. with commentary by I. Friedlaender in *JOAS*, 28 (1907), 1–80; 29 (1909), 1–183.

Ibn al-Nadim, Muhammad b. Abi Ya'qub:

Fihrist   *Kitab al-fihrist*. Ed. Gustav Flugel. Leipzig: F. C. W. Vogel, 1871–72.

Ibn Sa'd:

Tabaqat   *Tabaqat al-kabir*. Ed. E. Sachau. Leiden: E. J. Brill, 1905–06.

Ibn Shahr Ashub, Muhammad b. 'Ali:

Ma'alim   *Ma'alim al-'ulama'*. Najaf: al-Matba'at al-Haydariyya, 1961.

Ibn Tawus, 'Ali b. Musa:

Malahim   *al-Malahim wa al-fitan*. Najaf: al-matba'at al-Haydariyya, 1948.

Iji, 'Adad al-Din wa al-Milla al-:

Mawaqif   *Sharh al-mawaqif*, with commentaries by al-Jurjani et al. Cairo: Bulaq, 1325/1907.

Iqbal, 'Abbas:

Khwandan   *Khwandan-i nawbakhti*. Tehran: Kitabkhani-i Tahuri, 1345 Sh.

Irbili, 'Ali b. 'Isa b. Abu al-Fath al-:

Kashf   *Kashf al-ghumma fi ma'rifat al-a'imma*. Najaf: Matba'at al-Najaf, 1965.

Isfahani, Abu al-Faraj al-:
Maqatil   *Maqatil al-talibiyyin.* Ed. Kazim al-Muzaffar. Najaf: al-Matba'at al-Haydariyya, 1965.
Kanji al-Shafi'i, Muhammad b. Yusuf b. Muhammad al-:
Bayan   *al-Bayan fi akhbar sahib al-zaman,* printed at the end of his *Kifayat al-talib.* Najaf: al-Matba'at al-Haydariyya, 1970.
Kifayat   *Kifayat al-talib fi manaqib 'Ali b. Abi Talib.* Najaf: al-Matba'at al-Haydariyya, 1970.
Kashani, Mulla Fath Allah:
Tafsir   *Tafsir kabir minhaj al-sadiqin fi ilzam al-mukhalifin.* Tehran: Islamiyya, 1347/1928.
Kashshi, Muhammad b. 'Umar b. 'Abd al-'Aziz, al-:
Rijal   *Kitab al-rijal.* (Abridged version entitled *Ikhtiyar ma'rifat al-rijal* by Muhammad b. al-Hasan al-Tusi.) Ed. Hasan al-Mustafawi. Mashhad: Faculty of Theology, Univ. of Mashhad, 1348 Sh.
Kulayni, Muhammad b. Ya'qub b. Ishaq al-:
Kafi   *al-Usul min al-kafi.* Ed. and tr. into Persian Ayatullah Muhammad Baqir al-Kamrahyi, with a commentary of Muhammad Baqir Majlisi. 4th ed. 4 vols. Tehran: Is-lamiyya, 1392/1972.
Rawda   *al-Rawda min al-kafi.* Ed. 'Ali Akbar al-Ghaffari. Tehran: Islamiyya, n.d.
Lahiji, Mulla 'Abd al-Razzaq:
Gawhar   *Gawhar-i murad.* Tehran: Islamiyya, 1377/1957.
Majlisi, Muhammad Baqir.
Bihar   *Bihar al-anwar.* 102 vols. Tehran: Islamiyya, 1384/1964.
Bihar 2   *Mahdi-yi maw'ud.* Tr. of vol. 13 of *Bihar,* lith. ed. Tr. 'Ali Davani. 2nd ed. Qumm: Chap-i Hikmat, 1344 Sh.
Mas'udi, 'Ali b. al-Husayn al-:
Muruj   *Muruj al-dhahab wa ma'adin al-jawhar.* Ed. and tr. into French by C. Barbier de Meynard et al. Paris: Im-primerie Imperiale, 1891.
Tanbih   *al-Tanbih wa al-ishraf.* Ed. M. J. de Goeje. Leiden: E. J. Brill, 1894.
Mufid, Muhammad b. Muhammad al-Nu'man al-:
Amali   *Amali al-shaykh al-Mufid.* 3rd rev. ed. Najaf: al-Matba'at al-Haydariyya, n.d.

Awa'il   *Awa'il al-maqalat fi al-madhahib wa al-mukhtarat.* Also includes *Sharh 'aqa'id al-Saduq aw tashih al-i'tiqad.* Ed. 'Ab-
basquli Wa'iz Charandani. Tabriz: Rada'i, 1371/1951.

Fusul 'A   *al-Fusul al-'ashara fi al-ghayba.* Najaf: al-Matba'at al-
Haydariyya, 1951.
al-Fusul M al-mukhtara min al-'uyun wa al-mahasin. 2 vols.
continuous paging. Najaf: al-Matba'at al-Haydariyya,
1962.

Irshad   *al-Irshad.* Ed. and tr. into Persian by Muhammad Baqir
Sa'idi Khurasani. Tehran: Islamiyya, 1351 Sh.

Tashih   *Sharh 'aqa'id al-Saduq aw tashih al-i'tiqad.* Tabriz: Rada'i,
1371/1951.

Muttaqi al-Hindi al-:
Talkhis   *Talkhis al-bayan fi 'alamat mahdi akhir al-zaman.* MS Mecca
Library of the Haram, No. 34. Mfm. at Amir al-
Mu'minin Library, Najaf.

Muzaffar, Muhammad Rida al-:
Usul   *Usul al-fiqh.* 3 vols. in 2. Najaf: Dar al-Nu'man, 1967.

Najashi, Ahmad b. 'Ali b. Ahmad b. al-'Abbas al-:
Rijal   *Kitab al-rijal.* Tehran: Markaz-i Nashr-i Kitab, n.d.

Nawbakhti, al-Hasan b. Musa al-:
Firaq   *Firaq al-shi'a.* Ed. Helmut Ritter. Istanbul: Staats Druc-
kerci, 1931.

Nu'mani, Muhammad b. Ibrahim b. Ja'far al-:
Ghayba N   *Kitab al-ghayba.* Tabriz: Maktabat al-Sabiri, 1383/1963.

Sayyid Mir Lawhi:
Kifayat   *Kifayat al-muhtadi fi ma'rifat al-mahdi.* MS Tehran Univ.
Library, Mishkat Collection.

Shahid al-Awwal, Muhammad b. Jamal al-Din al-Makki al-'Amili al-:
Lum'a   *al-Lum'a al-damishqiyya,* including in al-Shahid al-Thani's
al-Rawdat al-bahiyya (see the following entry).

Shahid al-Thani, Zayn al-Din al-Jab'i al-'Amili al-:
Rawda   *al-Rawdat al-bahiyya fi sharh al-lum'a al-damishqiyya* of al-
Shahid al-Awwal. 9 vols. Religious Univ. of Najaf Publi-
cation No. 10. Najaf: Adab, 1967.

Shatr   *Shatr al-usul min kitab ma'alim al-din wa maladh al-
mujtahidin.* Tehran: Islamiyya, 1378/1958.

Shahrastani, Muhammad b. 'Abd al-Karim al-:

Milal   *Kitab al-milal wa al-nihal*. Ed. Ahmad Fahmi Mahmud. 3 vols. Cairo: Maktabat al-Husayn, 1948–49.

Sharif al-Murtada, Abu al-Qasim 'Ali b. al-Husayn al-Musawi al-:

Intisar   *Kitab al-intisar*. Najaf: al-Matba'at al-Haydariyya, 1971.

Shafi   *al-Shafi fi al-imama*, Tehran: Lith., n.d.

Treatise   *Risala fi al-ghayba*. Printed in the margins of *Fara'id al-usul* of Mulla Akhund. Tehran: Lith., 1302. Tr. A. Sachedina under the title of "A Treatise on the Occultation of the Twelfth Imamite Imam," in *SI*, 48 (1978), 109–24.

Tabari, Muhammad b. Jarir al-:

Ta'rikh   *Ta'rikh al-rusul wa al-muluk*. 10 vols. Cairo: Dar al-Ma'arif, 1960–68.

Tabarsi, Abu 'Ali al-Fadl b. al-Hasan al-:

I'lam   *I'lam al-wara' bi a'lam al-huda*. Tehran: Islamiyya, 1379/1959.

Tabarsi, Abu Mansur Ahmad b. 'Ali b. Abi Talib al-:

Ihtijaj   *al-Ihtijaj*. Ed. Sayyid Muhammad Baqir al-Khirsan. 2 vols. Beirut: Dar al-Nu'man, 1966.

Tusi, Muhammad b. al-Hasan al-:

Amali   *Amali al-Shaykh al-Tusi*. 2 vols. Najaf: Matba'at al-Nu'man, 1964.

Fihrist   *al-Fihrist*. 2nd ed. Najaf: al-Matba'at al-Haydariyya, 1961.

    Ikhtiyar ma'rifat al-rijal, known as *Rijal al-Kashshi* (see Kashshi).

Ghayba   *Kitab al-ghayba*. Najaf: Maktabat al-Sadiq, 1965.

Khilaf   *Kitab al-khilaf fi al-fiqh*. 2 vols. 2nd ed. Tehran: Chapkhana-i Taban, 1382/1962.

Rijal   *Rijal al-Tusi*. Ed. Muhammad Sadiq Al Bahr al-'Ulum. Najaf: al-Matba'at al-Haydariyya.

Talkhis   *Talkhis al-shafi fi al-imama*. Ed. Husayn Bahr al-'Ulum. 3rd ed. 4 vols. Najaf: Adab, 1963-.

Tamhid   *al-Tamhid fi al-usul*. MS at the Astana-i Quds Library in Mashhad, No. a.q.l. sh. 54.

Tibyan   *Tafsir al-tibyan*. 10 vols. Najaf: 'Ilmiyya, 1957.

Tusi, Nasir al-Din:

Fusul   *Fusul al-'aqa'id*. Baghdad, 1970.

Index

exposition of Imamate of Hidden Imam, 130–34;
their contribution, 149.
See also Imamite jurists
Imamite traditionists *(muhaddithun)*:
their method, 79;
early representatives of, 79;
ghayba, according to, 82–86;
vindication of *ghayba* by, 102–103;
reason for *ghayba*, according to, 103–106.
See also Imamite jurists
Imamites (Twelvers):
accommodation with the Sunnites, 13;
leadership of, during *ghayba*, 29–30;
their jurists in Baghdad, 30–38;
sub-divisions of, 42–53;
their position regarding al-Mahdi, 49–51;
safety of, depends on *ghayba*, 50;
early *qat'iyya*, 54;
messianic Imam, cornerstone of their belief, 68;
authority of *wakils* among, 76;
relation with Buyids, 80–81;
used to pay *khums* to *wakils*, 89–90;
during the rule of al-Mahdi, 173–79
Imamiyya. *See* Imamites
Islam, revolutionary challenge of, 2–4
'isma (infallibility):
early exposition of, 106;
relationship with *tawfiq*, 125;
kind of *lutf*, 135;
necessary in prophets and Imams, 135–38;
psychic power, 137;
required in *ijma'*, 138–40
Isma'il b. Ja'far al-Sadiq, 12, 49, 54, 153–54
Isma'ili Shi'ism:
beginnings of, 19,
concept of Mahdiism in, 13;
criticism of, 49, 51;
designated as *waqifiyya*, 54
Ja'far al-Sadiq. *See* Sadiq, al-
Ja'far b. 'Ali al-Hadi, 41–42; 44–45; 48–49; 52
Ja'fari, school of Islamic Law, 17:
concept of *ijma'* in, 139–48
Jafr, al-, 22
Jami'a, al-, 22
Jesus:
his appointment at childhood, 58;
comparison of, with al-Mahdi, 58, 74;

in Islamic eschatology, 171–72
Ka'ba, 76, 160, 162–64
kalam, Shi'i. *See* Imamite *kalam*
Karbala', 7, 15, 27, 159–60, 162, 165
Karbiyya (Shi'ite sect), 10
Karkh, al-, 29, 31–32, 38
Kaysaniyya (Shi'ite sect), 10.
See also Ibn al-Hanafiyya; Mukhtar
Kazim, Musa b. Ja'far, al- (seventh Imamite Imam):
Mahdiism of, 12;
imprisonment of, 25;
Imamate of, according to Fathiyya, 40, 44;
in Waqifite belief, 43;
Imamate of, discredited, 45;
his position concerning naming him, 50;
washes dead body of al-Sadiq, 52;
his messianism, 54;
bada' in his connection, 154
Khidr, al-, 104
khums (the fifth), 29, 87–88, 92–93
khuruj. See qiyam
Kufa:
center of early Shi'ites, 6;
Mukhtar's rebellion in, 9;
Fathiyya in, 44;
entry of al-Mahdi in, 159–60;
164–65
Kulyani, Muhammad b. Ya'qub, al-, 32–33, 35, 83–84
lutf:
theme of *kalam*, 111;
principle of, 120–22;
relationship of, with Imamate, 122–25;
governing principles of, 125–27;
kinds of, 128–30;
Imamate of al-Mahdi and, 130–34;
in *ijma'*, 142–44
Mahdi, al- (Twelfth Imam):
divinely guided savior, 3;
main function of, 6–7;
eschatological leader, 9;
righteous Islamic ruler, 9;
Sunnite concept of, 14;
eschatological Qa'im, 15–16;
messianic savior, 18;
Master of the Sword, 22;
unlawful to mention his name, 50;
Awaited Imam, 53;
belief in his death, 56;
Imamate of, according to al-Mufid,